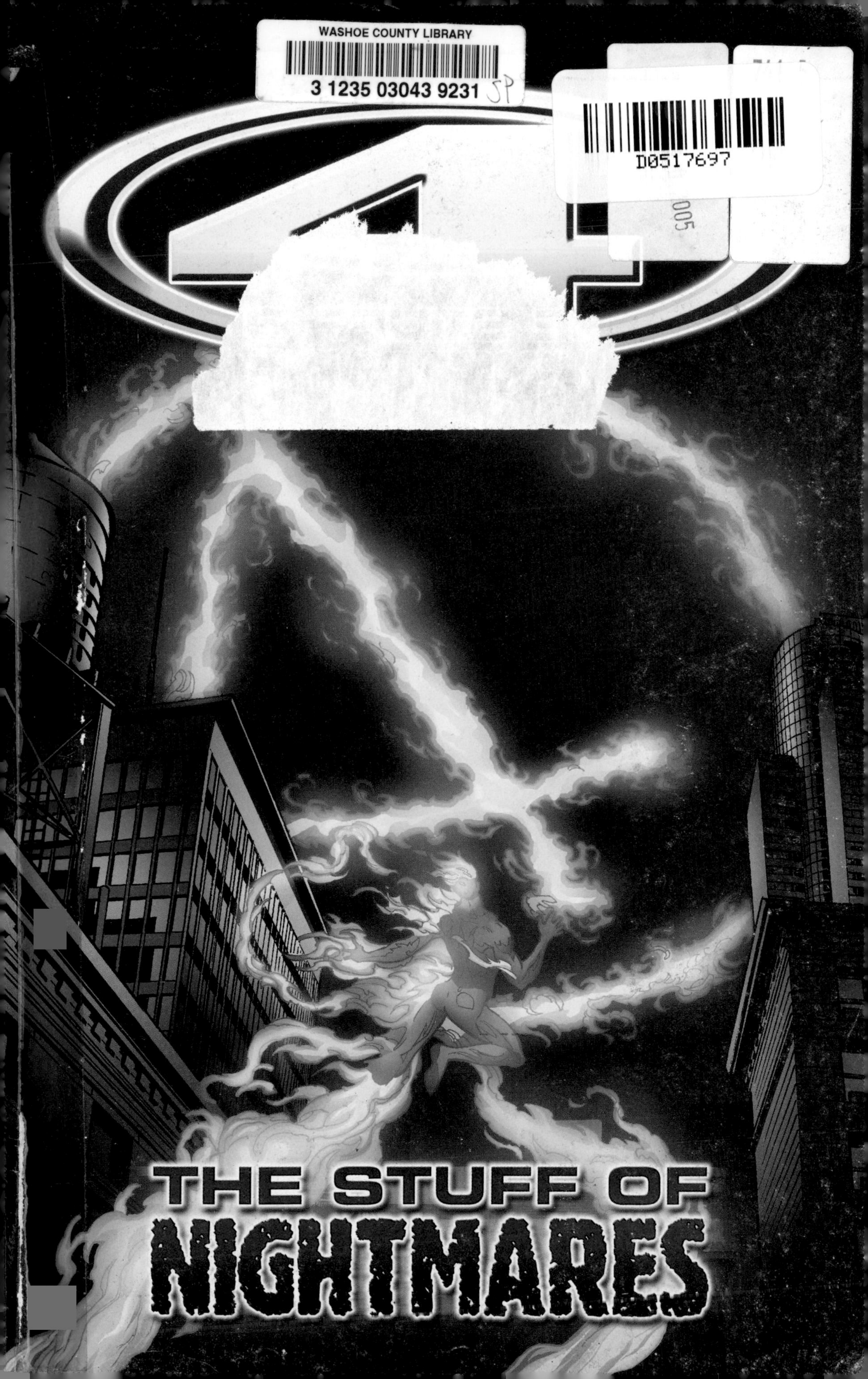
THE STUFF OF
NIGHTMARES

4

THE STUFF OF NIGHTMARES

Writer:
Roberto Aguirre-Sacasa

Penciler:
Jim Muniz
with Staz Johnson (ISSUE #11)

Inkers:
Scott Hanna
(Issue #10: Breakdowns by Jim Muniz & Finishes by Scott Hanna)

Colorists:
Brian Reber
with Morry Hollowell (Issue #8) & Sotocolor's J. Brown (Issue #9)

Letterers:
**Virtual Calligraphy's Randy Gentile,
Cory Petit & Dave Sharpe**

Cover Artist:
Steve McNiven

Editor:
Warren Simons

Executive Editor:
Axel Alonso

Collections Editor:
Jeff Youngquist

Assistant Editor:
Jennifer Grünwald

Book Designer:
Patrick McGrath

Creative Director:
Tom Marvelli

Editor in Chief:
Joe Quesada

Publisher:
Dan Buckley

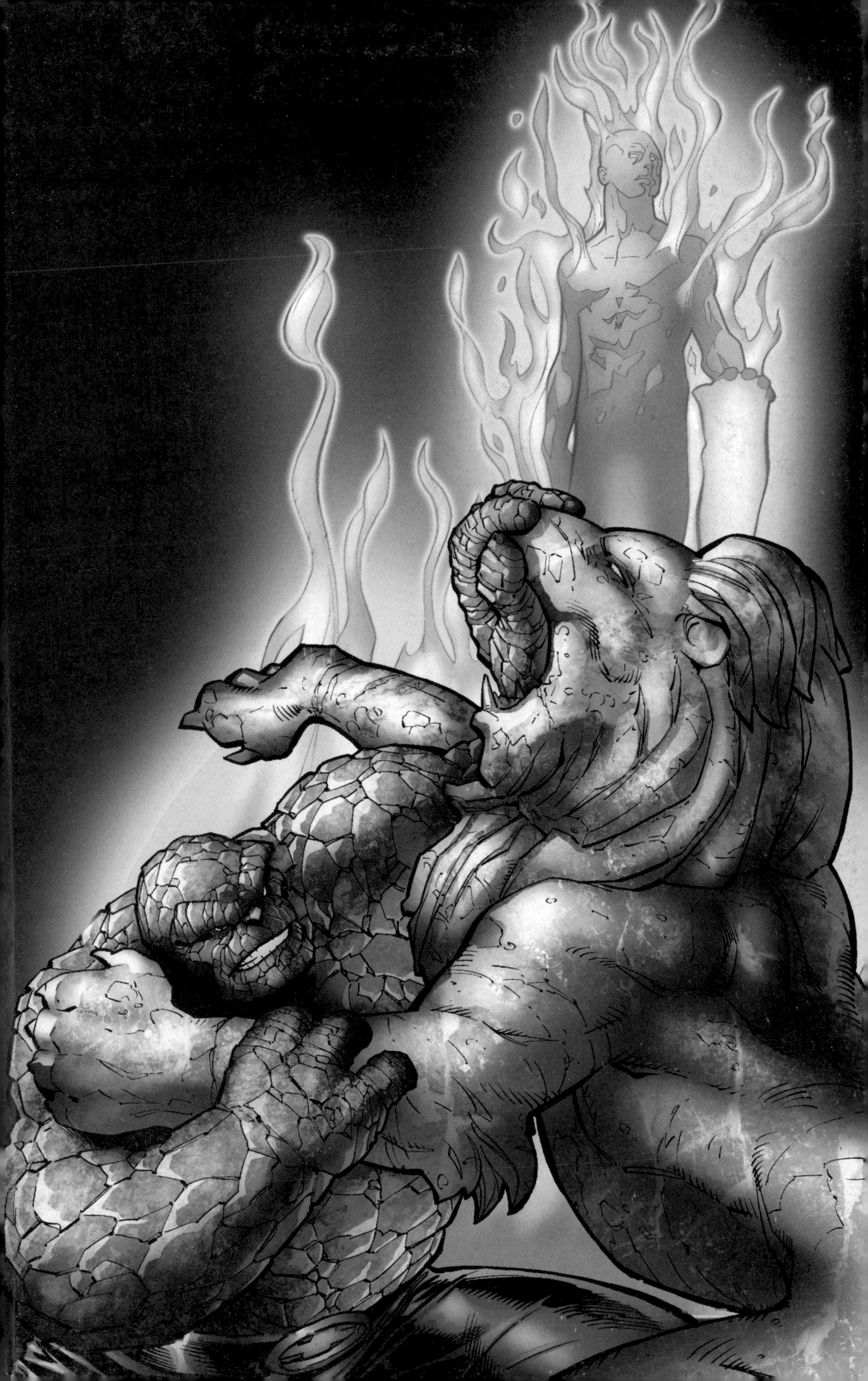

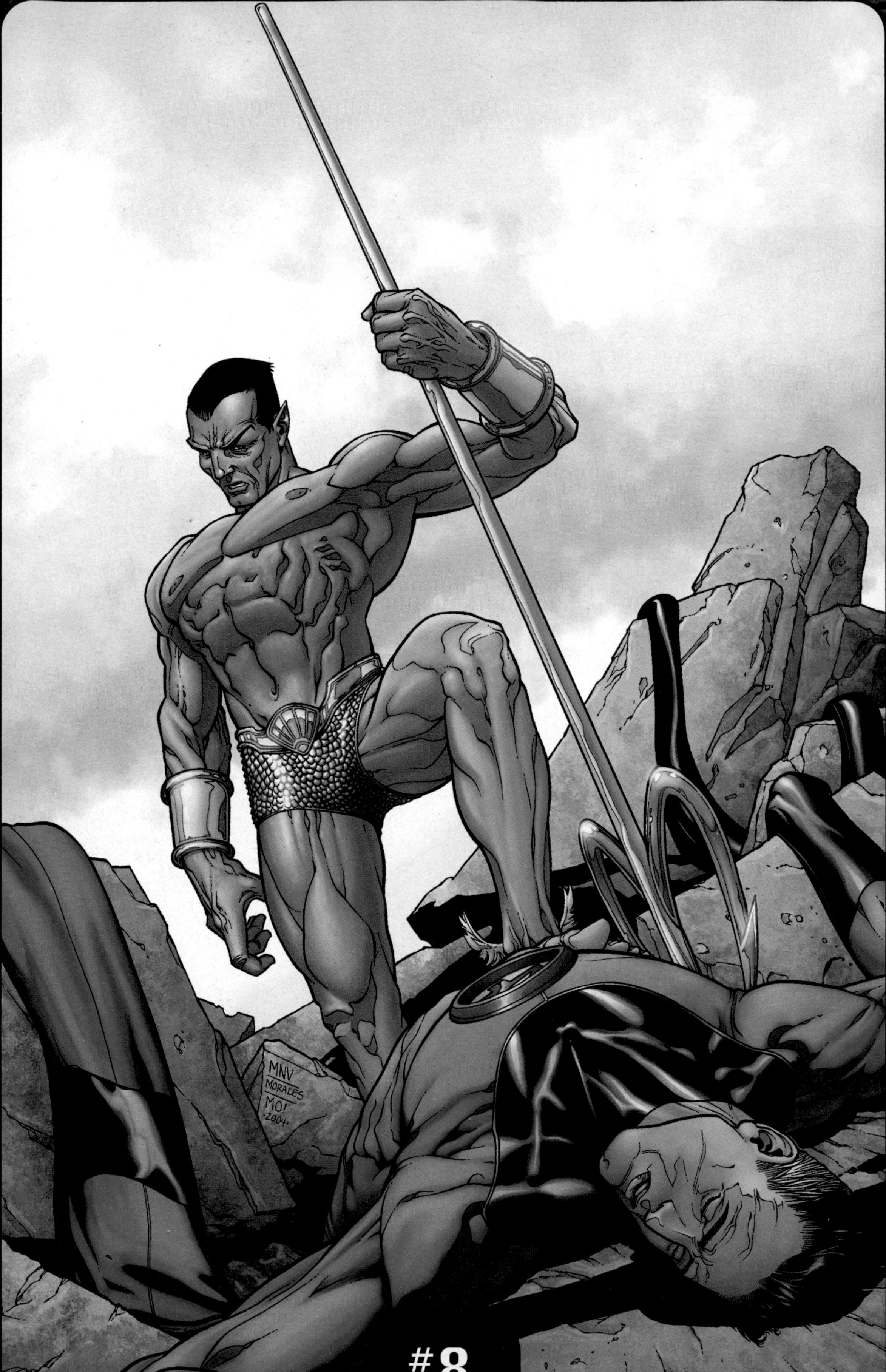
MNV
MORALES
MO!
2004

#8

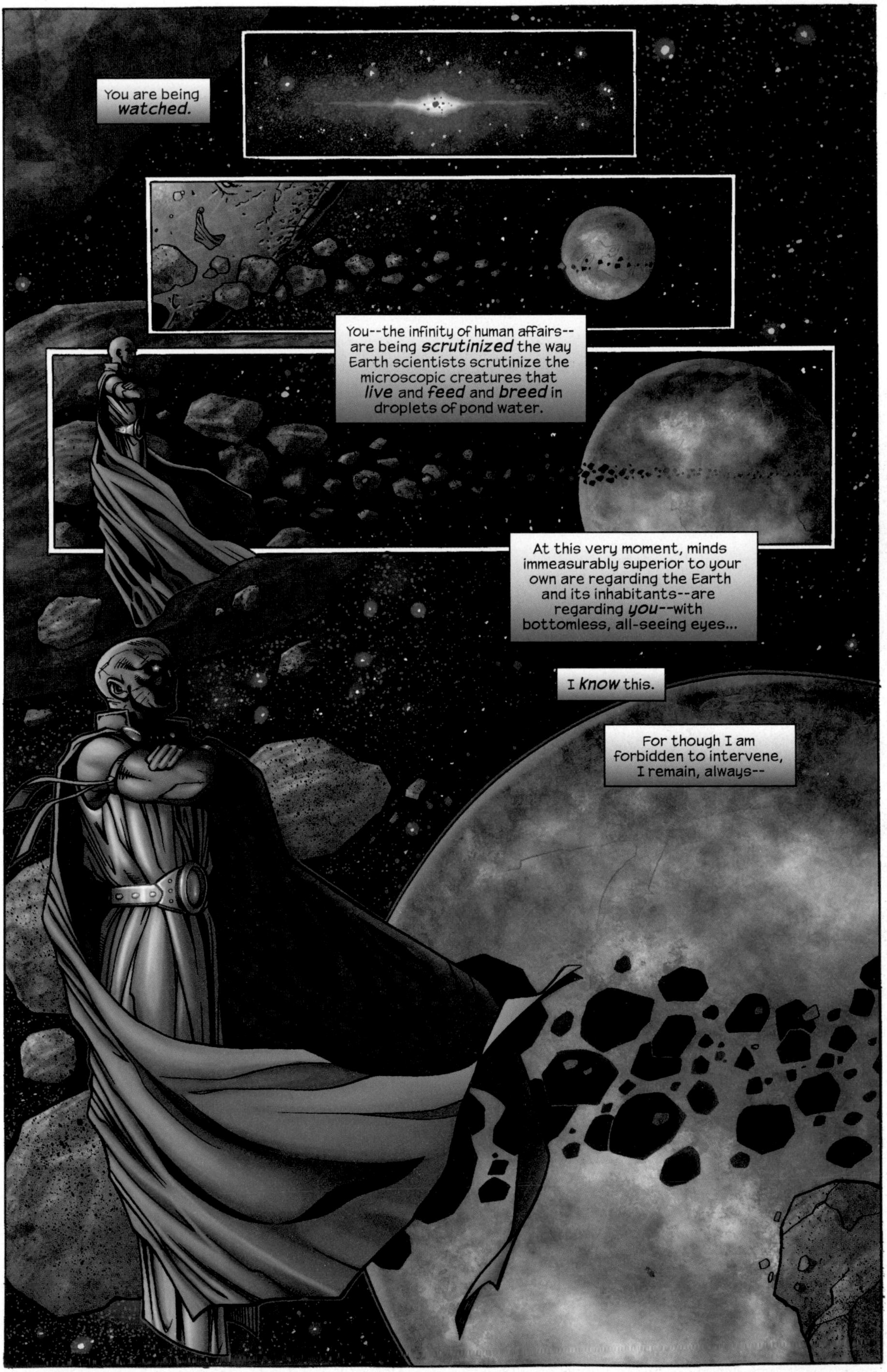
You are being *watched.*
You--the infinity of human affairs--are being *scrutinized* the way Earth scientists scrutinize the microscopic creatures that *live* and *feed* and *breed* in droplets of pond water.
At this very moment, minds immeasurably superior to your own are regarding the Earth and its inhabitants--are regarding *you*--with bottomless, all-seeing eyes...
I *know* this.
For though I am forbidden to intervene, I remain, always--

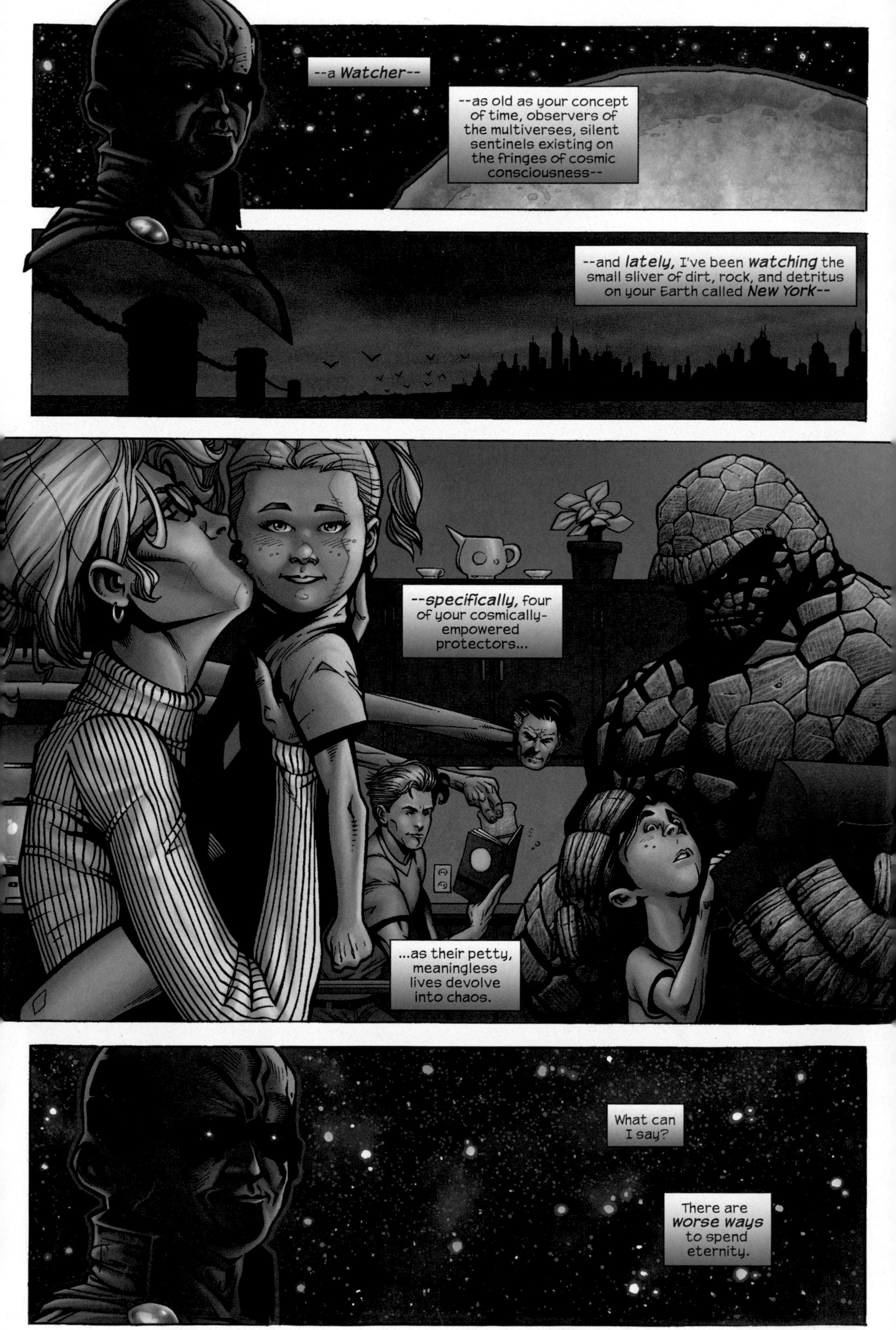
--a Watcher--
--as old as your concept of time, observers of the multiverses, silent sentinels existing on the fringes of cosmic consciousness--
--and lately, I've been watching the small sliver of dirt, rock, and detritus on your Earth called New York--
--specifically, four of your cosmically-empowered protectors...
...as their petty, meaningless lives devolve into chaos.
What can I say?
There are worse ways to spend eternity.

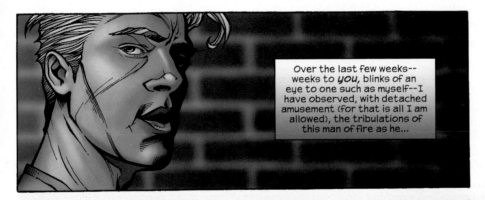

Over the last few weeks--weeks to *you*, blinks of an eye to one such as myself--I have observed, with detached amusement (for that is all I am allowed), the tribulations of this man of fire as he...

...well, *see* for yourself.

÷Whew÷

Finally.

Man, if I have to *mop* one more floor...

Oh--uh--hey, guys, what's up? How was...

...lunch?

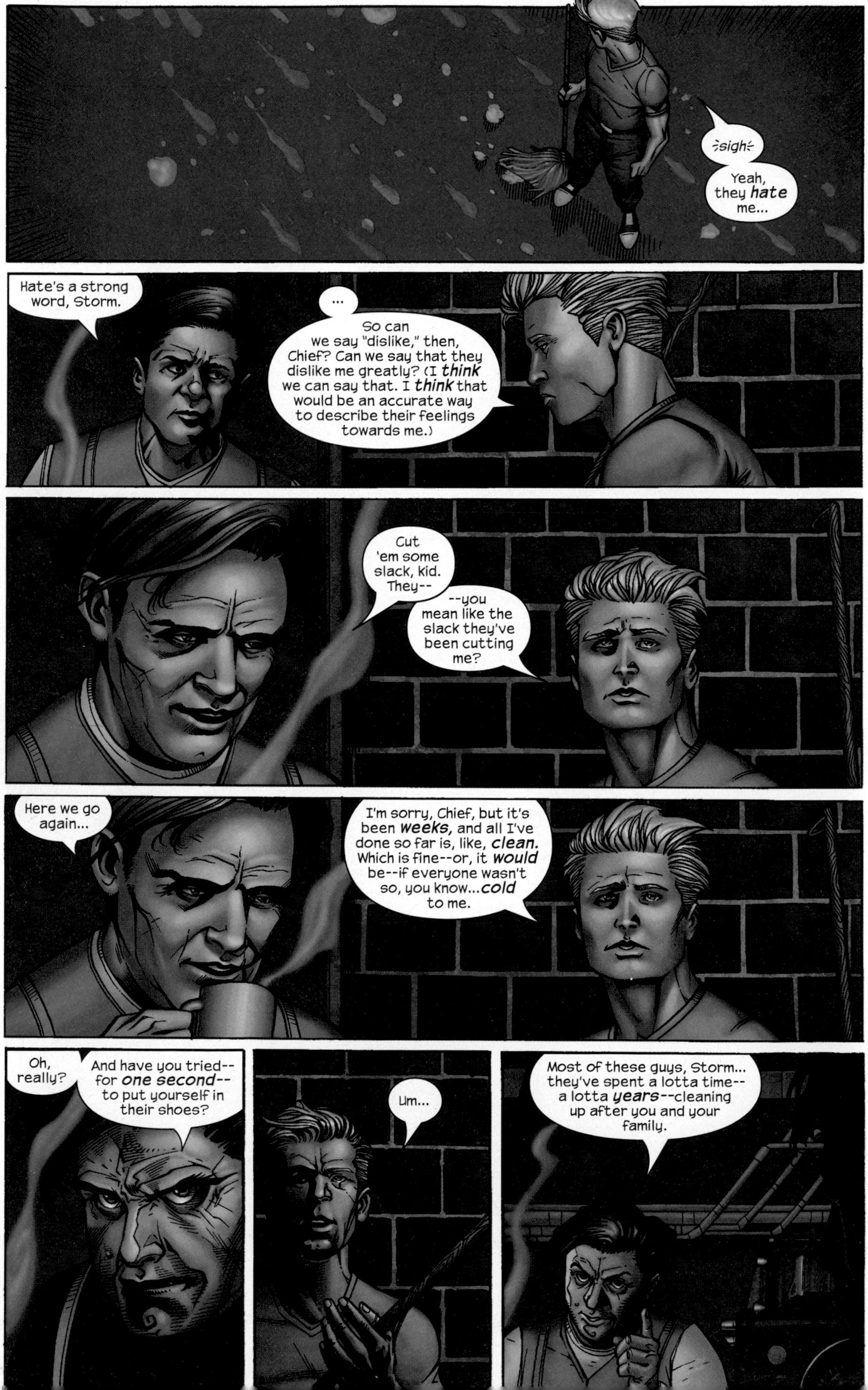

-sigh-
Yeah, they *hate* me...
Hate's a strong word, Storm.
...
So can we say "dislike," then, Chief? Can we say that they dislike me greatly? (I *think* we can say that. I *think* that would be an accurate way to describe their feelings towards me.)
Cut 'em some slack, kid. They--
--you mean like the slack they've been cutting me?
Here we go again...
I'm sorry, Chief, but it's been *weeks,* and all I've done so far is, like, *clean.* Which is fine--or, it *would* be--if everyone wasn't so, you know...*cold* to me.
Oh, really?
And have you tried--for *one second*--to put yourself in their shoes?
Um...
Most of these guys, Storm... they've spent a lotta time--a lotta *years*--cleaning up after you and your family.

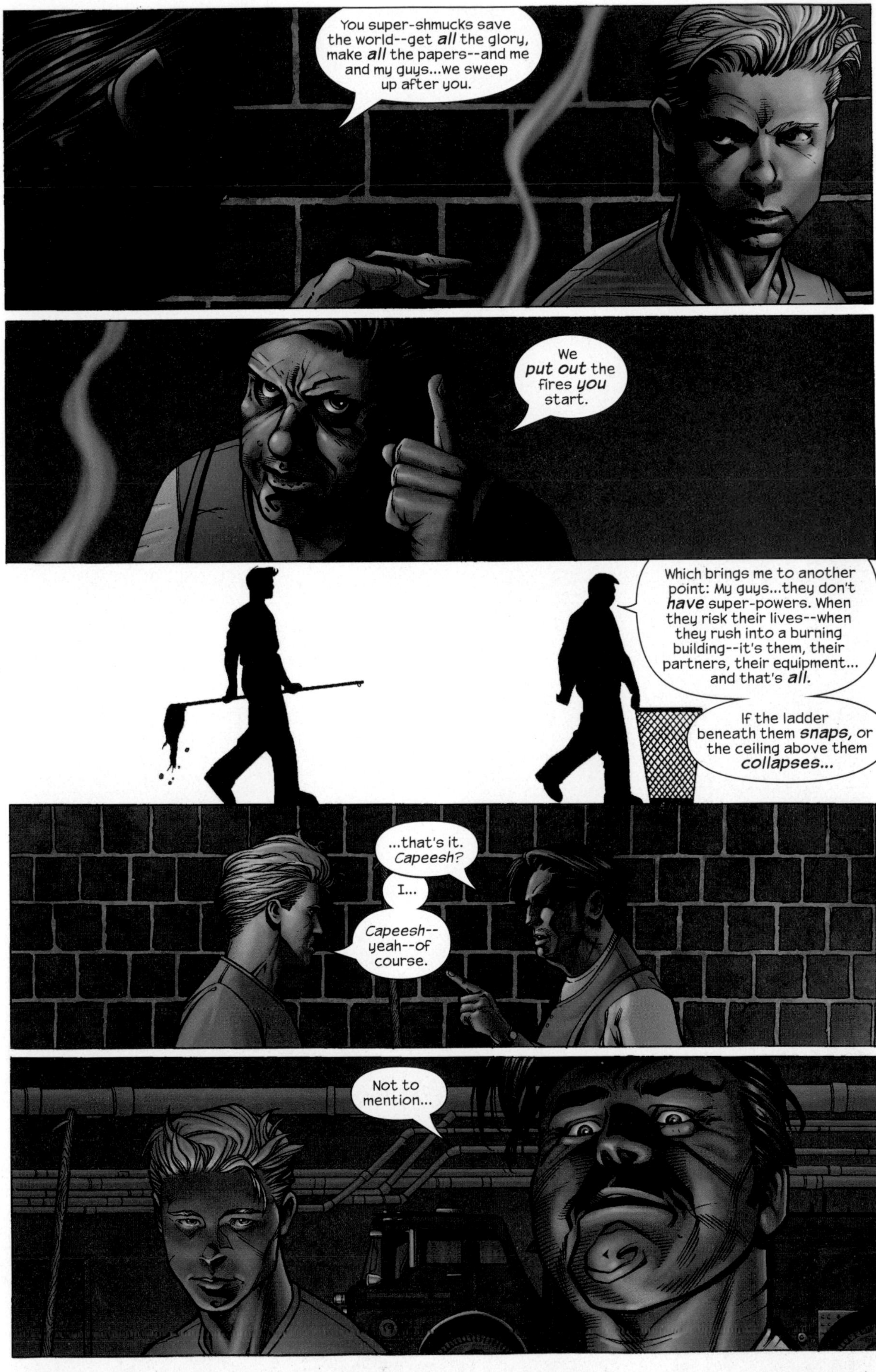
You super-shmucks save the world--get *all* the glory, make *all* the papers--and me and my guys...we sweep up after you.
We *put out* the fires *you* start.
Which brings me to another point: My guys...they don't *have* super-powers. When they risk their lives--when they rush into a burning building--it's them, their partners, their equipment... and that's *all.*
If the ladder beneath them *snaps,* or the ceiling above them *collapses...*
...that's it. *Capeesh?*
I...
Capeesh--yeah--of course.
Not to mention...

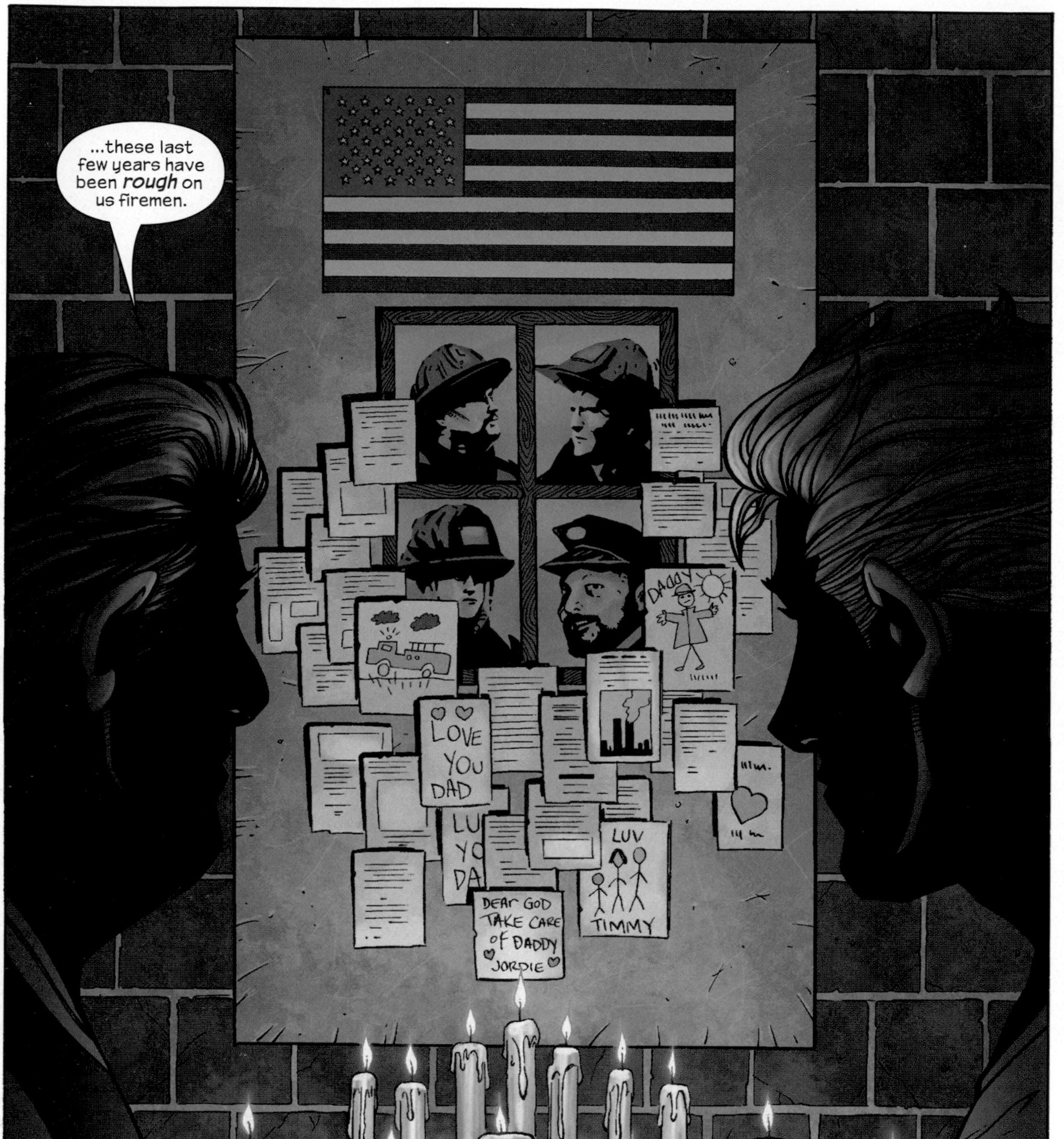
...these last few years have been *rough* on us firemen.
DADDY
LOVE YOU DAD
DEAR GOD TAKE CARE OF DADDY JORDIE
LUV TIMMY

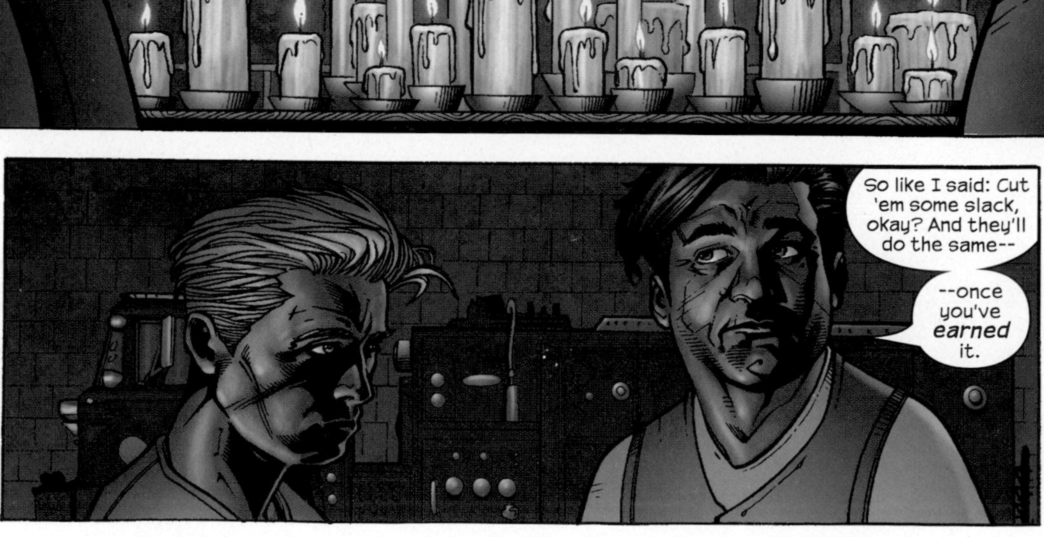
So like I said: Cut 'em some slack, okay? And they'll do the same--
--once you've *earned* it.

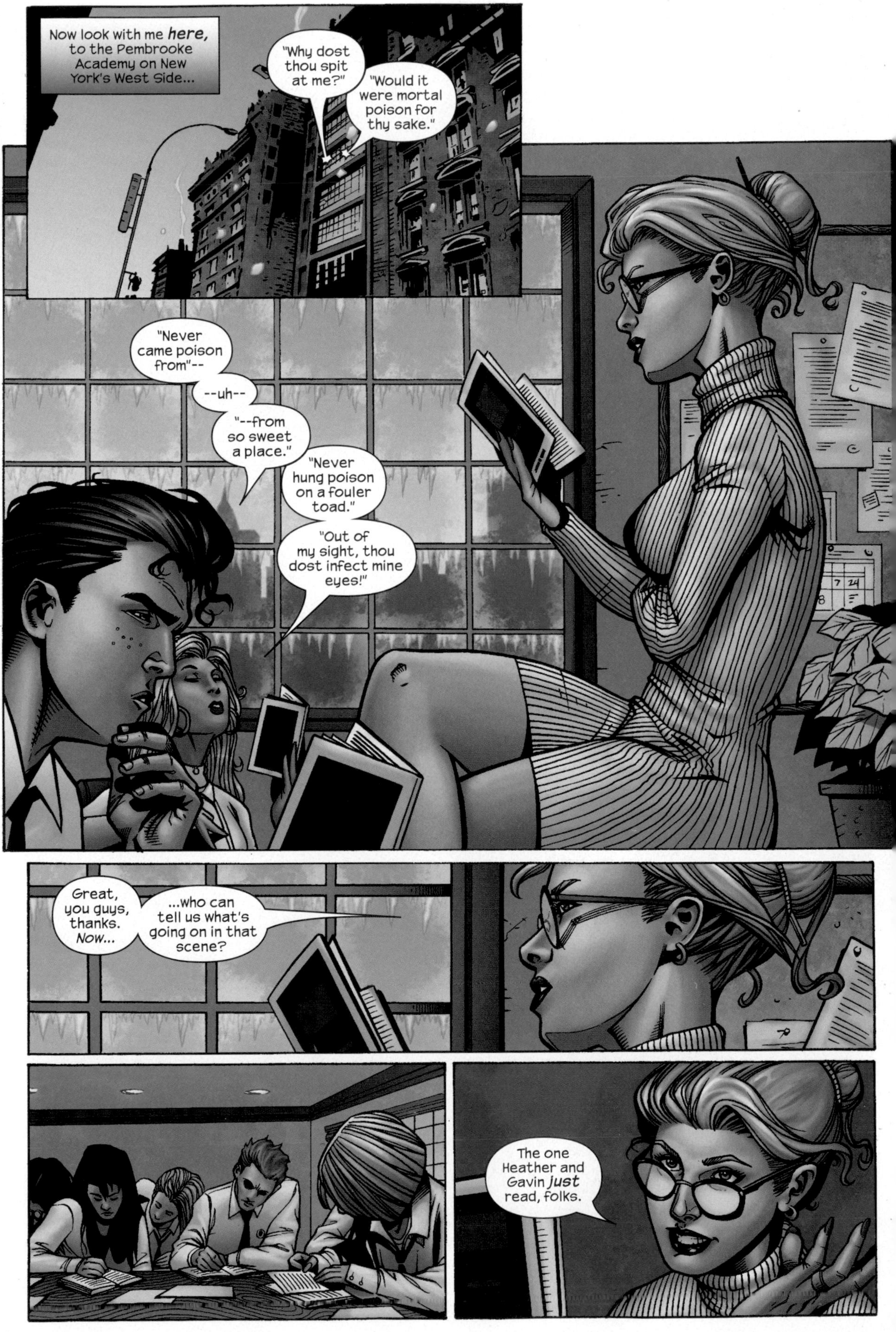

Now look with me *here*, to the Pembrooke Academy on New York's West Side...
"Why dost thou spit at me?"
"Would it were mortal poison for thy sake."
"Never came poison from"--
--uh--
"--from so sweet a place."
"Never hung poison on a fouler toad."
"Out of my sight, thou dost infect mine eyes!"
Great, you guys, thanks. *Now*...
...who can tell us what's going on in that scene?
The one Heather and Gavin *just* read, folks.

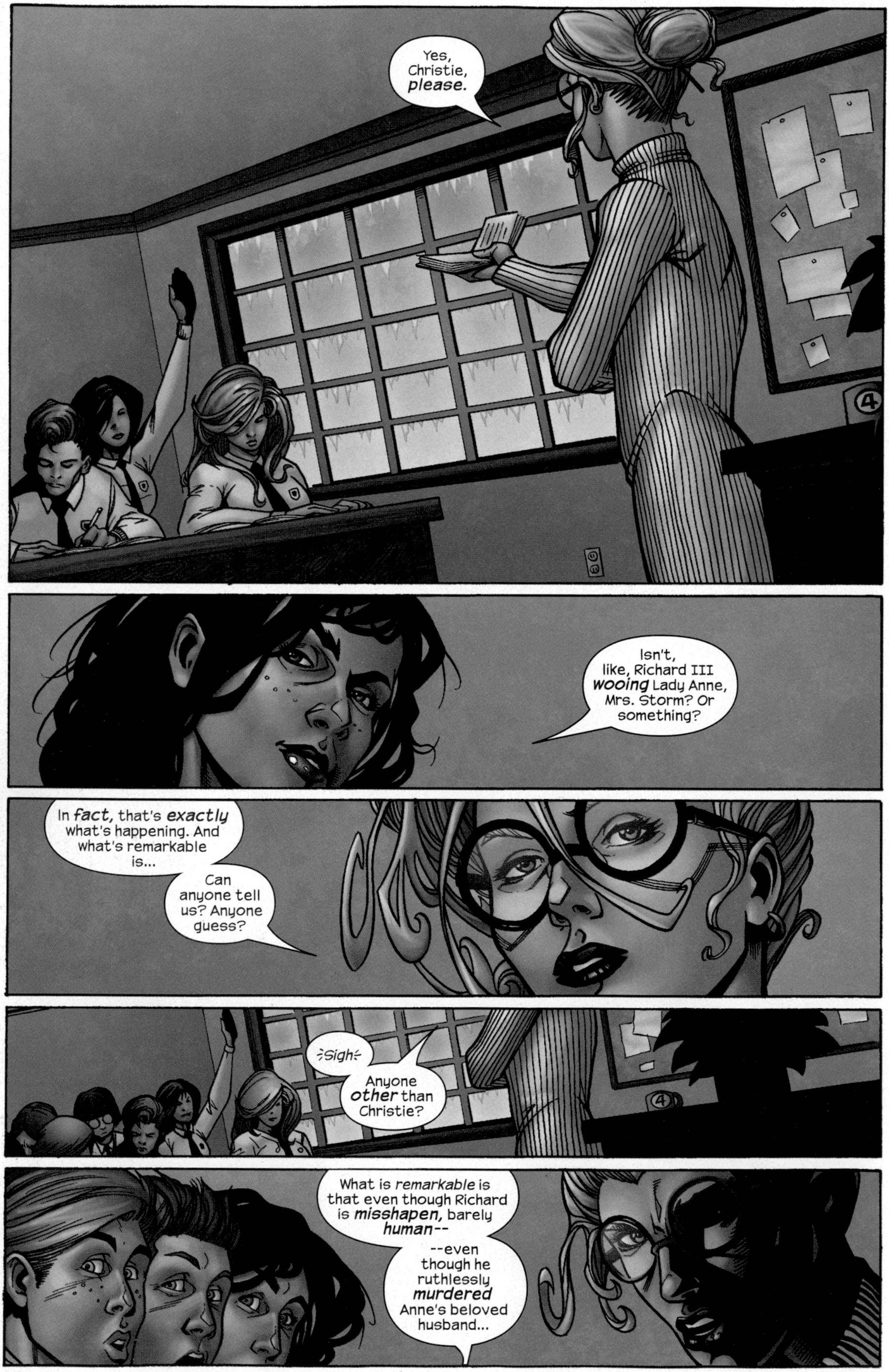
Yes, Christie, *please.*
Isn't, like, Richard III *wooing* Lady Anne, Mrs. Storm? Or something?
In *fact,* that's *exactly* what's happening. And what's remarkable is...
Can anyone tell us? Anyone guess?
Sigh
Anyone *other* than Christie?
What is *remarkable* is that even though Richard is *misshapen,* barely *human*--
--even though he ruthlessly *murdered* Anne's beloved husband...

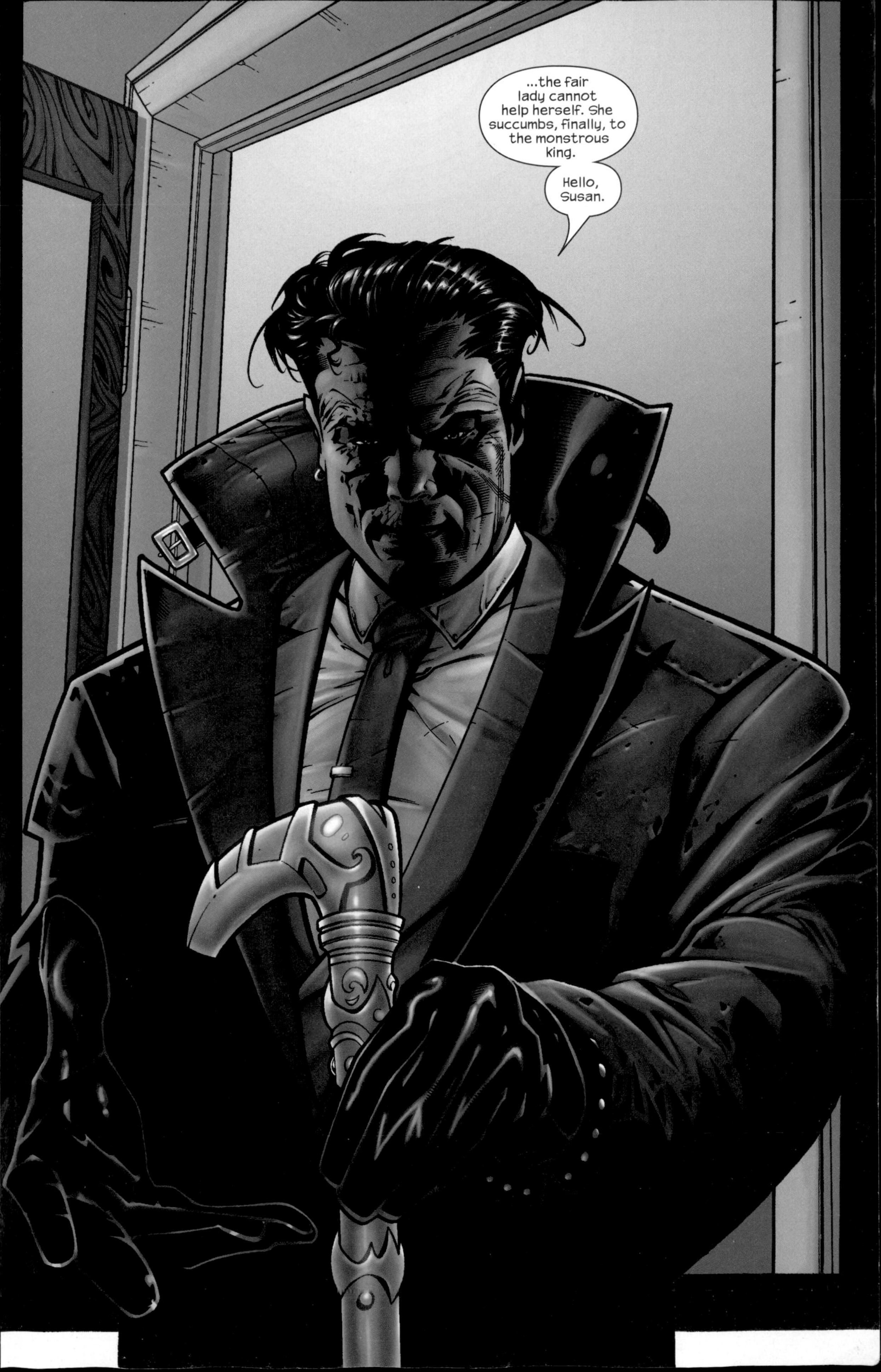
...the fair lady cannot help herself. She succumbs, finally, to the monstrous king.
Hello, Susan.

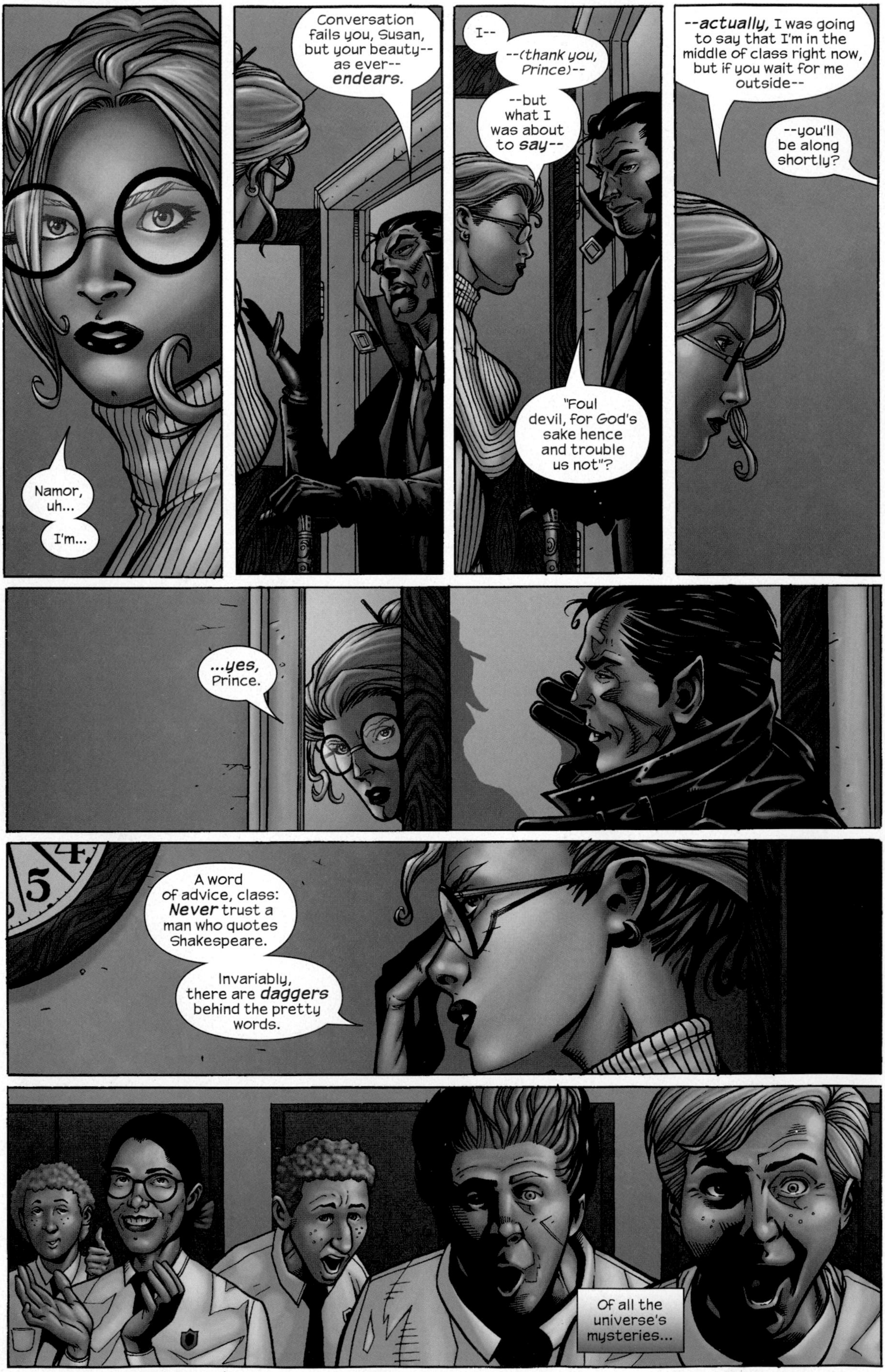
Namor, uh...
I'm...
Conversation fails you, Susan, but your beauty-- as ever-- *endears.*
I--
--(*thank you, Prince*)--
--but what I was about to *say*--
"Foul devil, for God's sake hence and trouble us not"?
--*actually,* I was going to say that I'm in the middle of class right now, but if you wait for me outside--
--you'll be along shortly?
...yes, Prince.
A word of advice, class: *Never* trust a man who quotes Shakespeare.
Invariably, there are *daggers* behind the pretty words.
Of all the universe's mysteries...

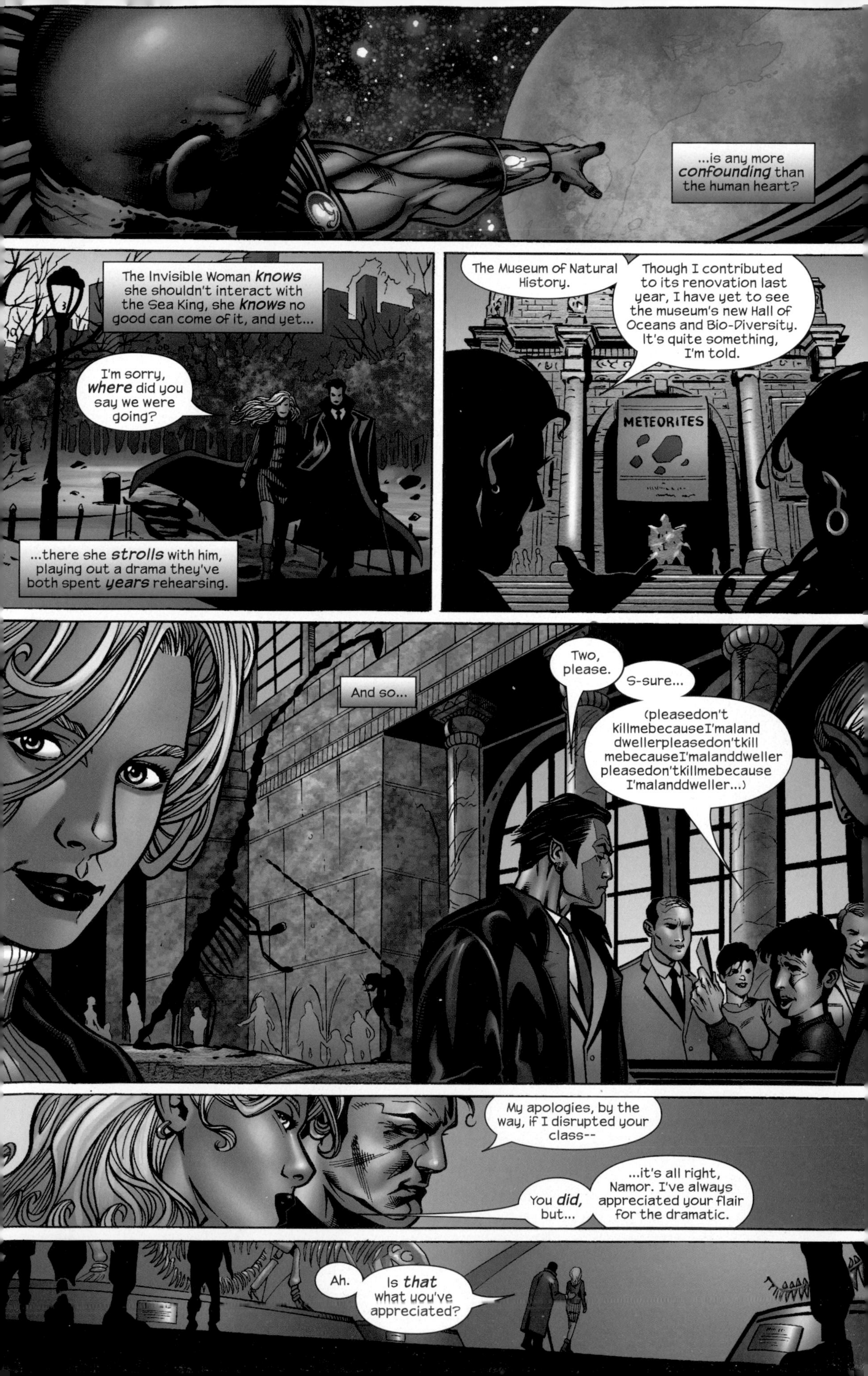
...is any more *confounding* than the human heart?
The Invisible Woman *knows* she shouldn't interact with the Sea King, she *knows* no good can come of it, and yet...
I'm sorry, *where* did you say we were going?
...there she *strolls* with him, playing out a drama they've both spent *years* rehearsing.
The Museum of Natural History.
Though I contributed to its renovation last year, I have yet to see the museum's new Hall of Oceans and Bio-Diversity. It's quite something, I'm told.
METEORITES
And so...
Two, please.
S-sure...
(pleasedon't killmebecauseI'maland dwellerpleasedon'tkill mebecauseI'malanddweller pleasedon'tkillmebecause I'malanddweller...)
My apologies, by the way, if I disrupted your class--
You *did,* but...
...it's all right, Namor. I've always appreciated your flair for the dramatic.
Ah.
Is *that* what you've appreciated?

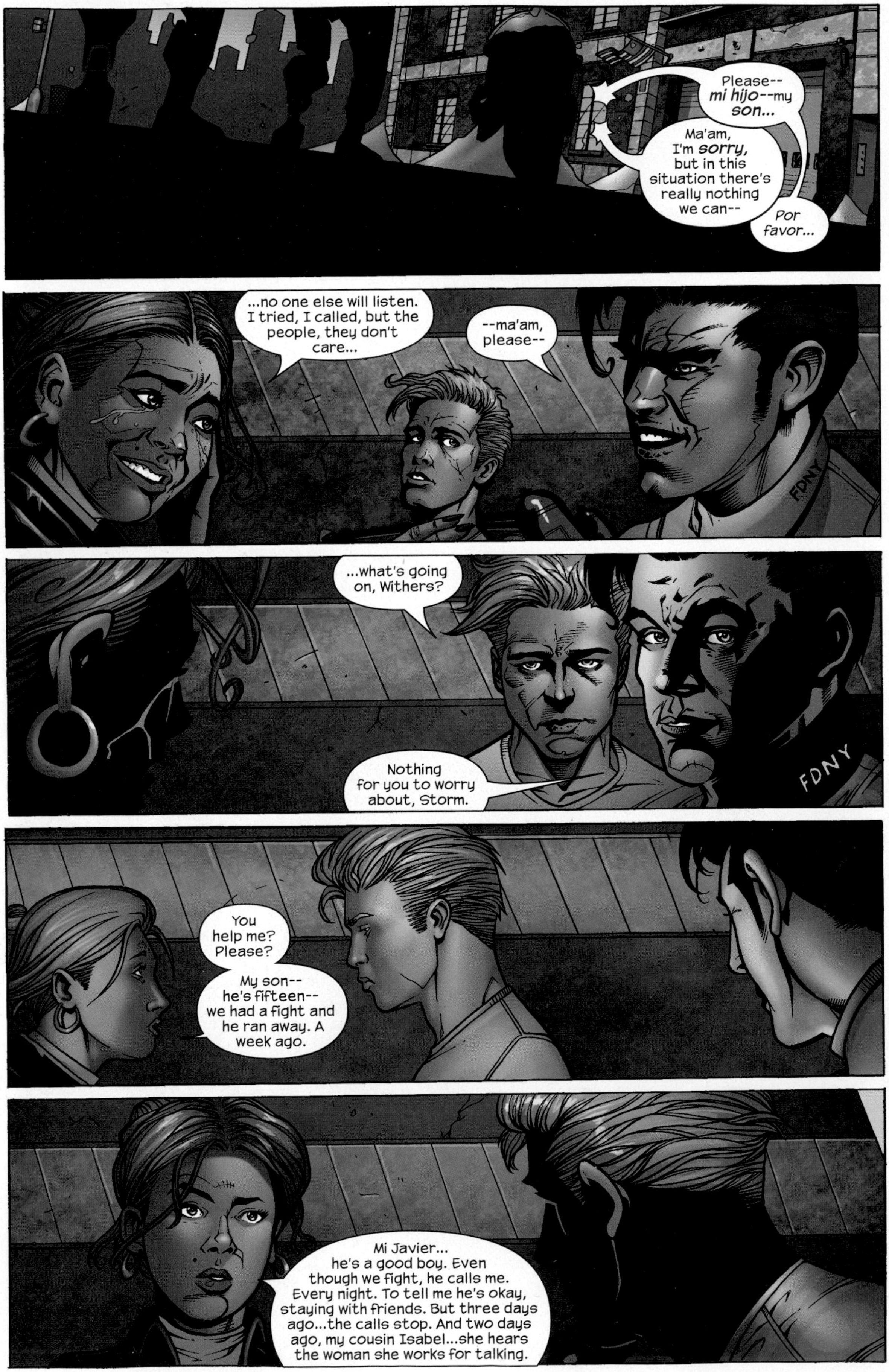
Please-- *mi hijo*--my *son...*
Ma'am, I'm *sorry,* but in this situation there's really nothing we can--
Por favor...
...no one else will listen. I tried, I called, but the people, they don't care...
--ma'am, please--
...what's going on, Withers?
Nothing for you to worry about, Storm.
FDNY
You help me? Please?
My son-- he's fifteen-- we had a fight and he ran away. A week ago.
Mi Javier... he's a good boy. Even though we fight, he calls me. Every night. To tell me he's okay, staying with friends. But three days ago...the calls stop. And two days ago, my cousin Isabel...she hears the woman she works for talking.

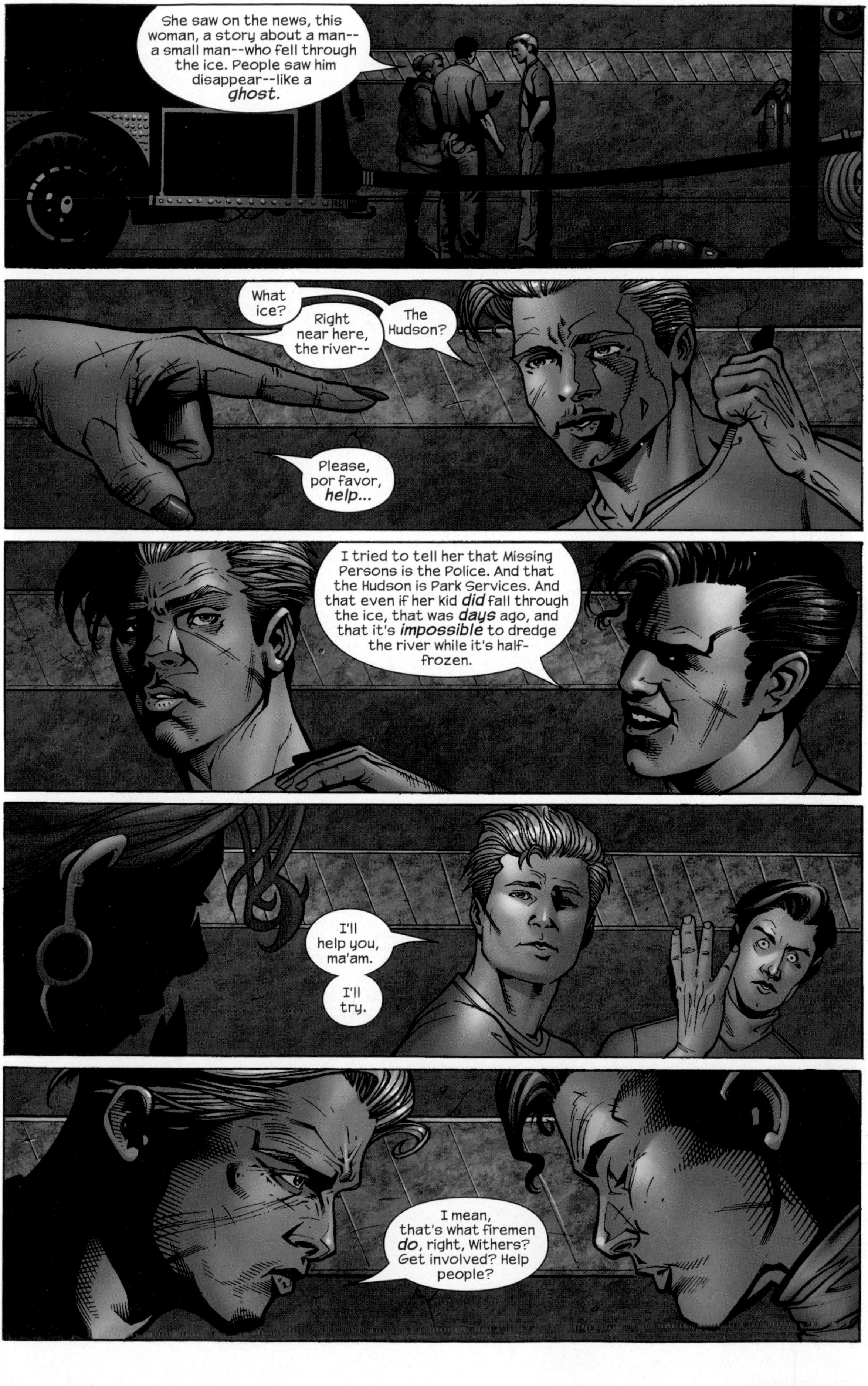
She saw on the news, this woman, a story about a man-- a small man--who fell through the ice. People saw him disappear--like a ghost.
What ice?
Right near here, the river--
The Hudson?
Please, por favor, help...
I tried to tell her that Missing Persons is the Police. And that the Hudson is Park Services. And that even if her kid did fall through the ice, that was days ago, and that it's impossible to dredge the river while it's half-frozen.
I'll help you, ma'am.
I'll try.
I mean, that's what firemen do, right, Withers? Get involved? Help people?

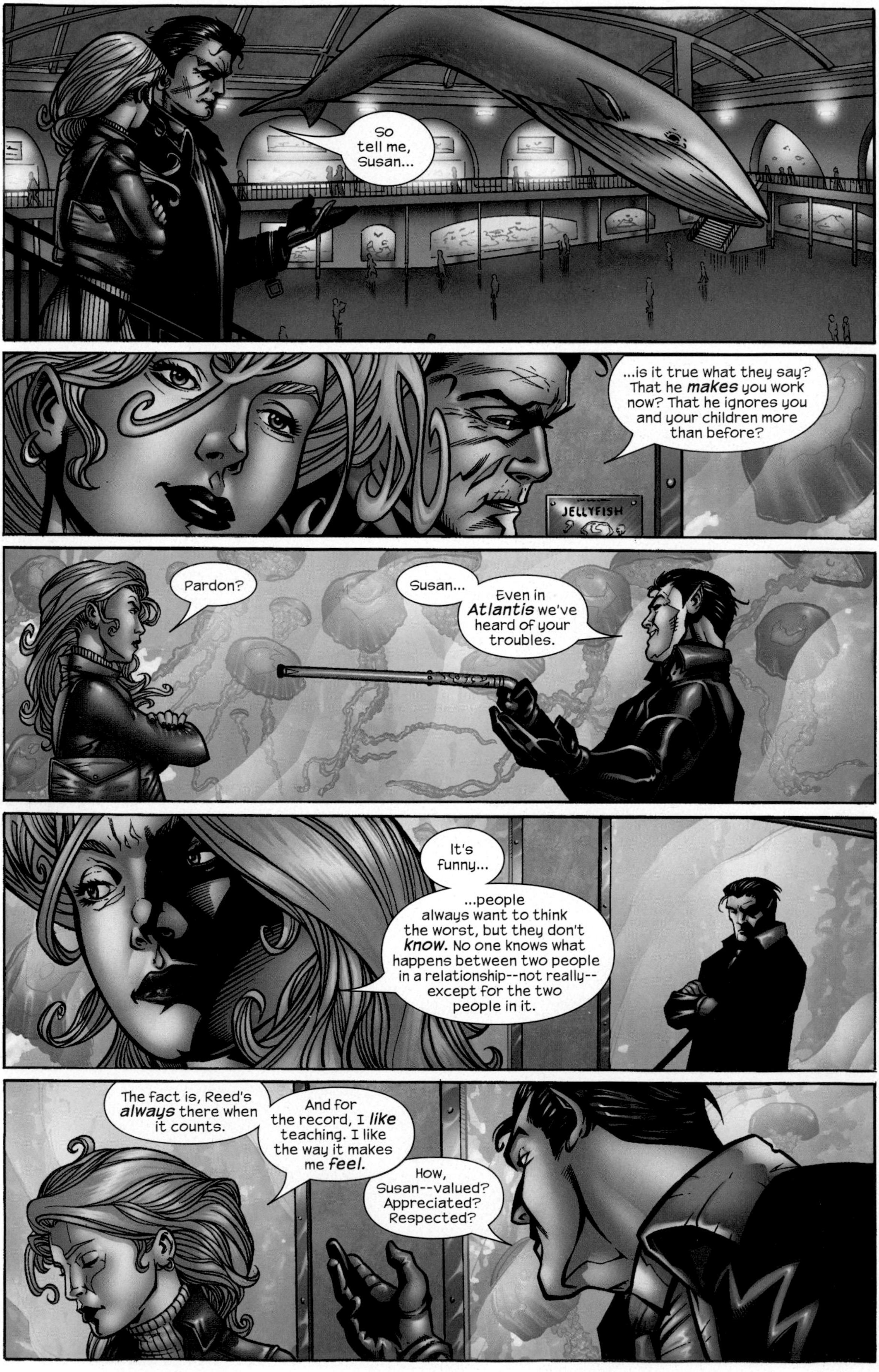
So tell me, Susan...
...is it true what they say? That he *makes* you work now? That he ignores you and your children more than before?
JELLYFISH
Pardon?
Susan...
Even in *Atlantis* we've heard of your troubles.
It's funny...
...people always want to think the worst, but they don't *know.* No one knows what happens between two people in a relationship--not really--except for the two people in it.
The fact is, Reed's *always* there when it counts.
And for the record, I *like* teaching. I like the way it makes me *feel.*
How, Susan--valued? Appreciated? Respected?

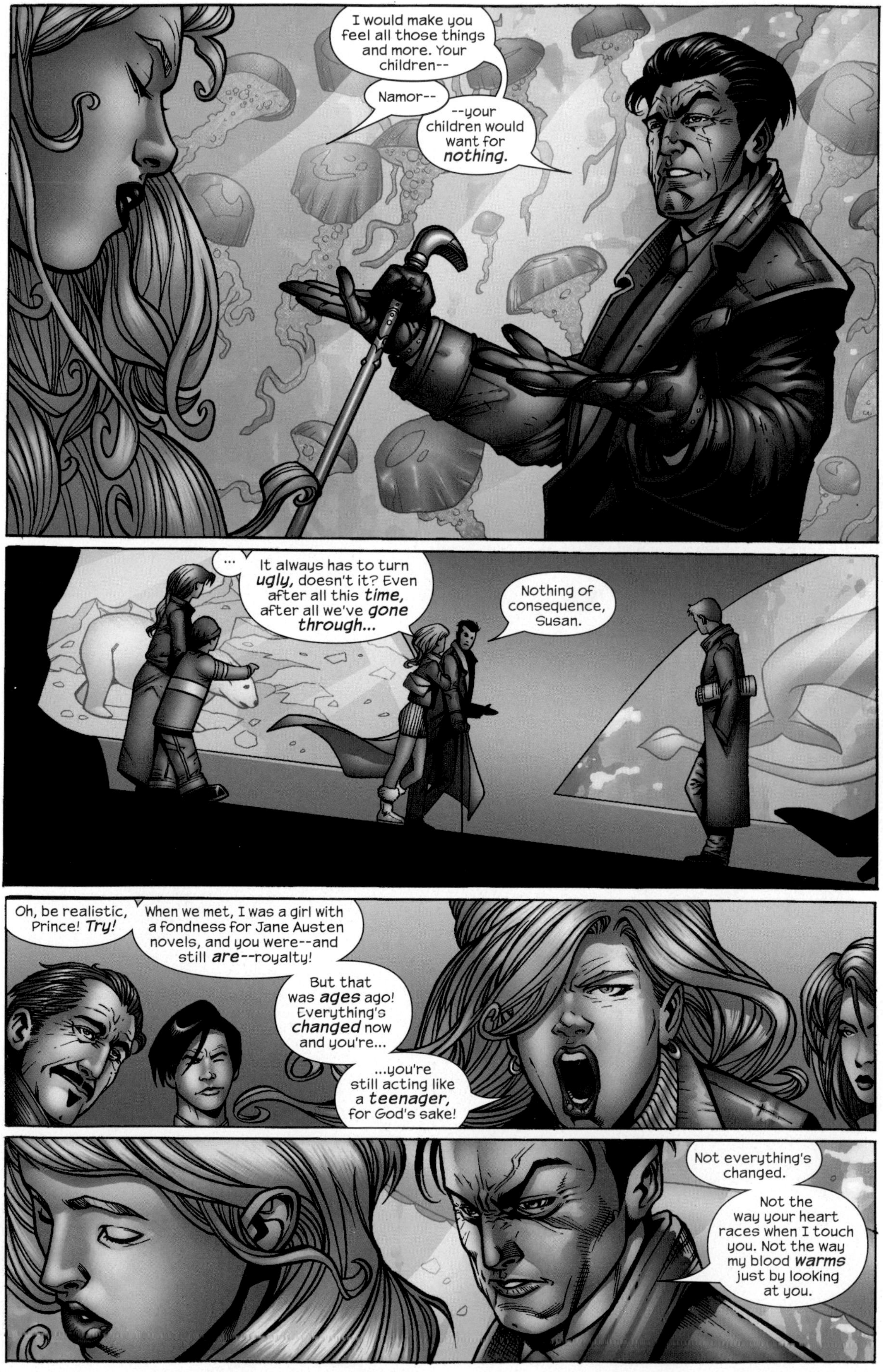

I would make you feel all those things and more. Your children--
Namor--
--your children would want for *nothing.*
...
It always has to turn *ugly,* doesn't it? Even after all this *time,* after all we've *gone through...*
Nothing of consequence, Susan.
Oh, be realistic, Prince! *Try!*
When we met, I was a girl with a fondness for Jane Austen novels, and you were--and still *are*--royalty!
But that was *ages* ago! Everything's *changed* now and you're...
...you're still acting like a *teenager,* for God's sake!
Not everything's changed.
Not the way your heart races when I touch you. Not the way my blood *warms* just by looking at you.

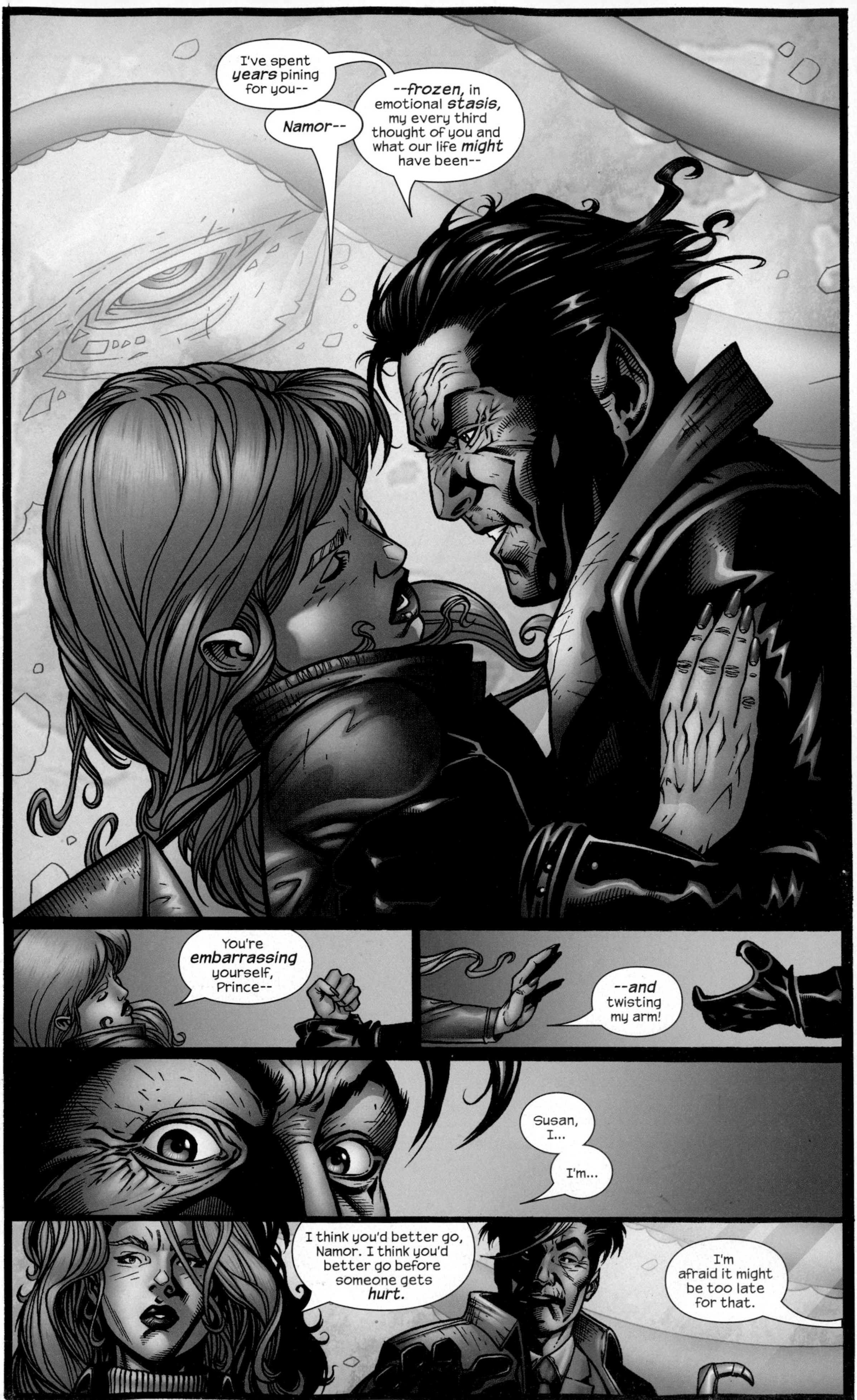
I've spent *years* pining for you--
Namor--
--frozen, in emotional *stasis,* my every third thought of you and what our life *might* have been--
You're *embarrassing* yourself, Prince--
--and twisting my arm!
Susan, I...
I'm...
I think you'd better go, Namor. I think you'd better go before someone gets *hurt.*
I'm afraid it might be too late for that.

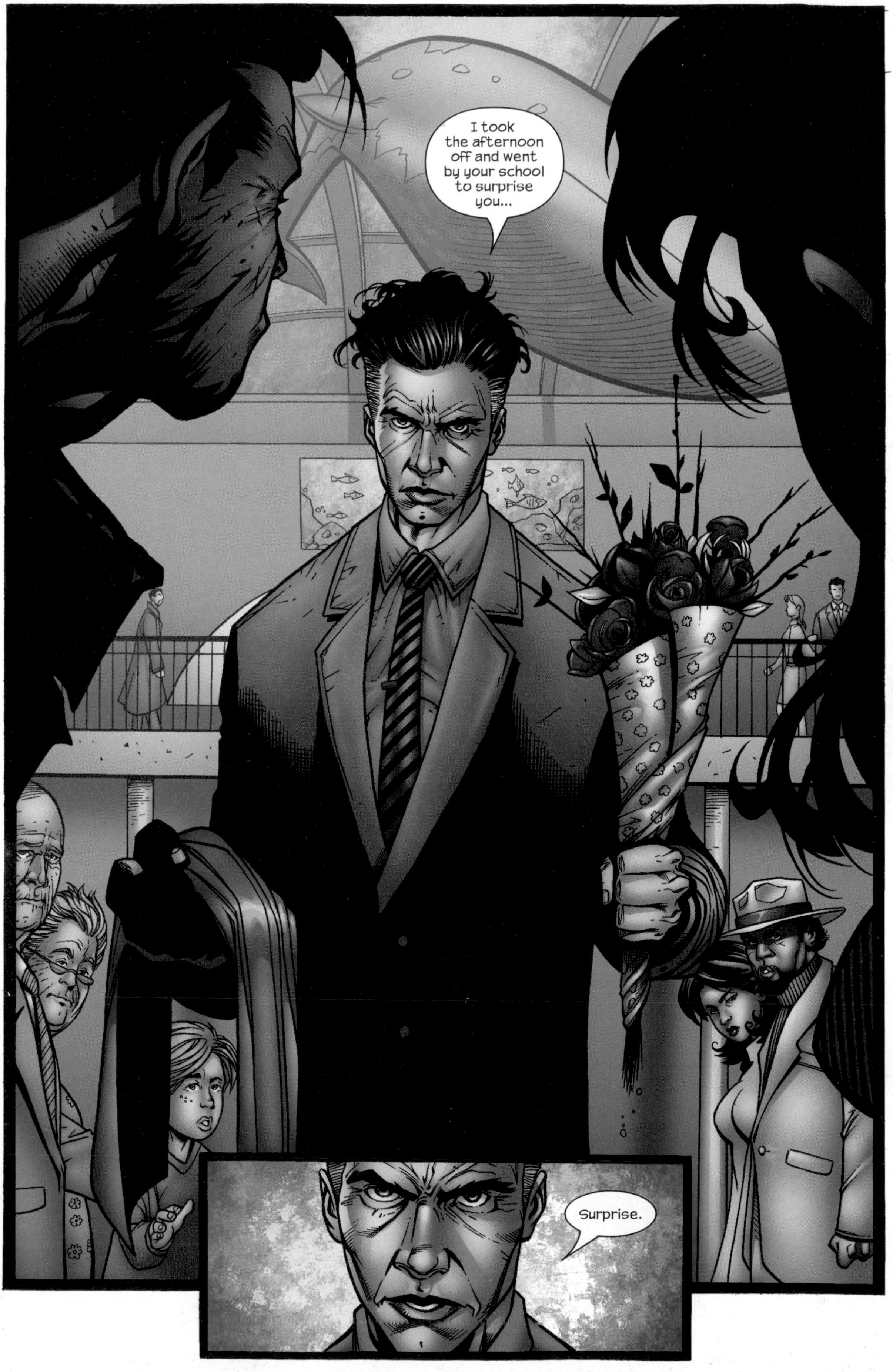
I took the afternoon off and went by your school to surprise you...
Surprise.

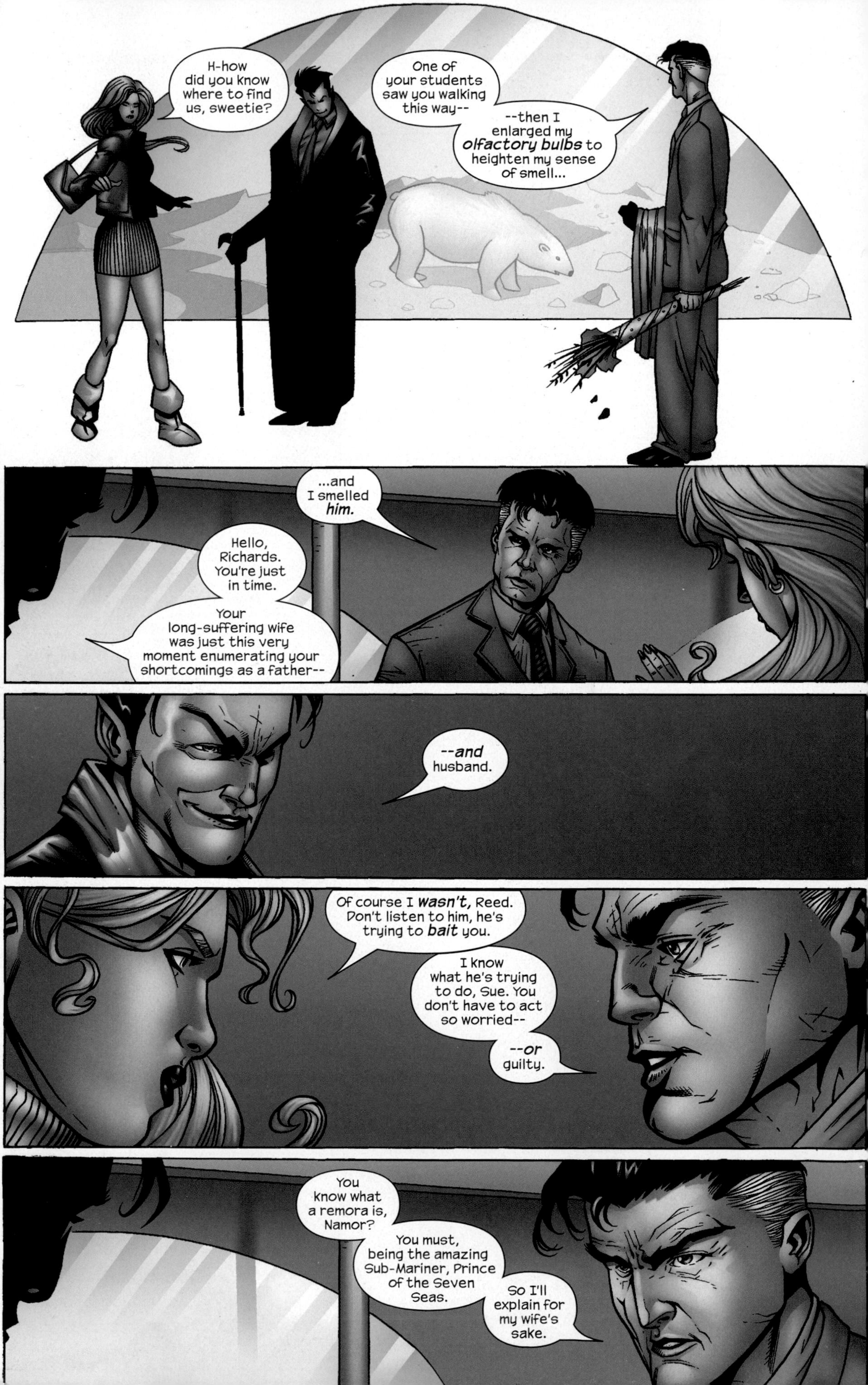
H-how did you know where to find us, sweetie?
One of your students saw you walking this way--
--then I enlarged my olfactory bulbs to heighten my sense of smell...
...and I smelled him.
Hello, Richards. You're just in time.
Your long-suffering wife was just this very moment enumerating your shortcomings as a father--
--and husband.
Of course I wasn't, Reed. Don't listen to him, he's trying to bait you.
I know what he's trying to do, Sue. You don't have to act so worried--
--or guilty.
You know what a remora is, Namor?
You must, being the amazing Sub-Mariner, Prince of the Seven Seas.
So I'll explain for my wife's sake.

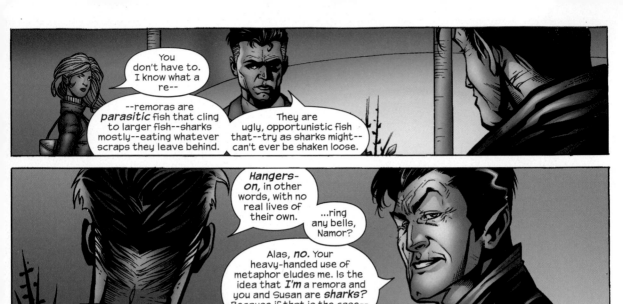

You don't have to. I know what a re--

--remoras are *parasitic* fish that cling to larger fish--sharks mostly--eating whatever scraps they leave behind.

They are ugly, opportunistic fish that--try as sharks might--can't ever be shaken loose.

Hangers-*on*, in other words, with no real lives of their own.

...ring any bells, Namor?

Alas, *no.* Your heavy-handed use of metaphor eludes me. Is the idea that *I'm* a remora and you and Susan are *sharks*? Because if that is the case--

Please, Reed...

Oh, yes? From what?

To tell you the truth, more than anything, the idea is--*was*--to distract you.

From the fact that I've redistributed 70% of my body's density into my right fist.

...you have nothing to prove.

Listen to her, Richards. You truly *don't* want me humiliating you in front of your *female.*

"Female"...?

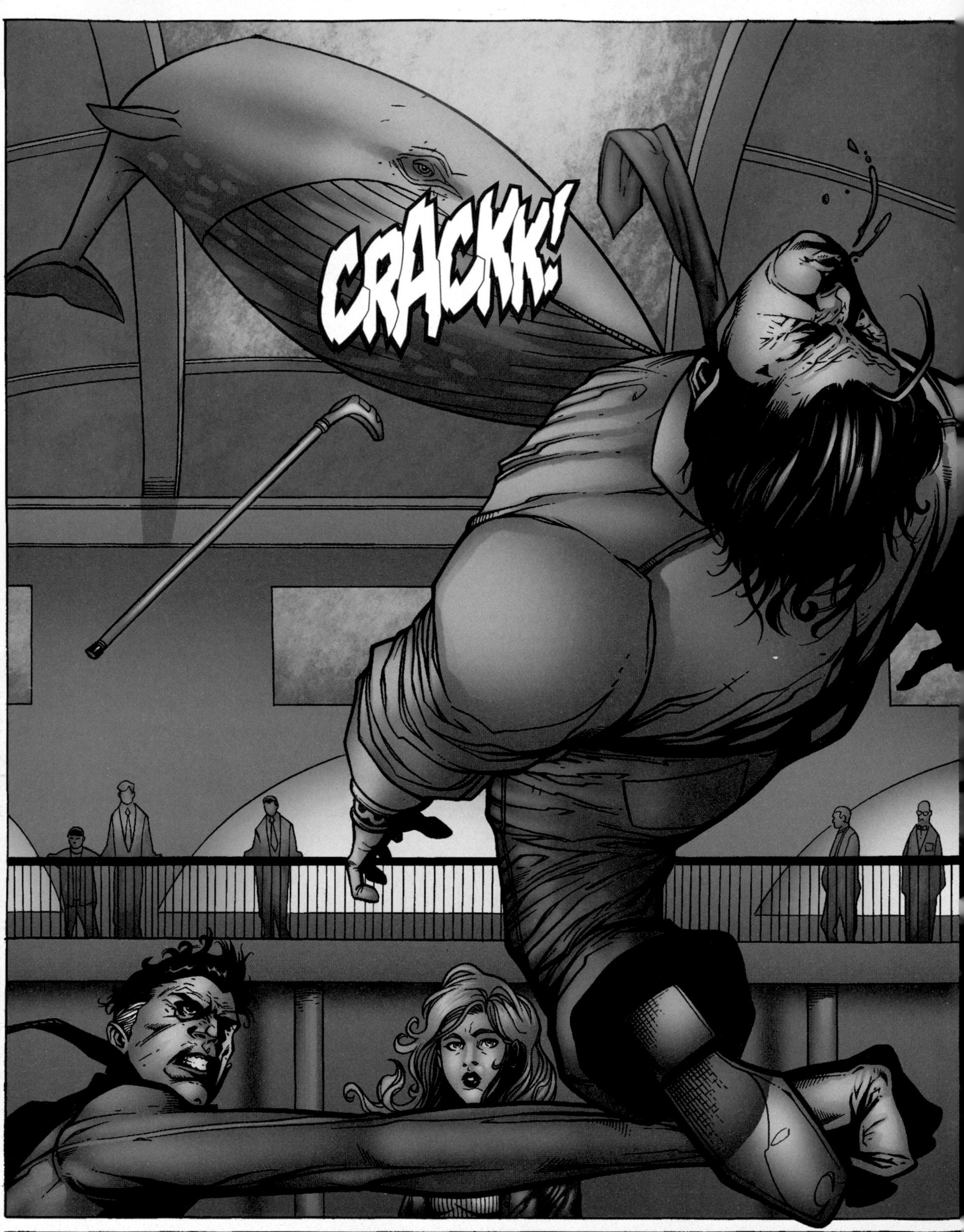
CRACKK!
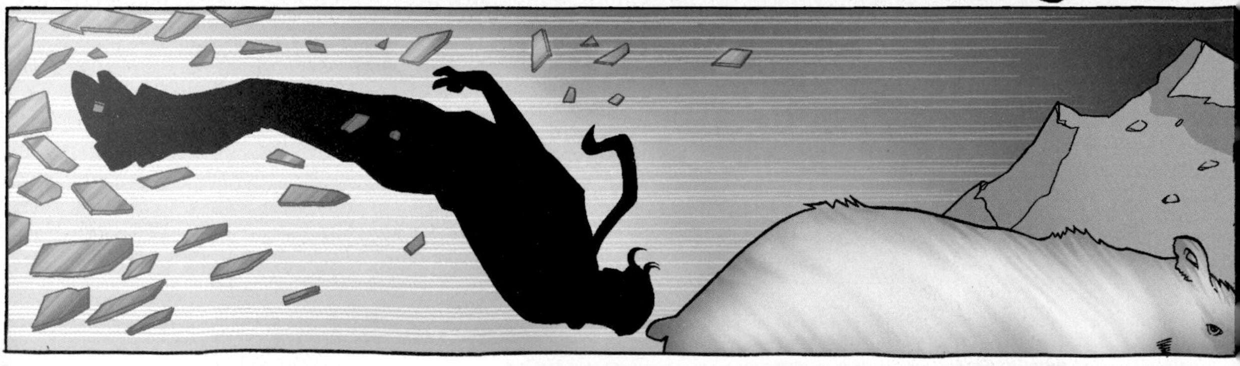

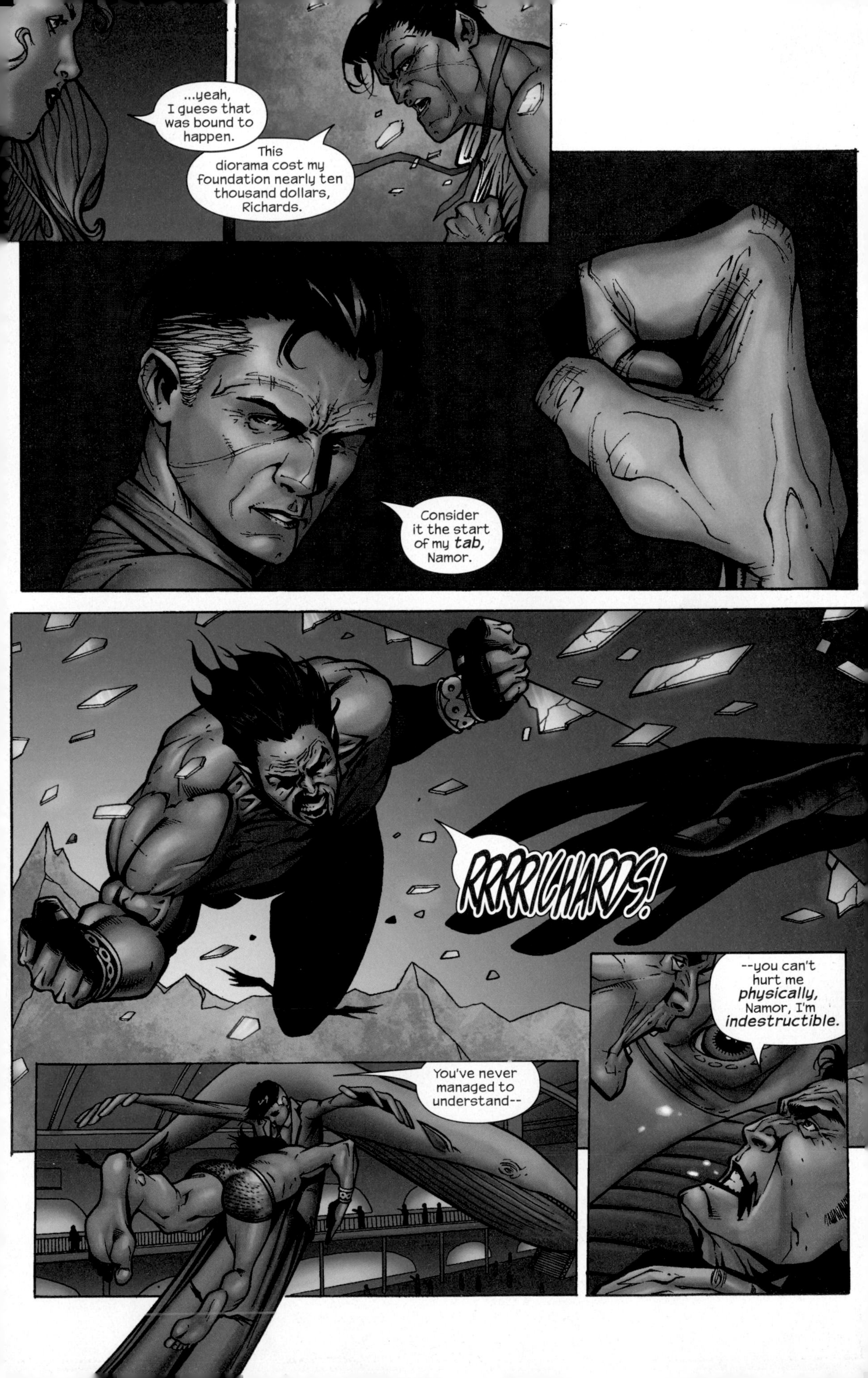

...yeah, I guess that was bound to happen.
This diorama cost my foundation nearly ten thousand dollars, Richards.
Consider it the start of my tab, Namor.
RRRRICHARDS!
You've never managed to understand--
--you can't hurt me physically, Namor, I'm indestructible.

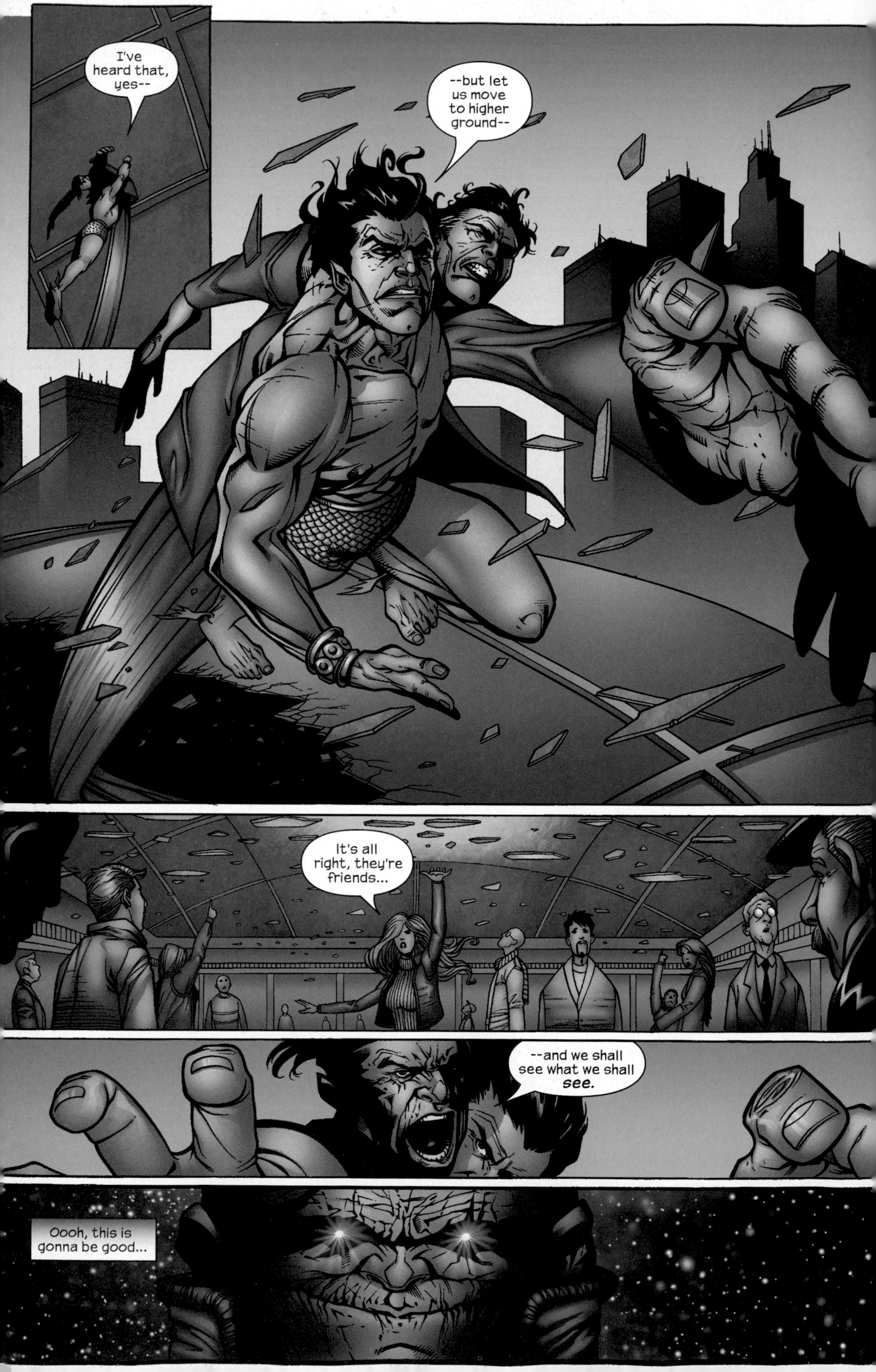
I've heard that, yes--
--but let us move to higher ground--
It's all right, they're friends...
--and we shall see what we shall *see.*
Oooh, this is gonna be good...

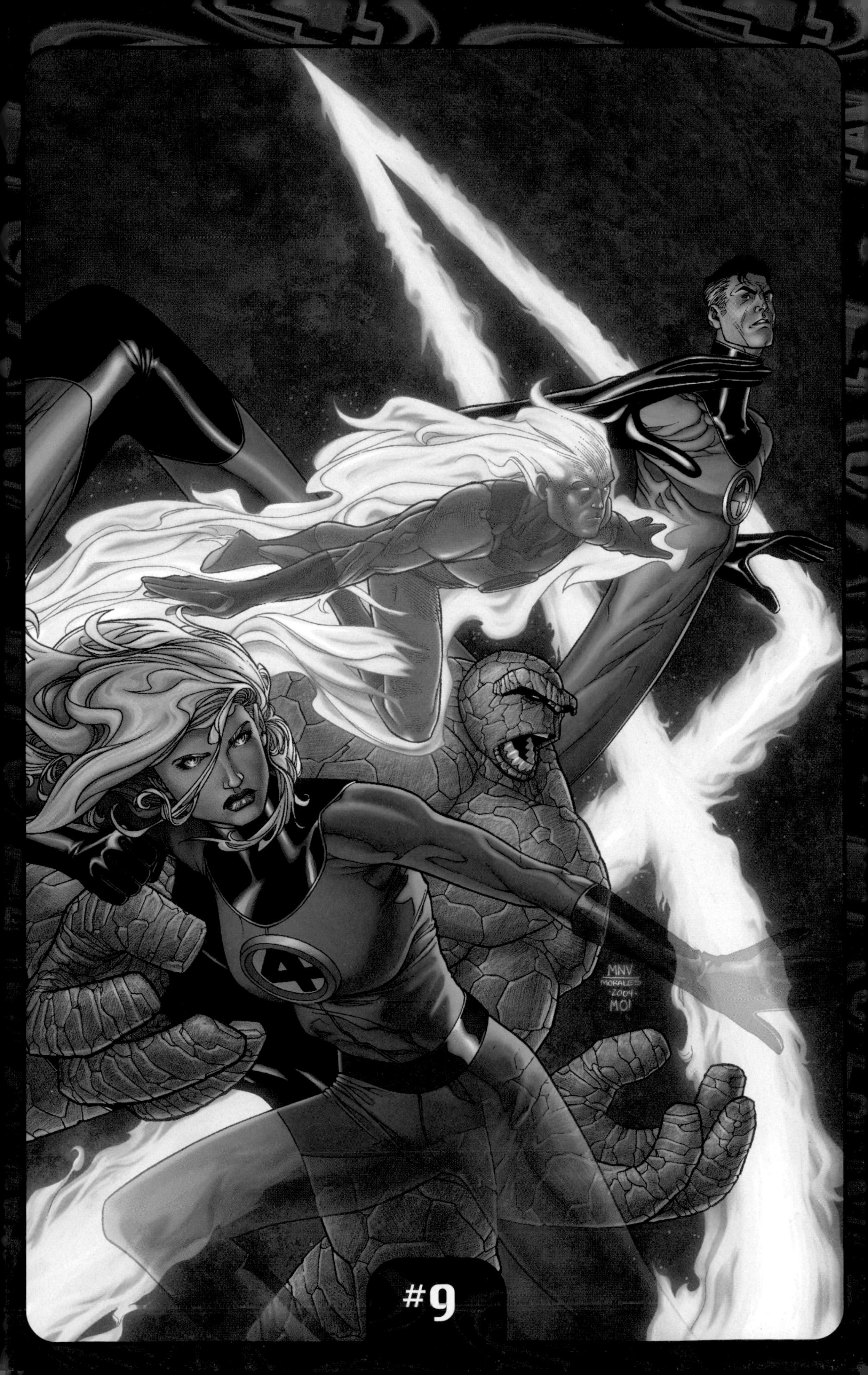
MNV
MORALES
2004
MO!
#9

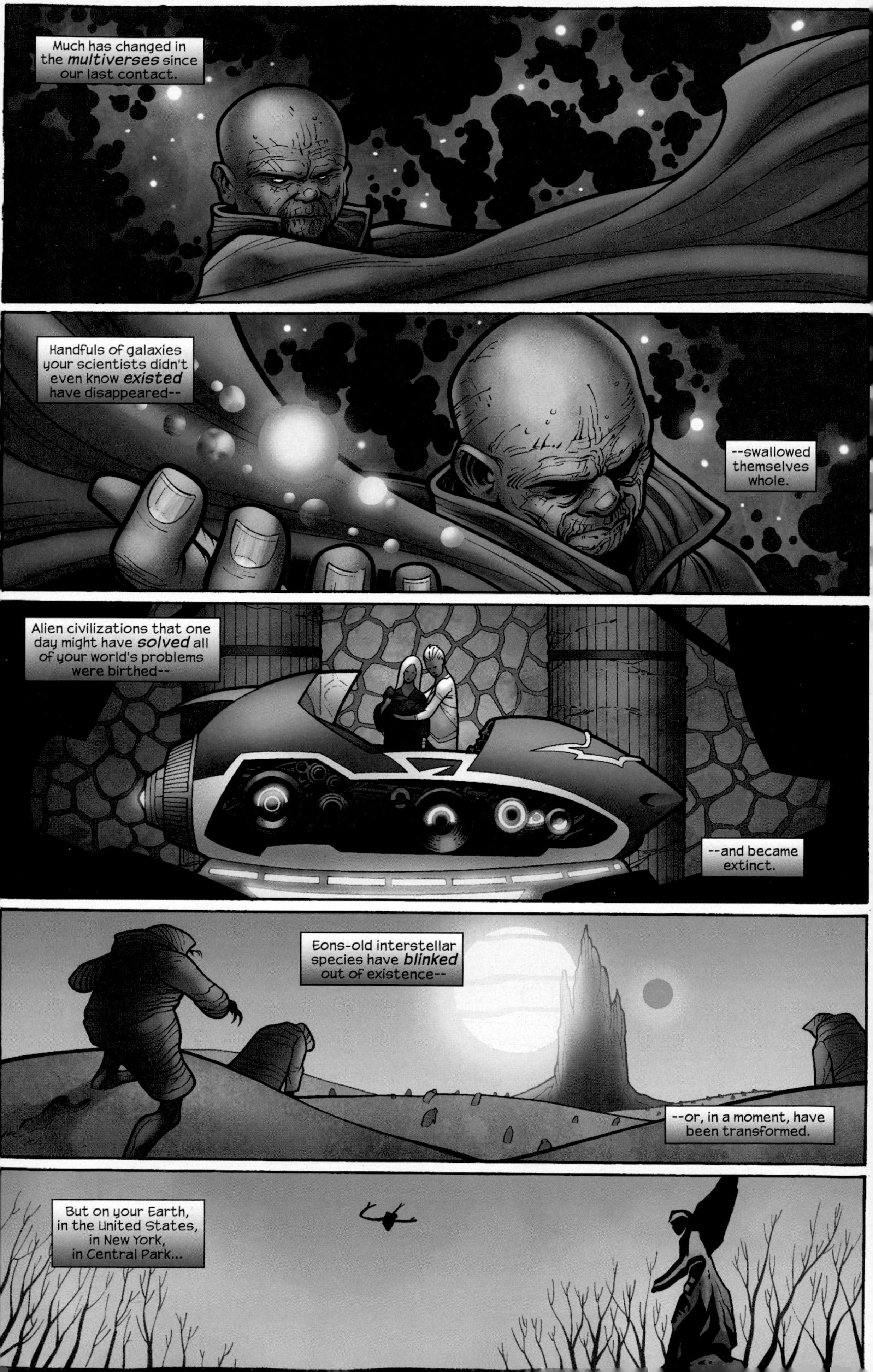
Much has changed in the *multiverses* since our last contact.
Handfuls of galaxies your scientists didn't even know *existed* have disappeared--
--swallowed themselves whole.
Alien civilizations that one day might have *solved* all of your world's problems were birthed--
--and became extinct.
Eons-old interstellar species have *blinked* out of existence--
--or, in a moment, have been transformed.
But on your Earth, in the United States, in New York, in Central Park...

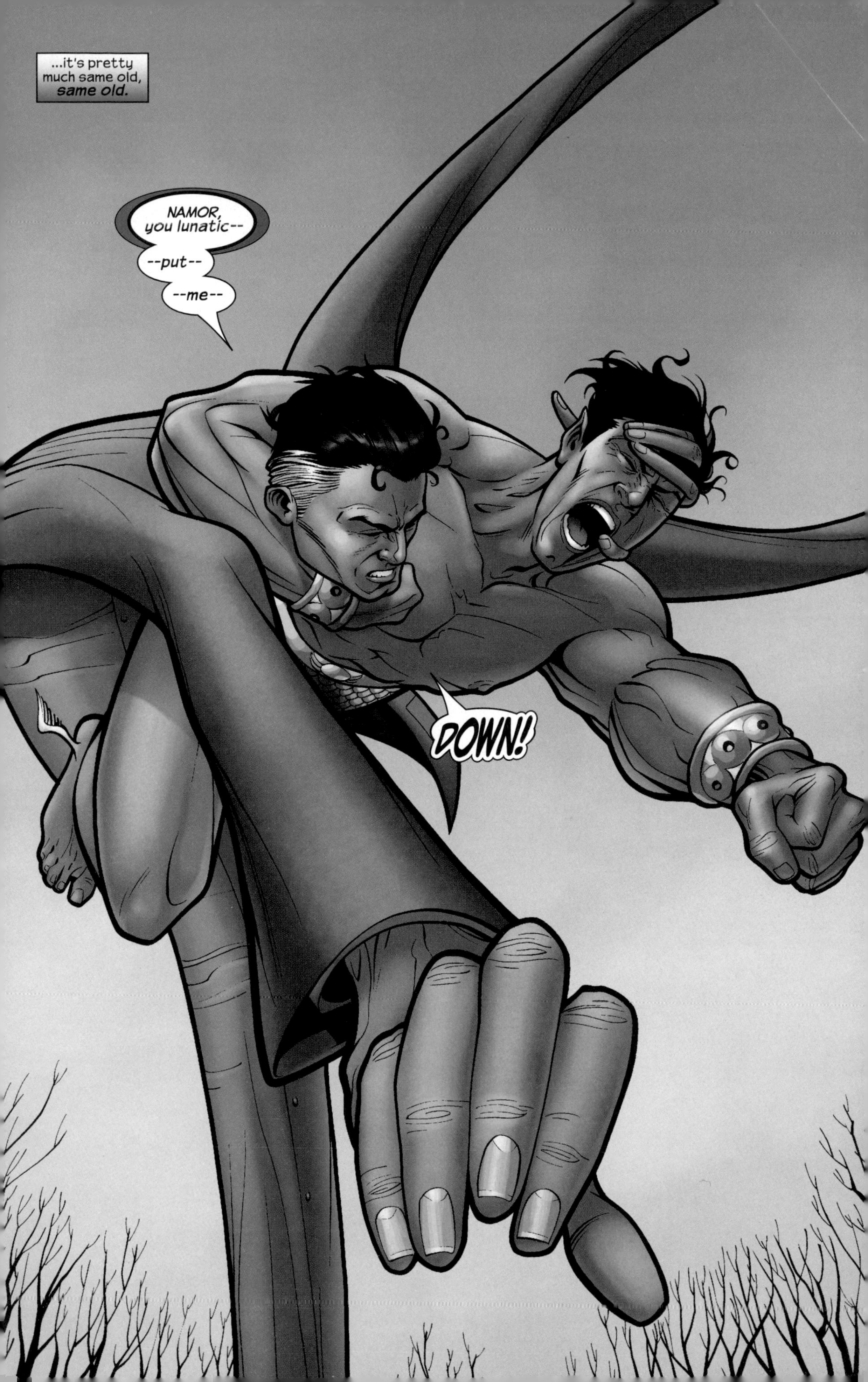
...it's pretty much same old, *same old.*
NAMOR, you lunatic--
--put--
--me--
DOWN!

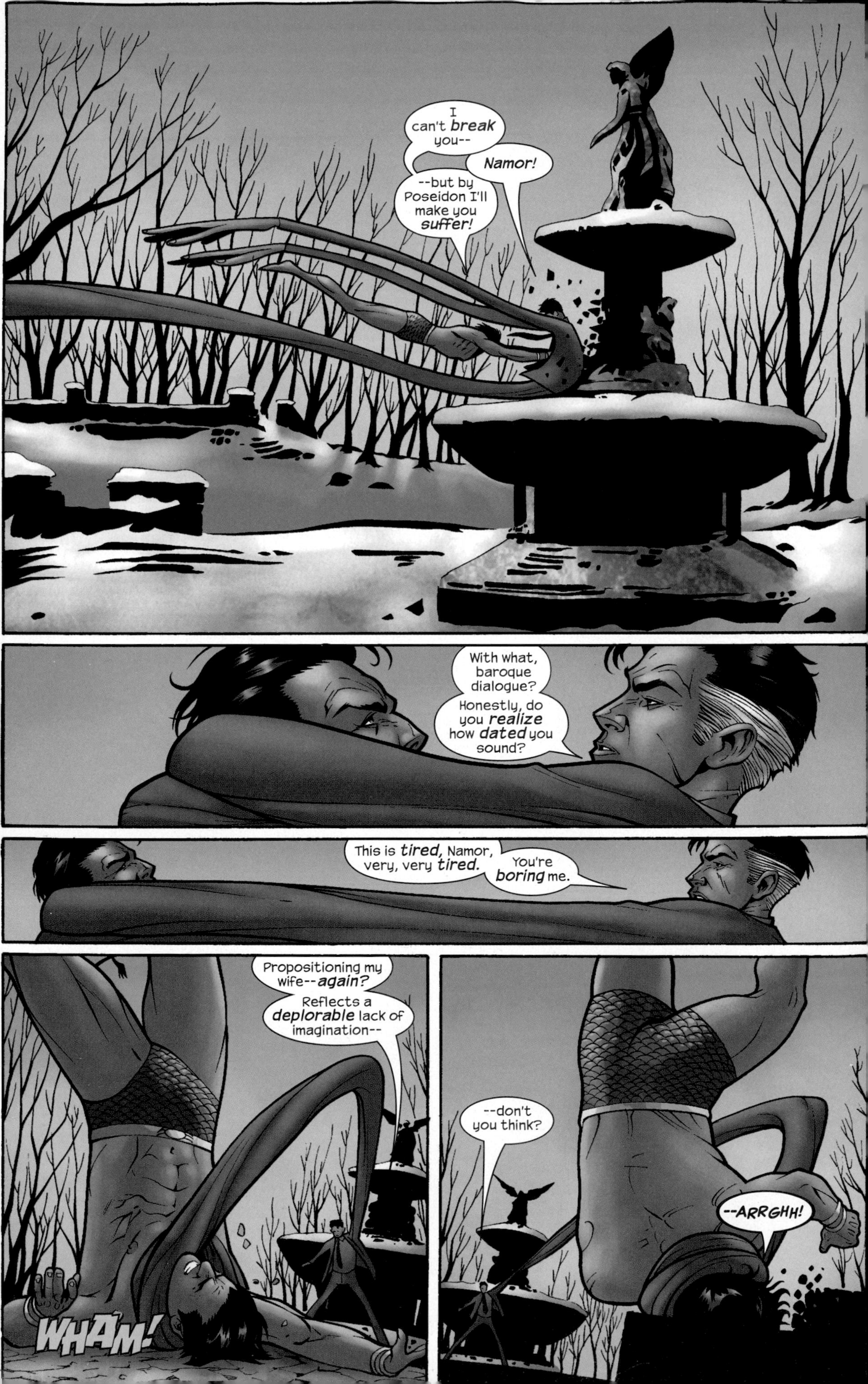
I can't break you--
Namor!
--but by Poseidon I'll make you suffer!
With what, baroque dialogue?
Honestly, do you realize how dated you sound?
This is tired, Namor, very, very tired.
You're boring me.
Propositioning my wife--again?
Reflects a deplorable lack of imagination--
WHAM!
--don't you think?
--ARRGHH!

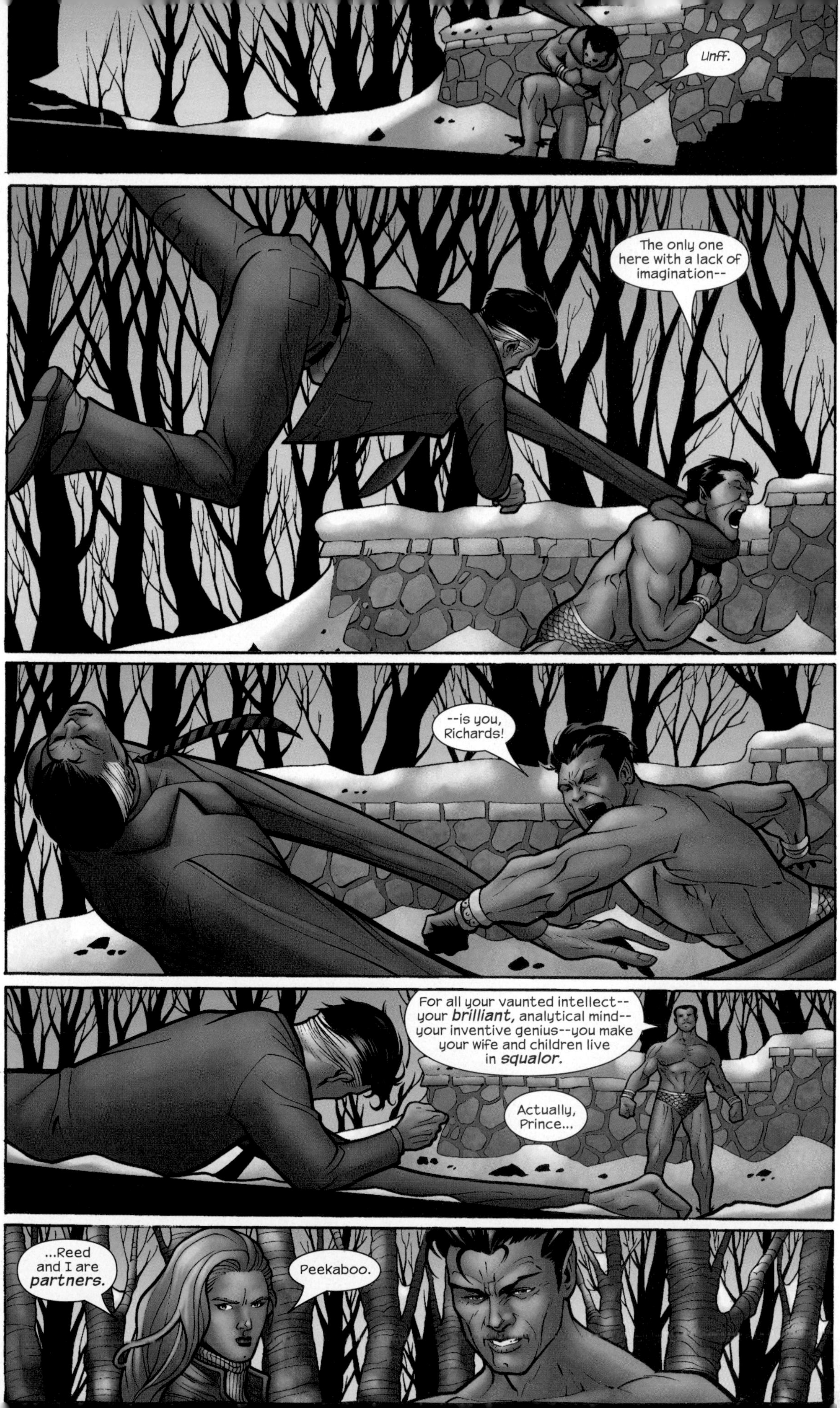
Unff.
The only one here with a lack of imagination--
--is you, Richards!
For all your vaunted intellect-- your brilliant, analytical mind-- your inventive genius--you make your wife and children live in squalor.
Actually, Prince...
...Reed and I are partners.
Peekaboo.

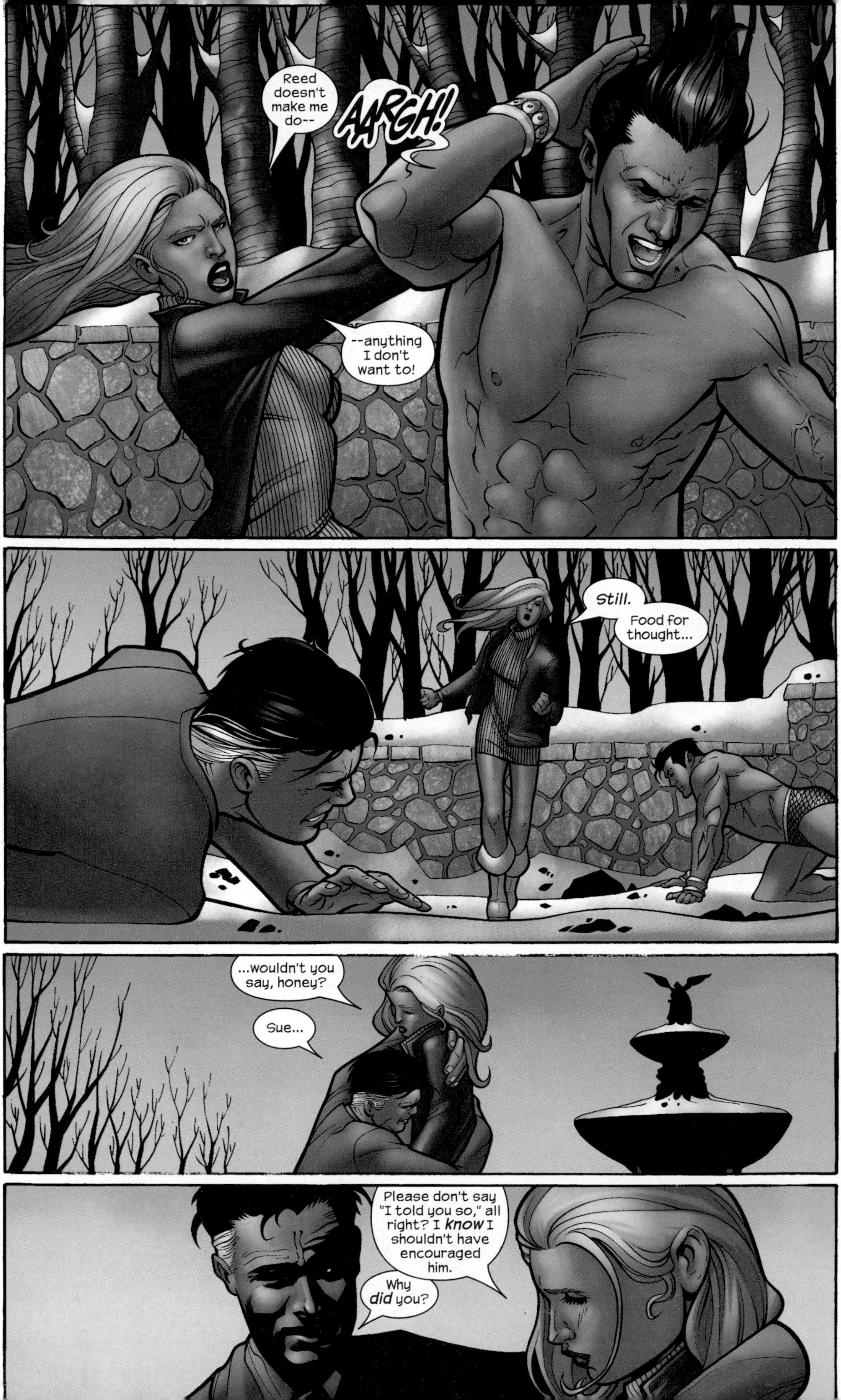

Reed doesn't make me do--
AARGH!
--anything I don't want to!
Still.
Food for thought...
...wouldn't you say, honey?
Sue...
Please don't say "I told you so," all right? I *know* I shouldn't have encouraged him.
Why *did* you?

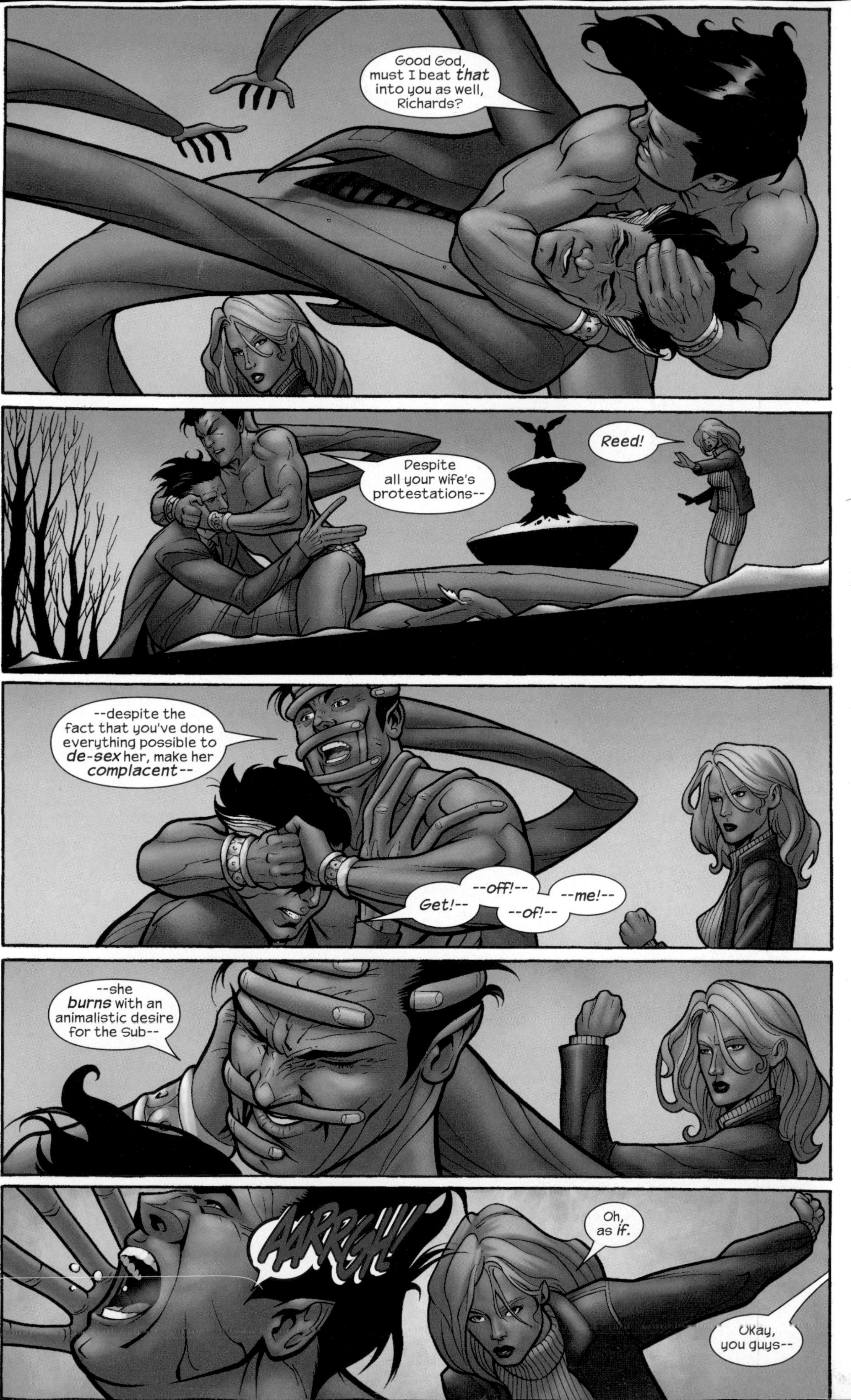
Good God, must I beat *that* into you as well, Richards?
Reed!
Despite all your wife's protestations--
--despite the fact that you've done everything possible to *de-sex* her, make her *complacent*--
Get!--
--off!--
--of!--
--me!--
--she *burns* with an animalistic desire for the Sub--
AARRGH!
Oh, as *if*.
Okay, you guys--

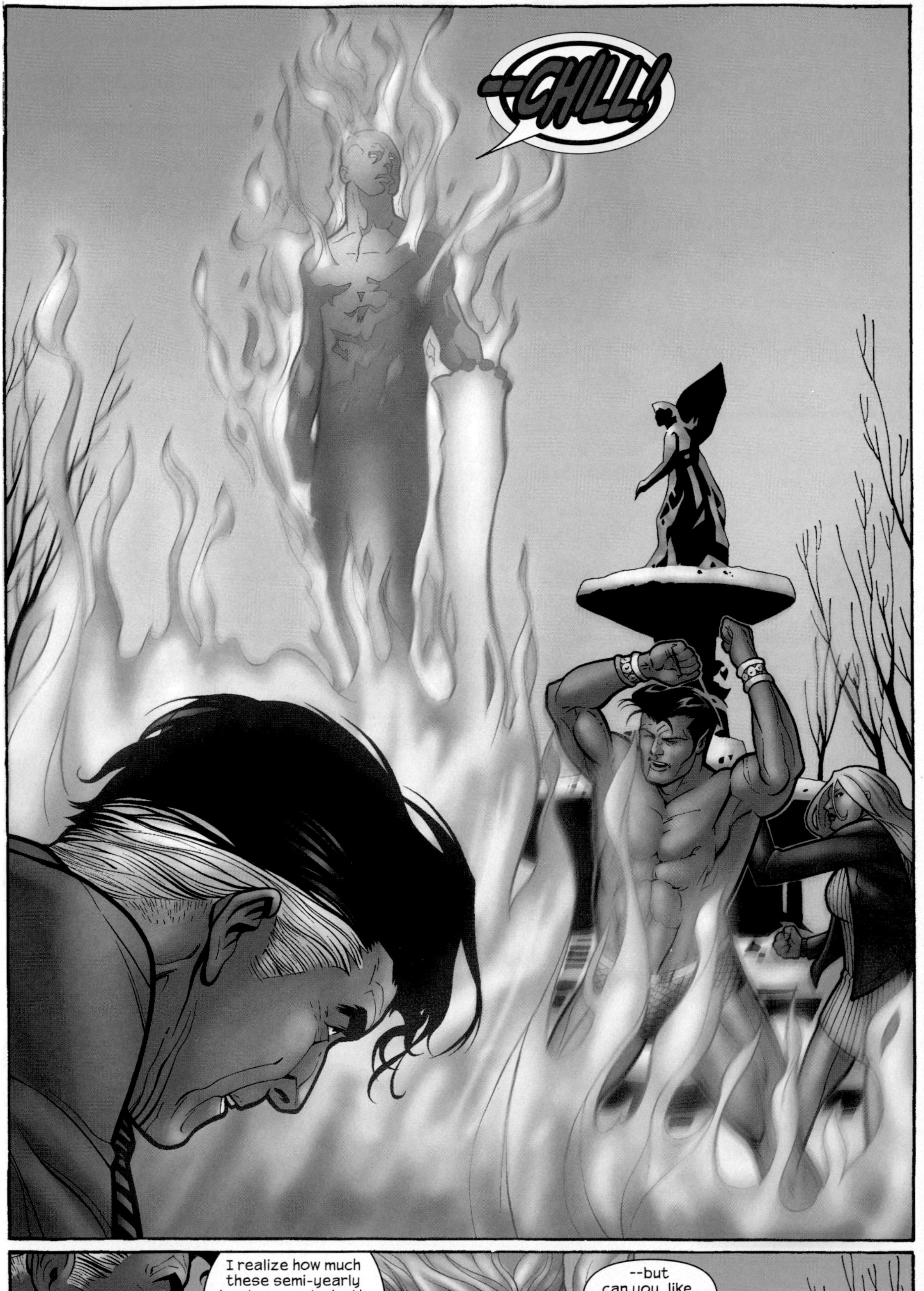
--CHILL!
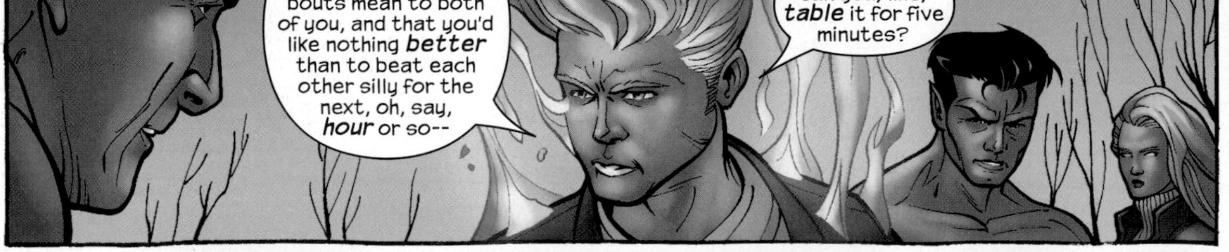
I realize how much these semi-yearly bouts mean to both of you, and that you'd like nothing **better** than to beat each other silly for the next, oh, say, **hour** or so--
--but can you, like, **table** it for five minutes?

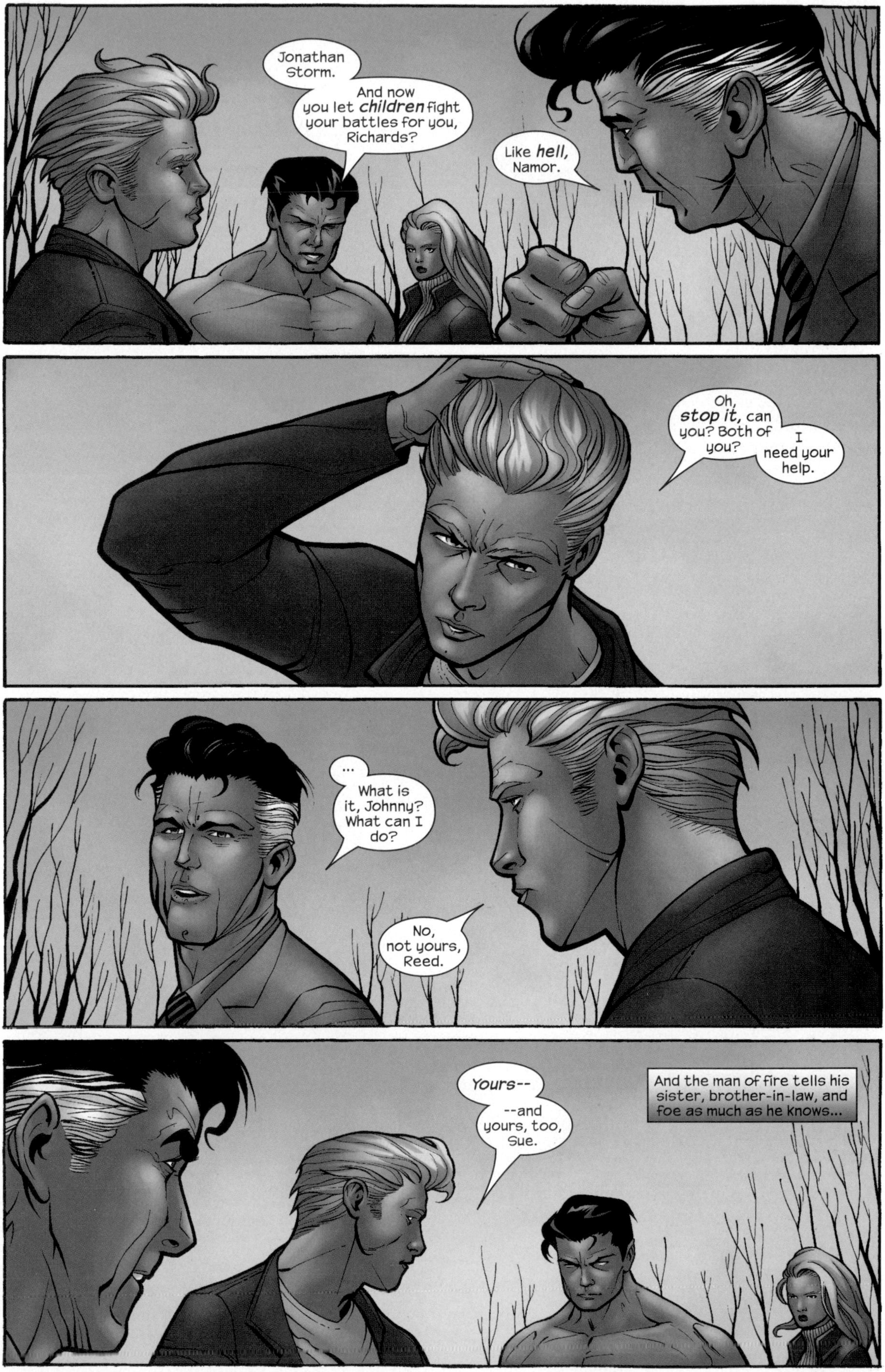
Jonathan Storm.
And now you let children fight your battles for you, Richards?
Like hell, Namor.
Oh, stop it, can you? Both of you?
I need your help.
...
What is it, Johnny? What can I do?
No, not yours, Reed.
Yours--
--and yours, too, Sue.
And the man of fire tells his sister, brother-in-law, and foe as much as he knows...

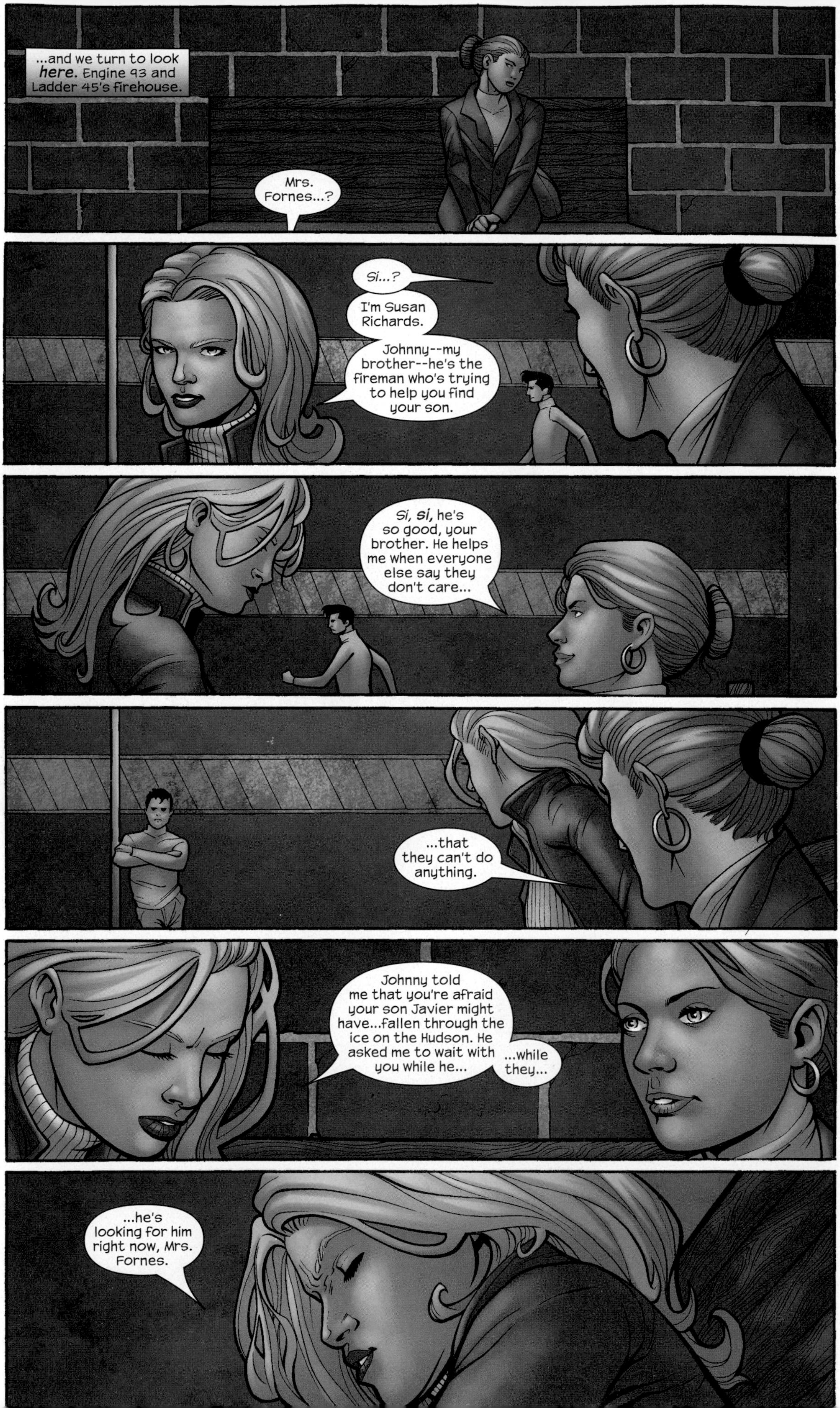
...and we turn to look *here*. Engine 93 and Ladder 45's firehouse.
Mrs. Fornes...?
Si...?
I'm Susan Richards.
Johnny--my brother--he's the fireman who's trying to help you find your son.
Si, **si**, he's so good, your brother. He helps me when everyone else say they don't care...
...that they can't do anything.
Johnny told me that you're afraid your son Javier might have...fallen through the ice on the Hudson. He asked me to wait with you while he...
...while they...
...he's looking for him right now, Mrs. Fornes.

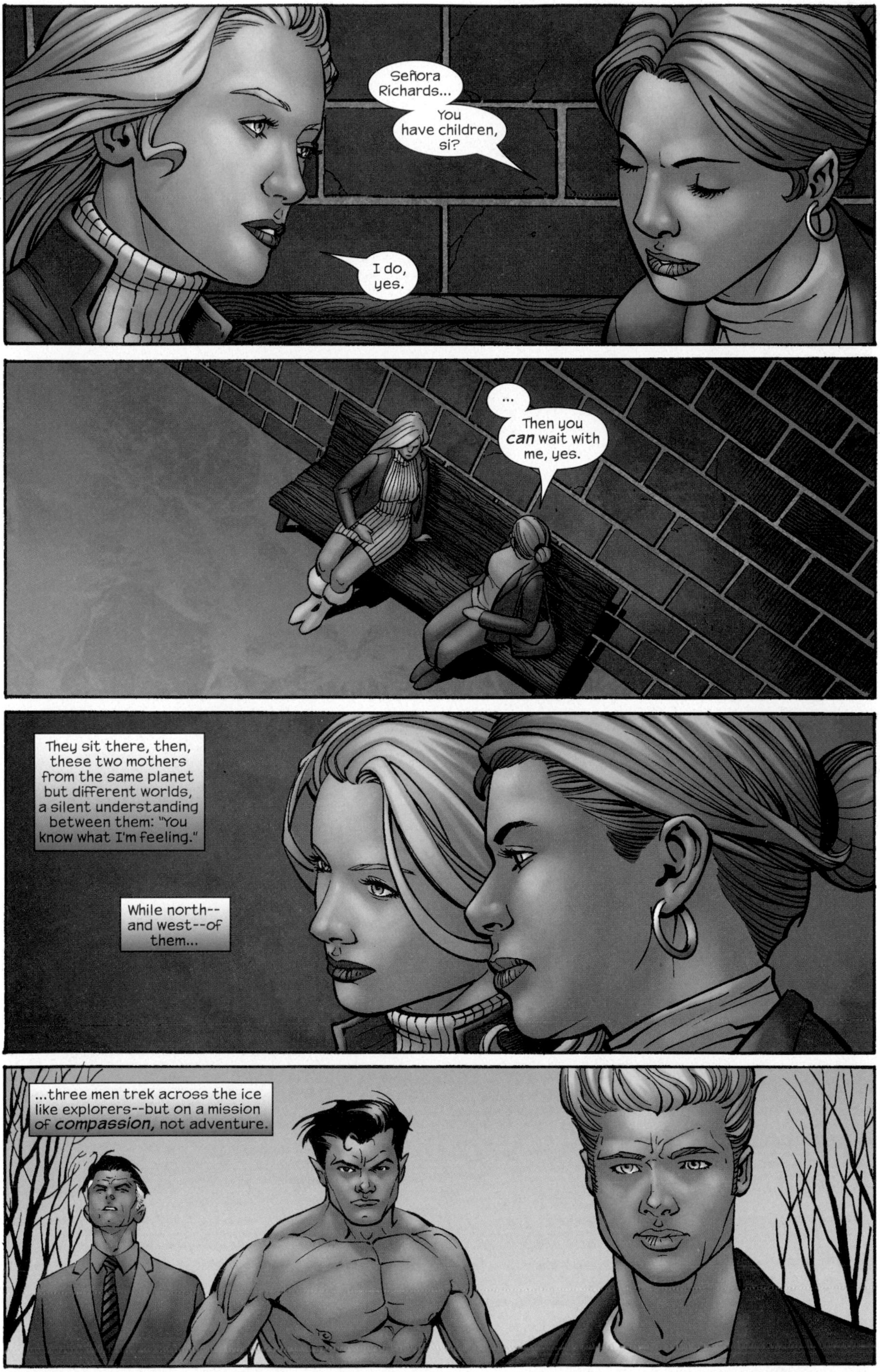
Señora Richards...
You have children, si?
I do, yes.
...
Then you *can* wait with me, yes.
They sit there, then, these two mothers from the same planet but different worlds, a silent understanding between them: "You know what I'm feeling."
While north-- and west--of them...
...three men trek across the ice like explorers--but on a mission of *compassion,* not adventure.

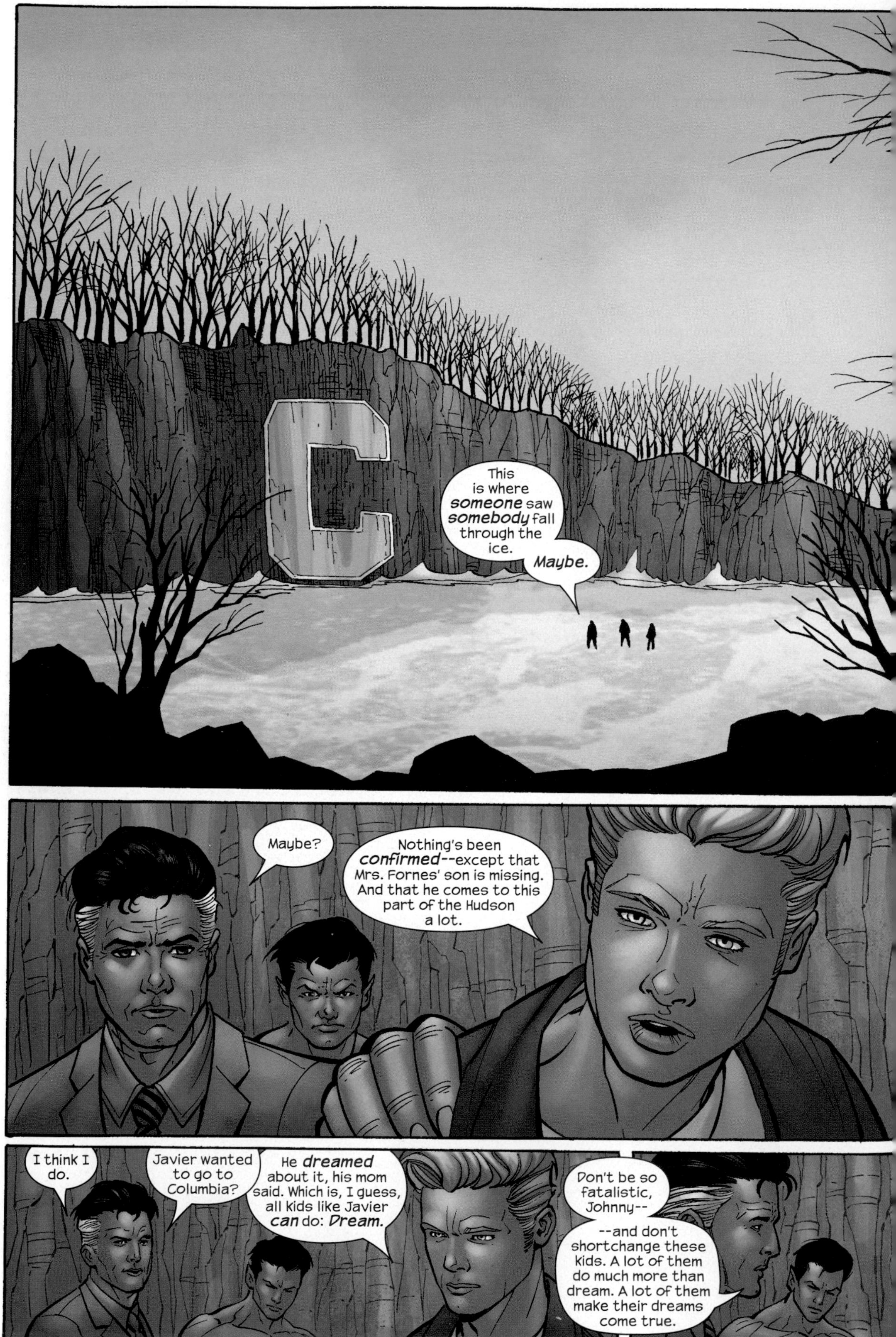

This is where *someone* saw *somebody* fall through the ice.
Maybe.
Maybe?
Nothing's been *confirmed*--except that Mrs. Fornes' son is missing. And that he comes to this part of the Hudson a lot.
I think I do.
Javier wanted to go to Columbia?
He *dreamed* about it, his mom said. Which is, I guess, all kids like Javier *can* do: *Dream.*
Don't be so fatalistic, Johnny--
--and don't shortchange these kids. A lot of them do much more than dream. A lot of them make their dreams come true.

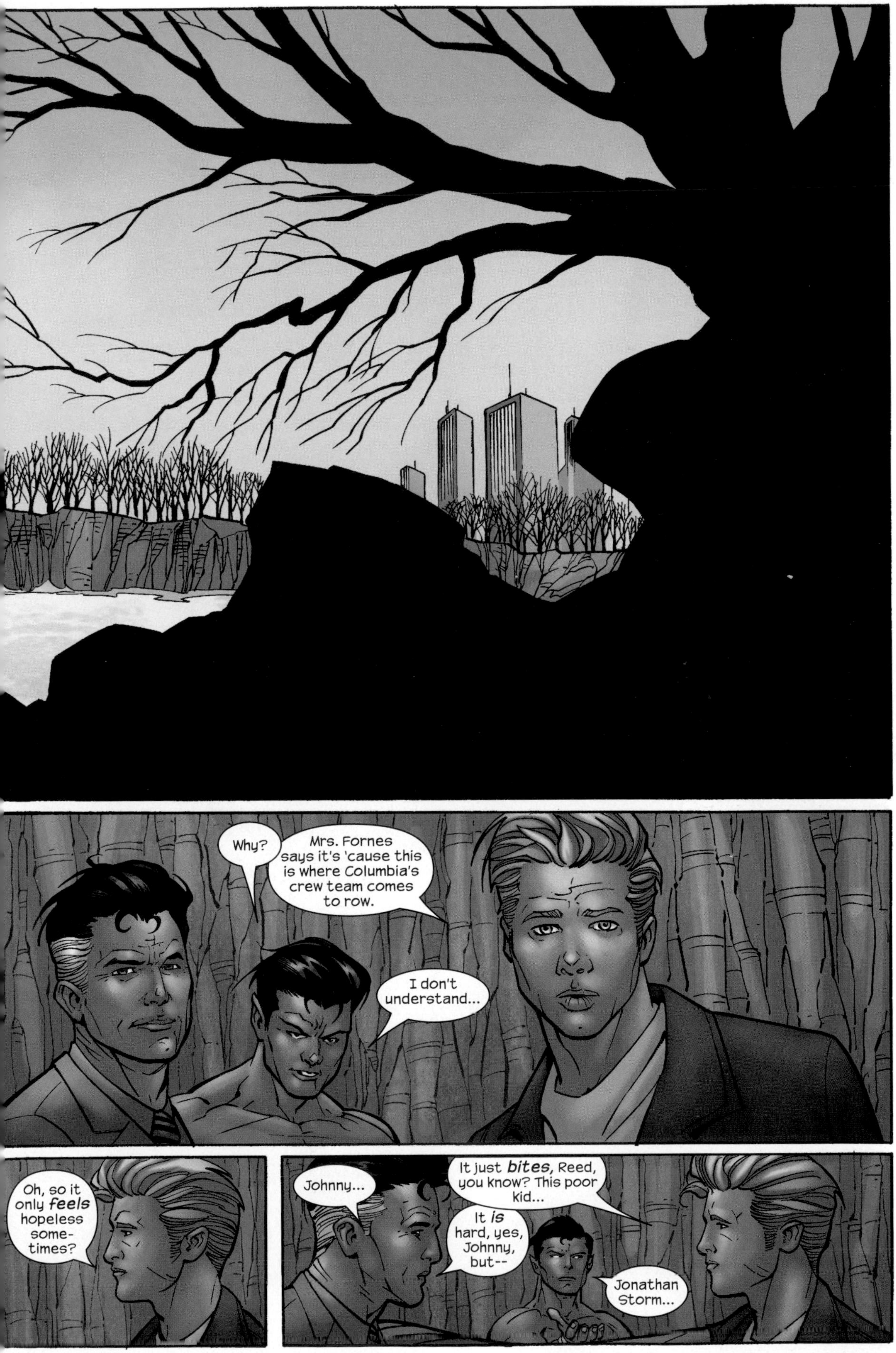
Why?
Mrs. Fornes says it's 'cause this is where Columbia's crew team comes to row.
I don't understand...
Oh, so it only *feels* hopeless some-times?
Johnny...
It just *bites*, Reed, you know? This poor kid...
It *is* hard, yes, Johnny, but--
Jonathan Storm...

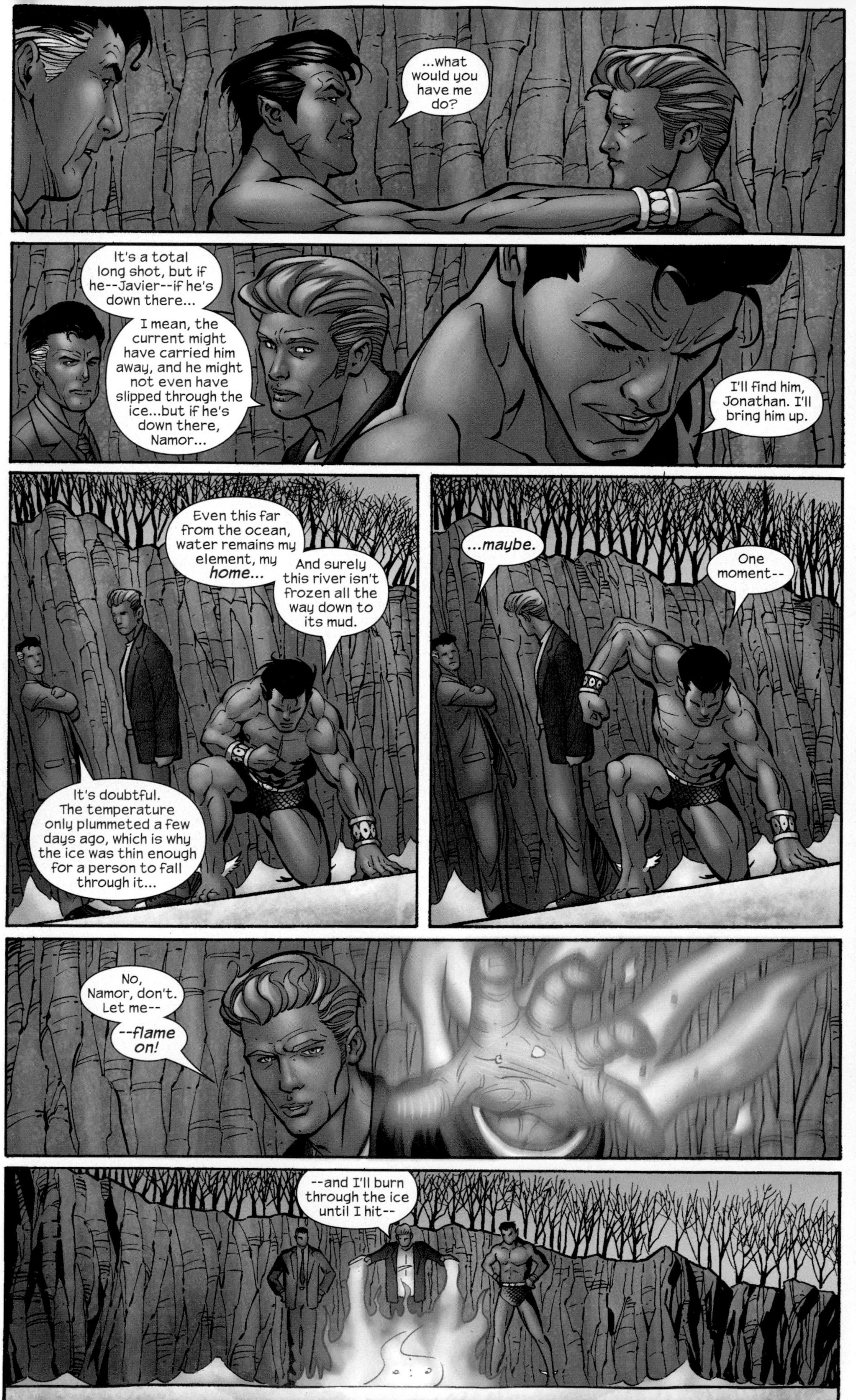
...what would you have me do?
It's a total long shot, but if he--Javier--if he's down there...
I mean, the current might have carried him away, and he might not even have slipped through the ice...but if he's down there, Namor...
I'll find him, Jonathan. I'll bring him up.
Even this far from the ocean, water remains my element, my *home*...
And surely this river isn't frozen all the way down to its mud.
It's doubtful. The temperature only plummeted a few days ago, which is why the ice was thin enough for a person to fall through it...
...*maybe.*
One moment--
No, Namor, don't. Let me--
--*flame on!*
--and I'll burn through the ice until I hit--

"--water."

What does the sea king feel--*experience*--as he plunges into the river's icy depths?

The sensation of slipping between cold sheets on the hottest summer night? Of putting on a second, *tighter* skin?

Those things, yes, but also...

...*relief.*

As though he'd slowly been going *mad* breathing air, and now the tempest in his mind-- and lungs--was quieted.

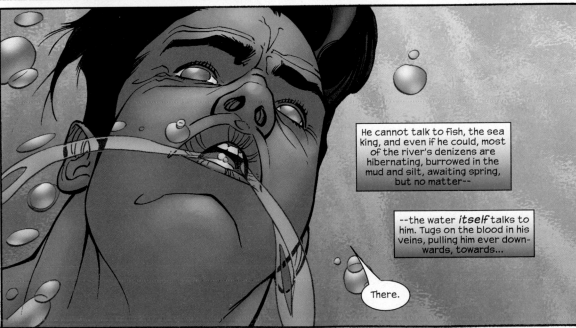

He cannot talk to fish, the sea king, and even if he could, most of the river's denizens are hibernating, burrowed in the mud and silt, awaiting spring, but no matter--

--the water *itself* talks to him. Tugs on the blood in his veins, pulling him ever down-wards, towards...

There.

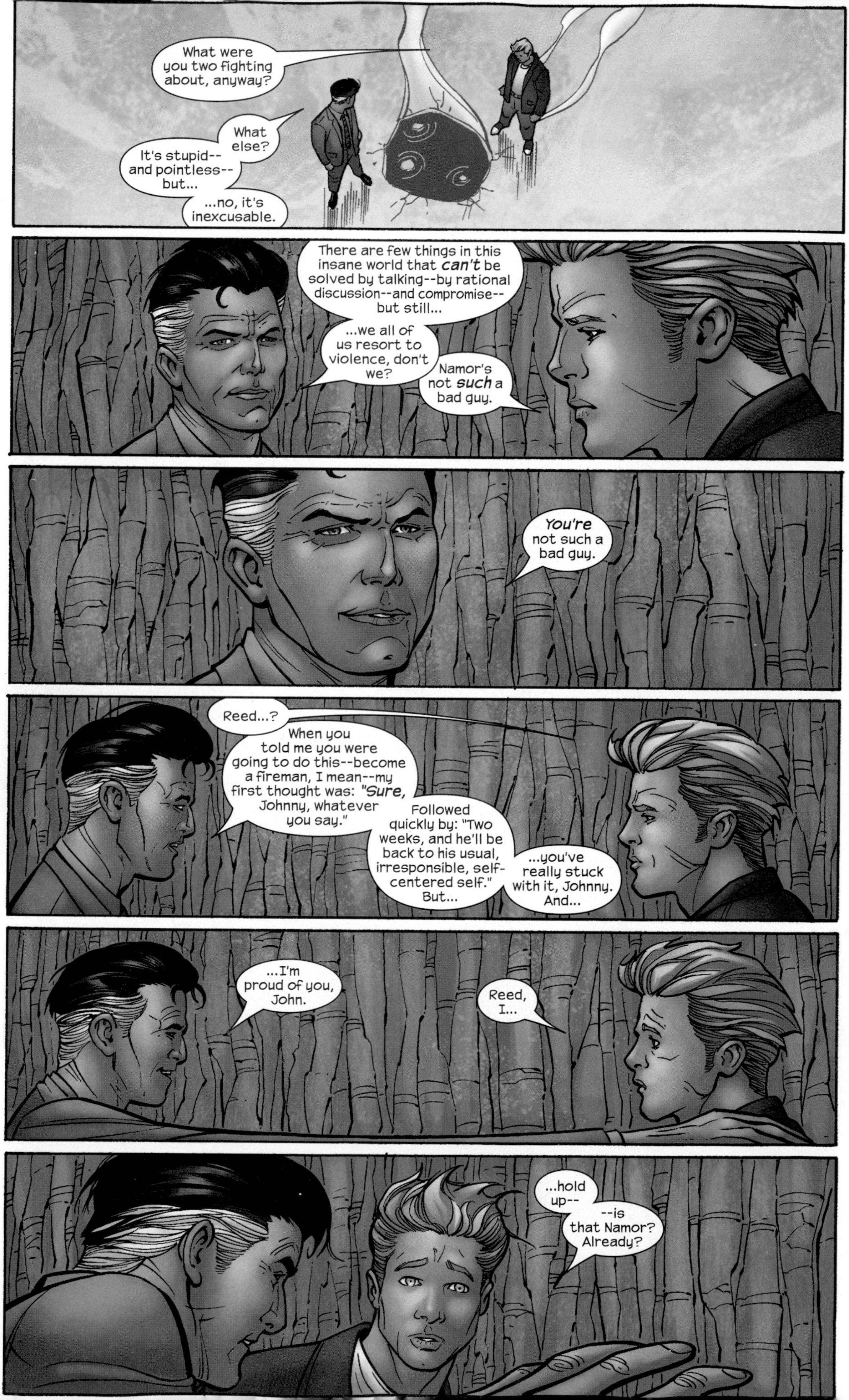
What were you two fighting about, anyway?
What else?
It's stupid--and pointless--but...
...no, it's inexcusable.
There are few things in this insane world that can't be solved by talking--by rational discussion--and compromise--but still...
...we all of us resort to violence, don't we?
Namor's not such a bad guy.
You're not such a bad guy.
Reed...?
When you told me you were going to do this--become a fireman, I mean--my first thought was: "Sure, Johnny, whatever you say."
Followed quickly by: "Two weeks, and he'll be back to his usual, irresponsible, self-centered self." But...
...you've really stuck with it, Johnny. And...
...I'm proud of you, John.
Reed, I...
...hold up--
--is that Namor? Already?

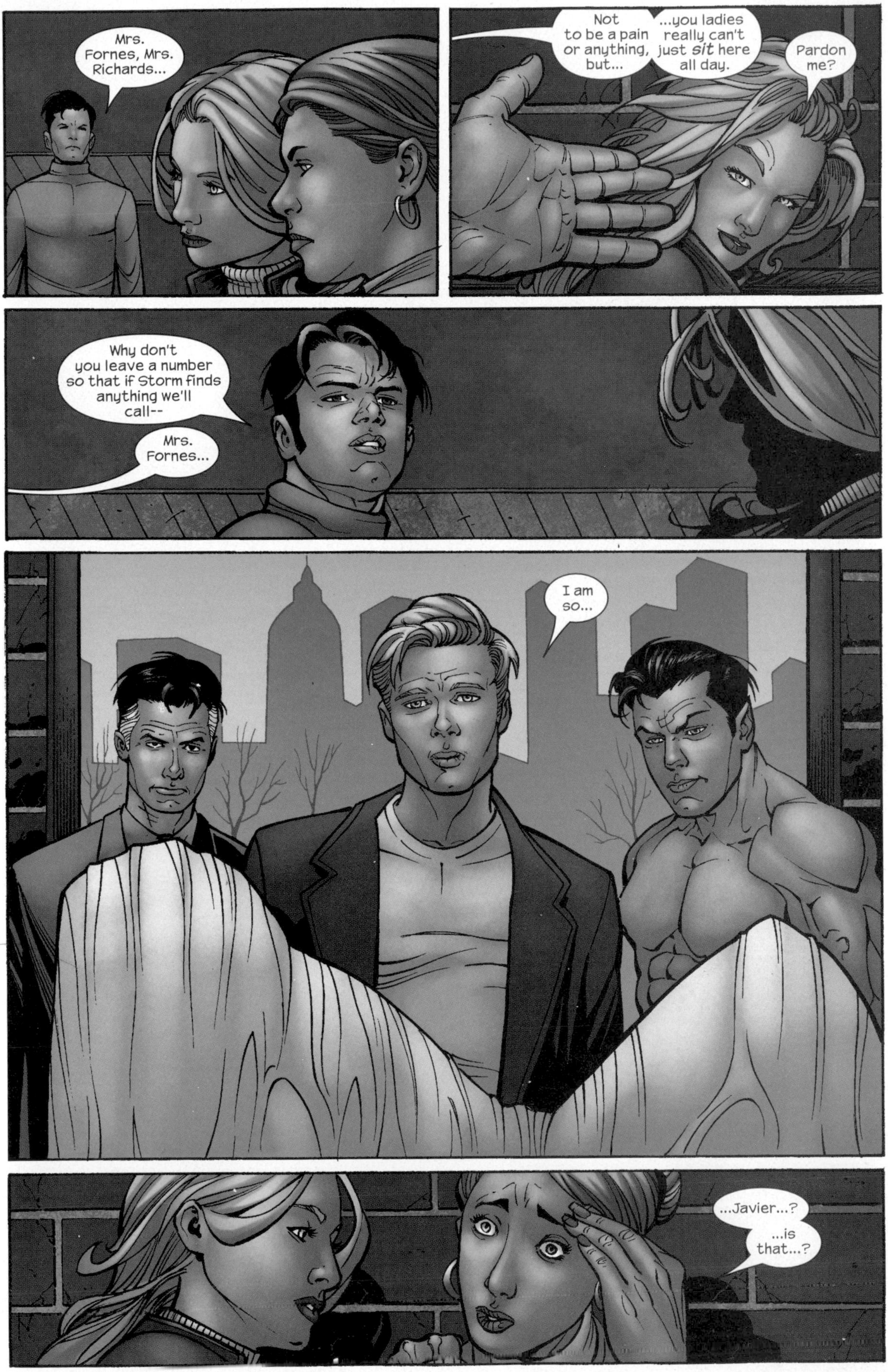
Mrs. Fornes, Mrs. Richards...
Not to be a pain or anything, but...
...you ladies really can't just *sit* here all day.
Pardon me?
Why don't you leave a number so that if Storm finds anything we'll call--
Mrs. Fornes...
I am so...
...Javier...?
...is that...?

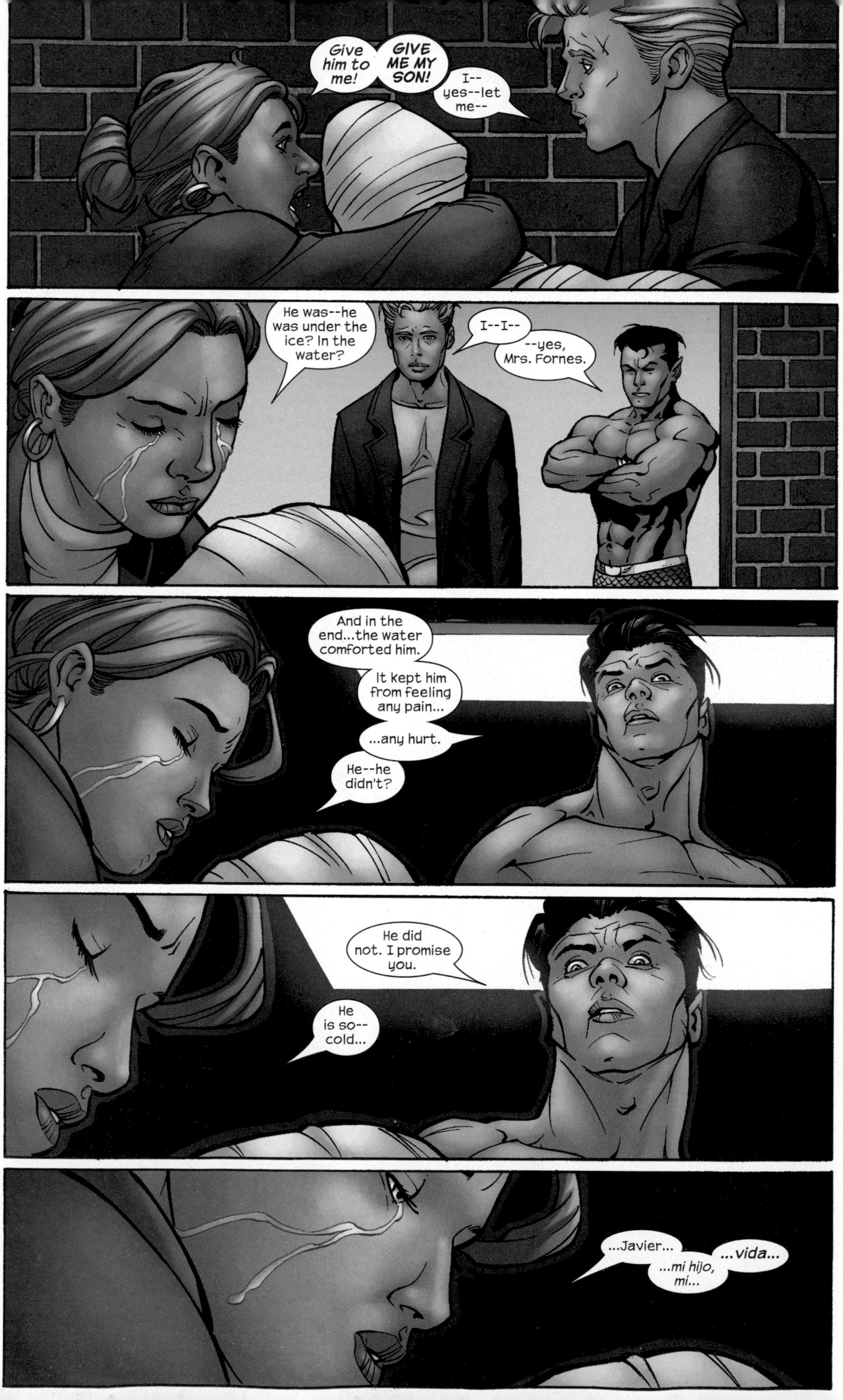
Give him to me!
GIVE ME MY SON!
I-- yes--let me--
He was--he was under the ice? In the water?
I--I--
--yes, Mrs. Fornes.
And in the end...the water comforted him.
It kept him from feeling any pain...
...any hurt.
He--he didn't?
He did not. I promise you.
He is so-- cold...
...Javier...
...mi hijo, mi...
...vida...

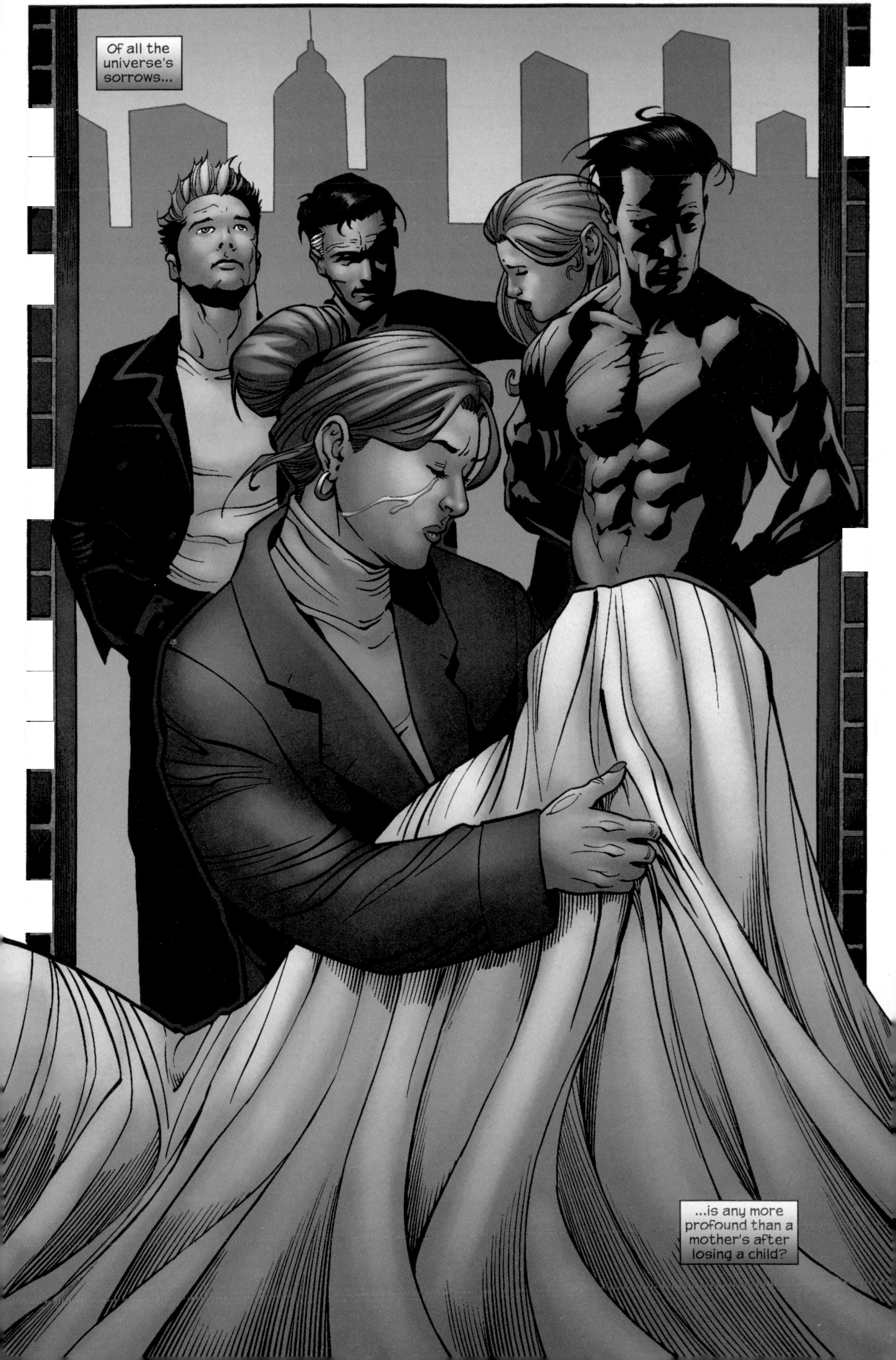
Of all the universe's sorrows...
...is any more profound than a mother's after losing a child?

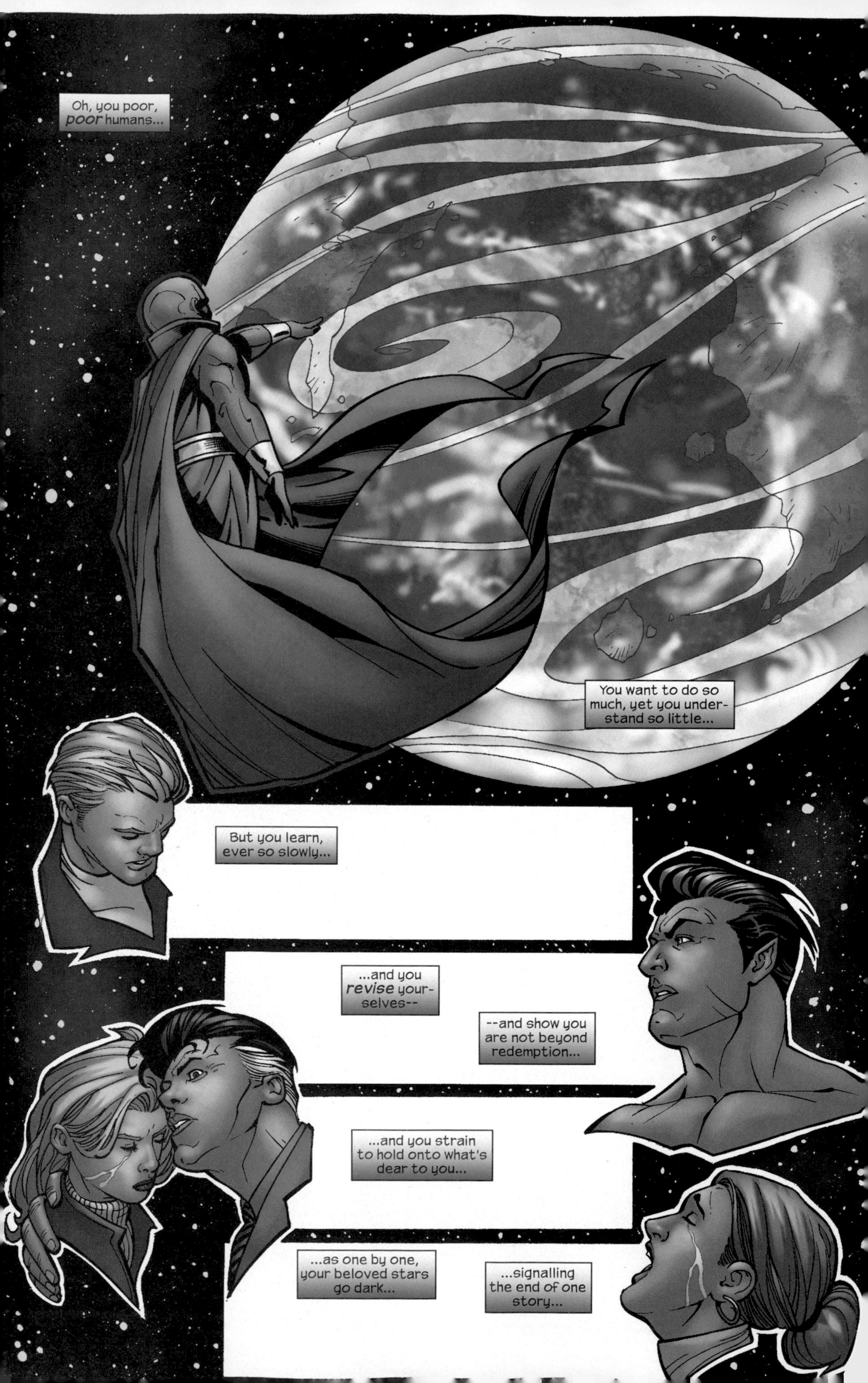
Oh, you poor, *poor* humans...
You want to do so much, yet you understand so little...
But you learn, ever so slowly...
...and you *revise* yourselves--
--and show you are not beyond redemption...
...and you strain to hold onto what's dear to you...
...as one by one, your beloved stars go dark...
...signalling the end of one story...

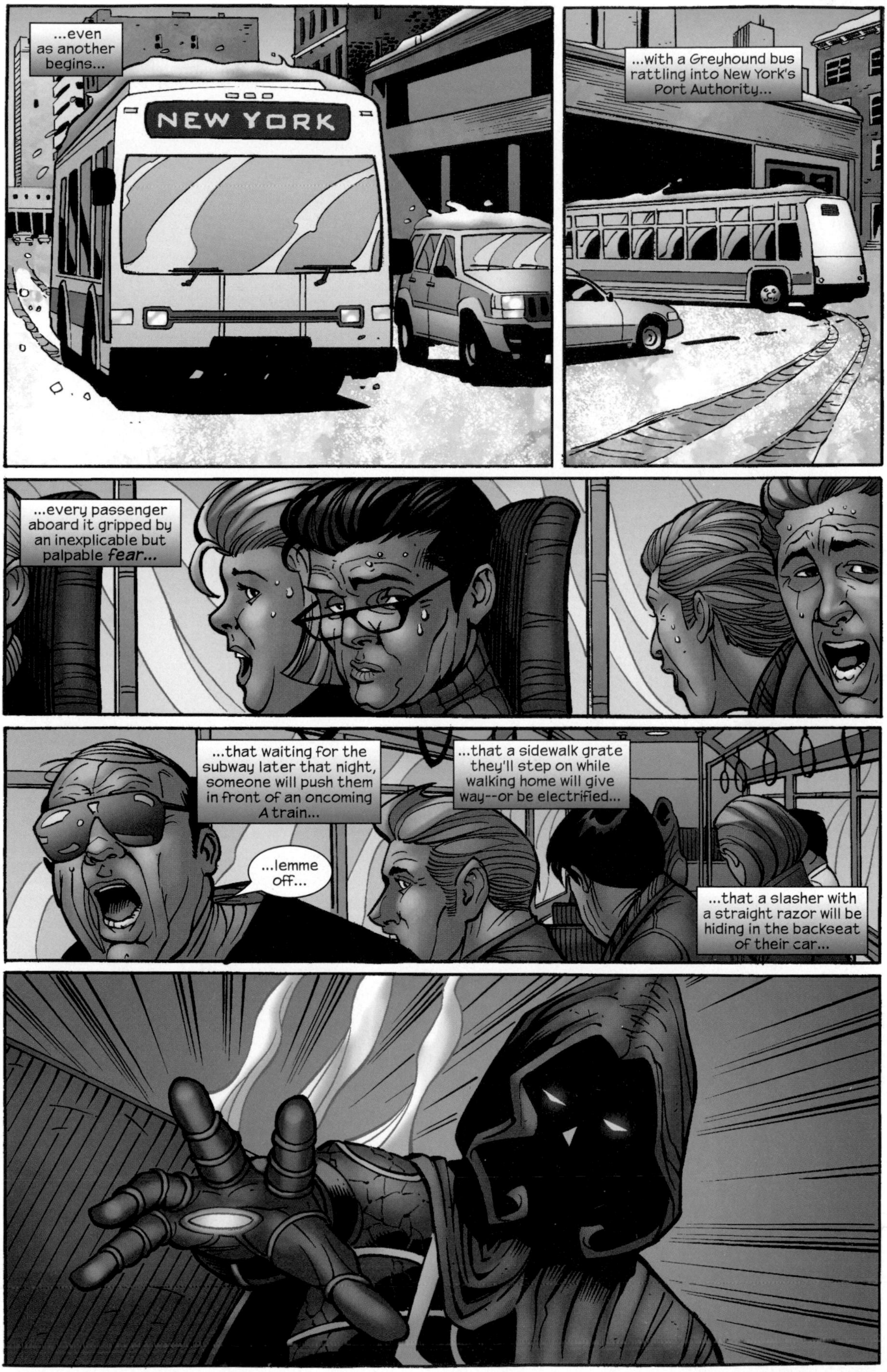
...even as another begins...
NEW YORK
...with a Greyhound bus rattling into New York's Port Authority...
...every passenger aboard it gripped by an inexplicable but palpable *fear...*
...that waiting for the subway later that night, someone will push them in front of an oncoming A train...
...lemme off...
...that a sidewalk grate they'll step on while walking home will give way--or be electrified...
...that a slasher with a straight razor will be hiding in the backseat of their car...

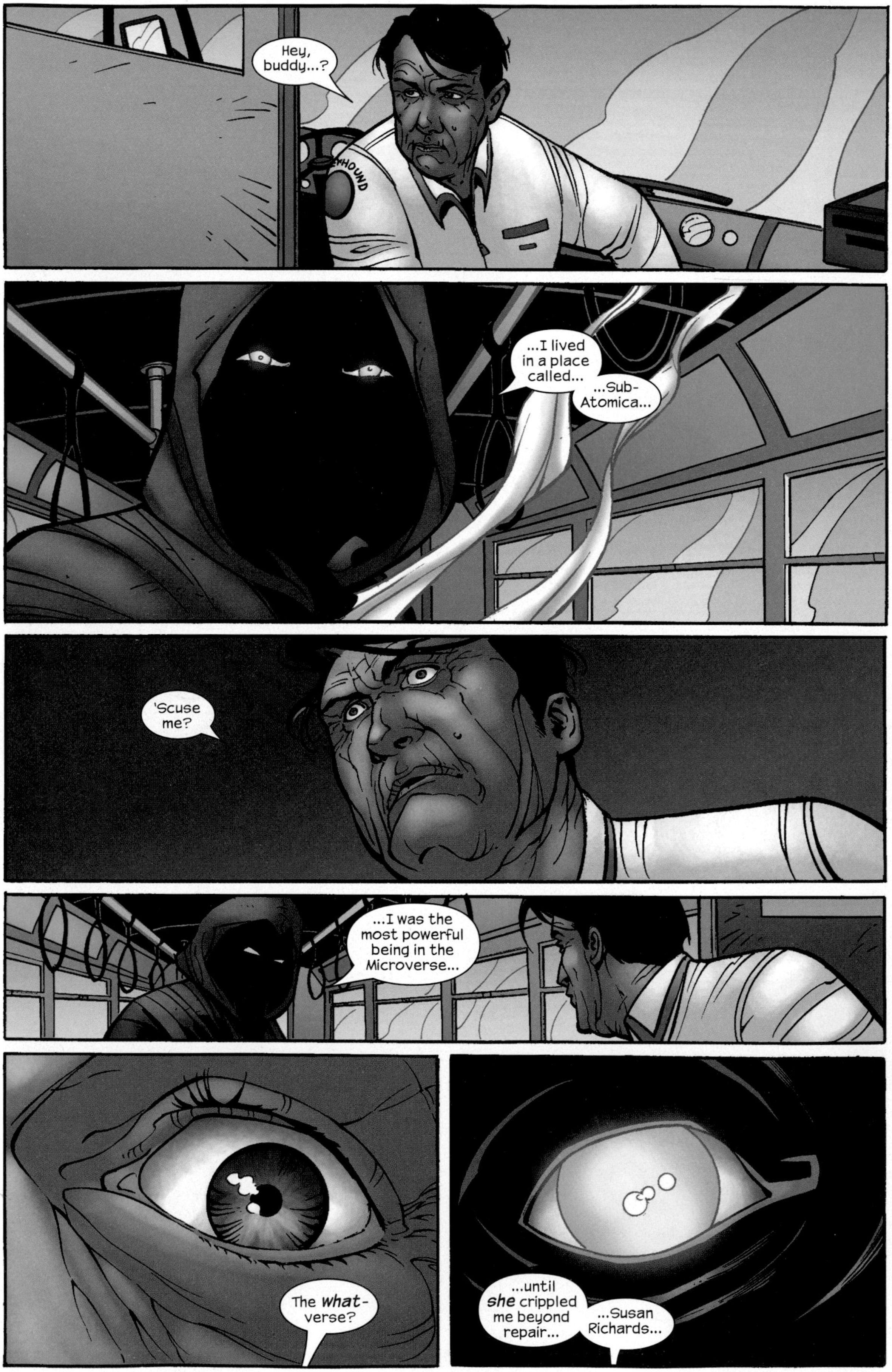
Hey, buddy...?
...I lived in a place called...
...Sub-Atomica...
'Scuse me?
...I was the most powerful being in the Microverse...
The *what*-verse?
...until *she* crippled me beyond repair...
...Susan Richards...

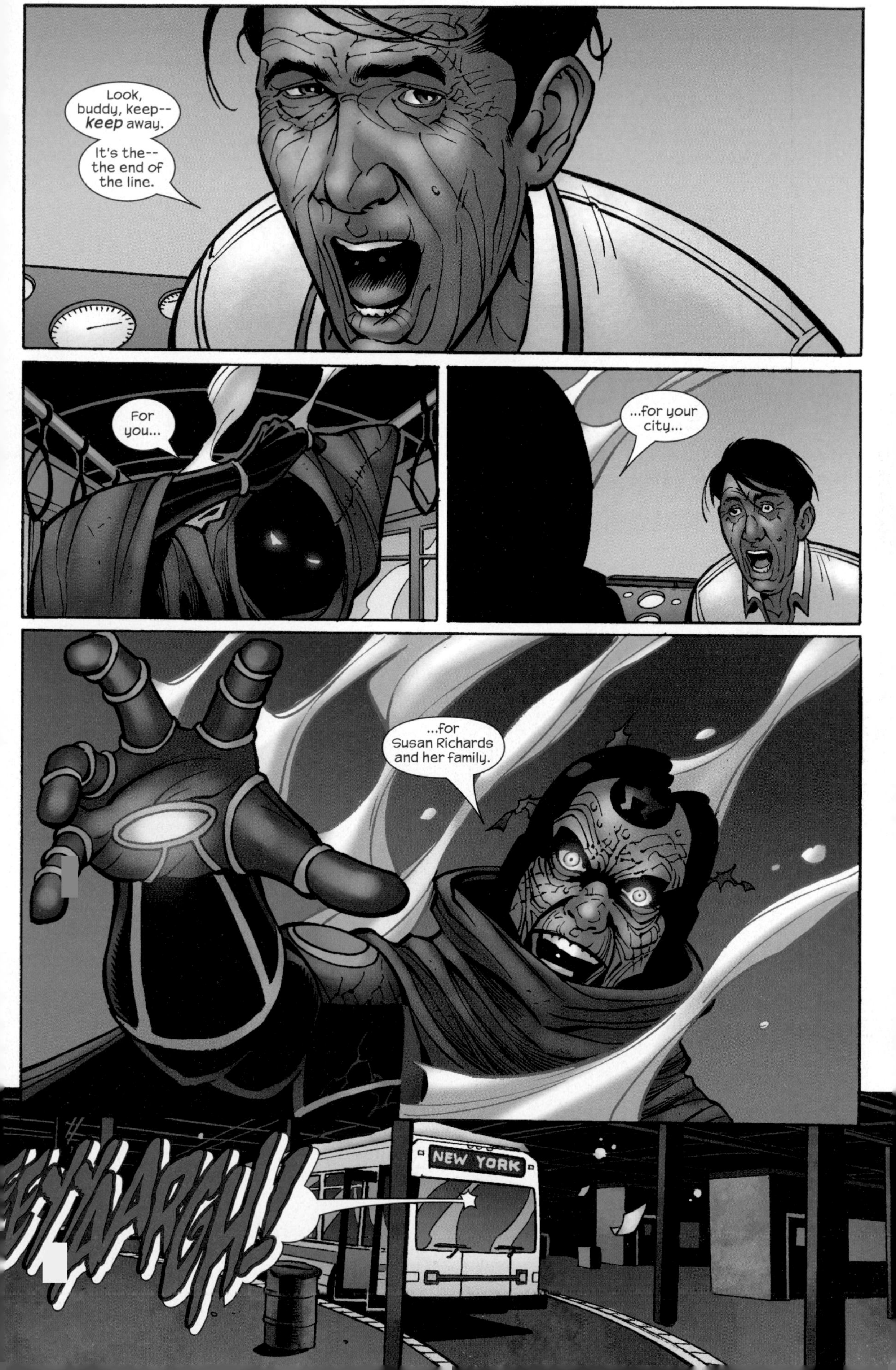
Look, buddy, keep-- *keep* away.
It's the-- the end of the line.
For you...
...for your city...
...for Susan Richards and her family.
NEW YORK

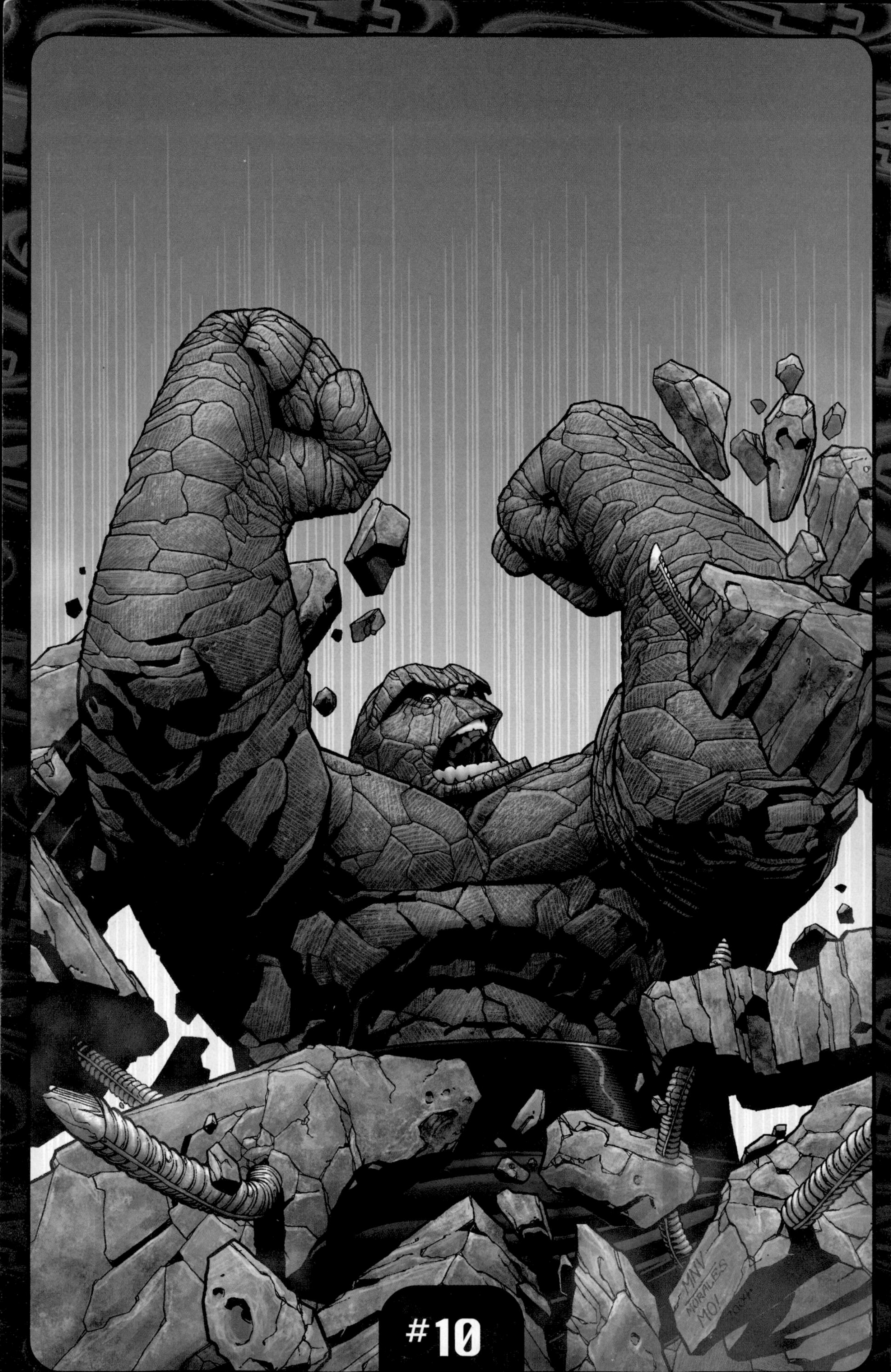
#10

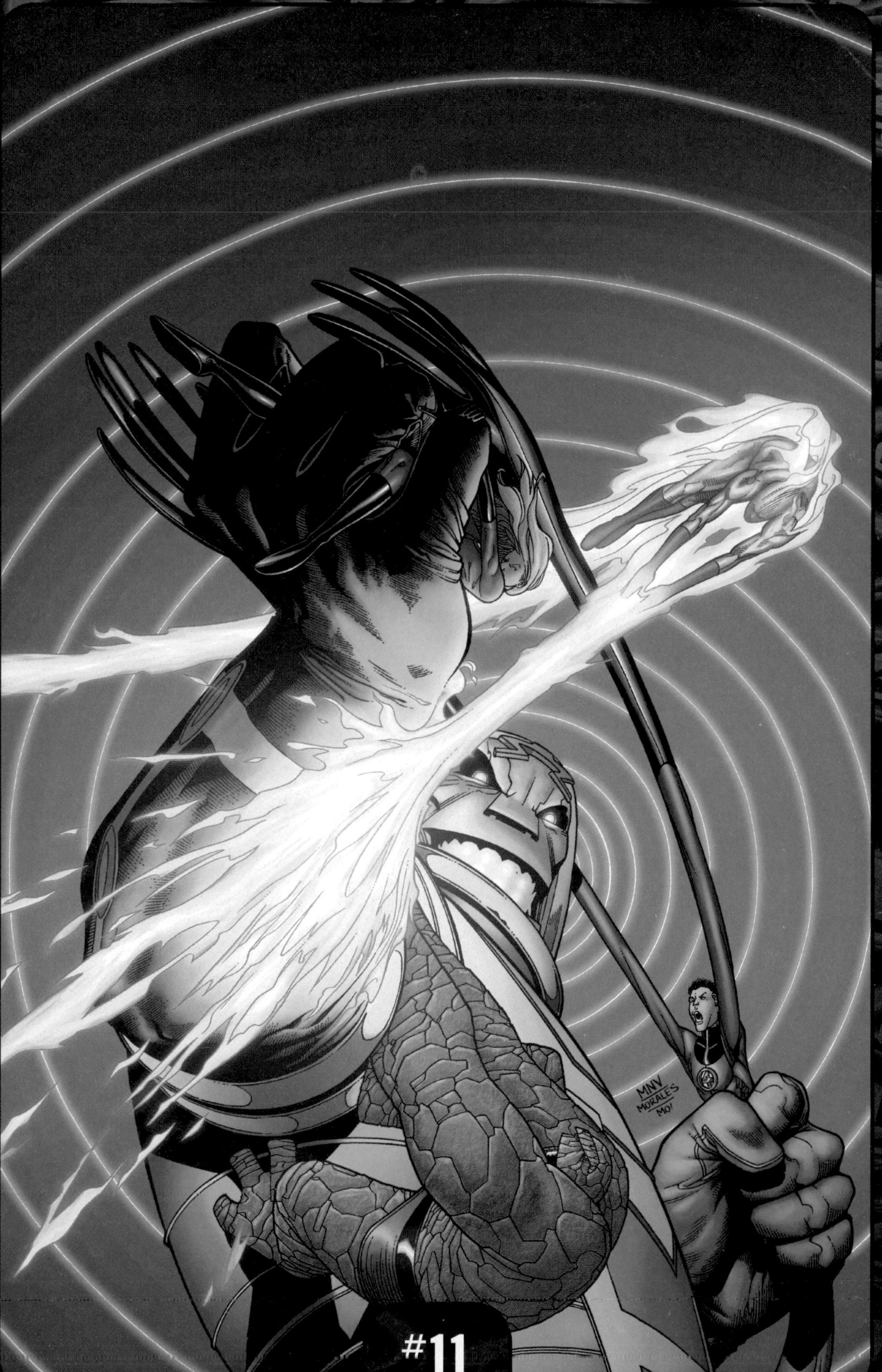
MNV
MORALES
MO!
#11

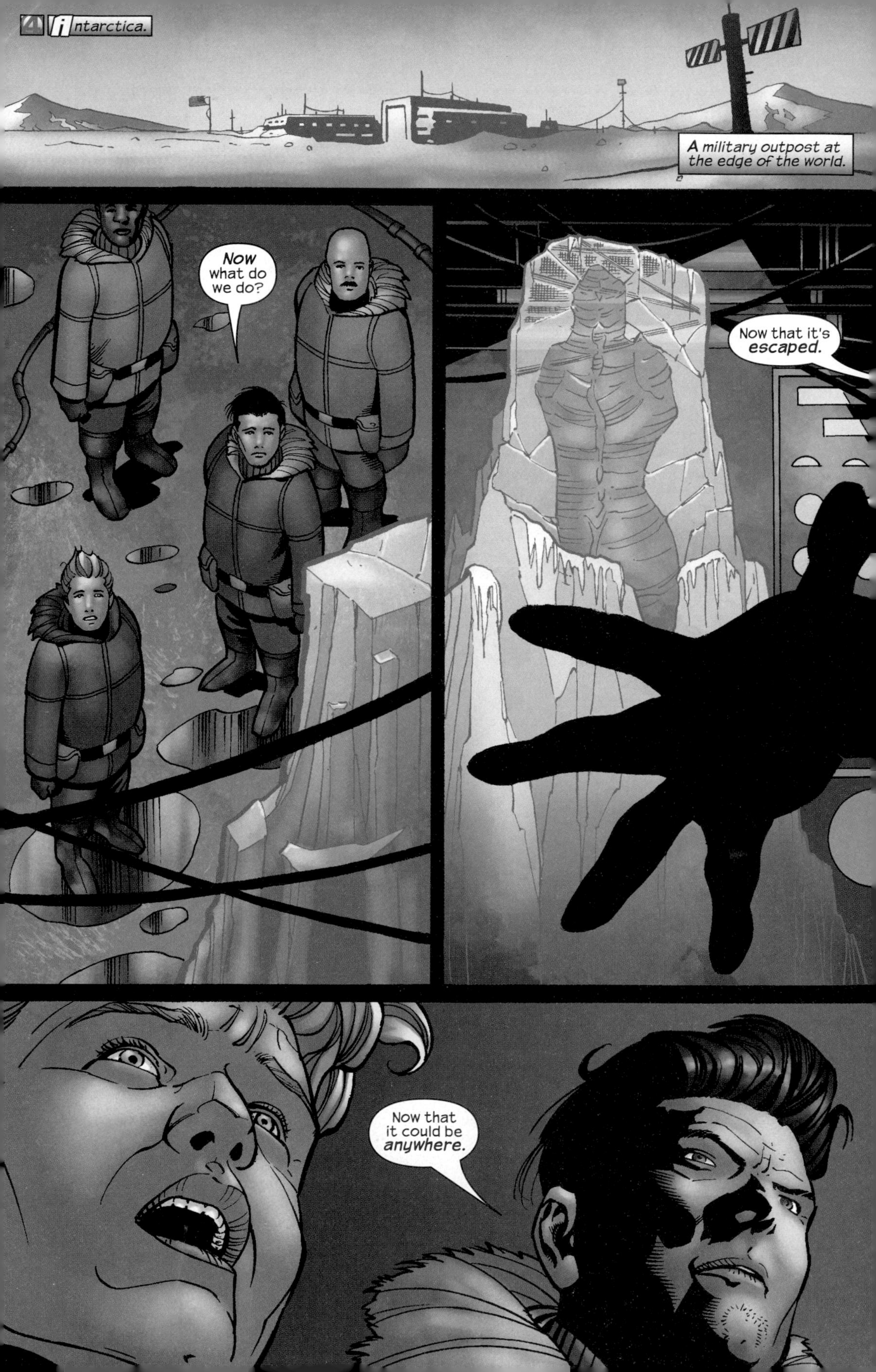
Antarctica.
A military outpost at the edge of the world.
Now what do we do?
Now that it's escaped.
Now that it could be anywhere.

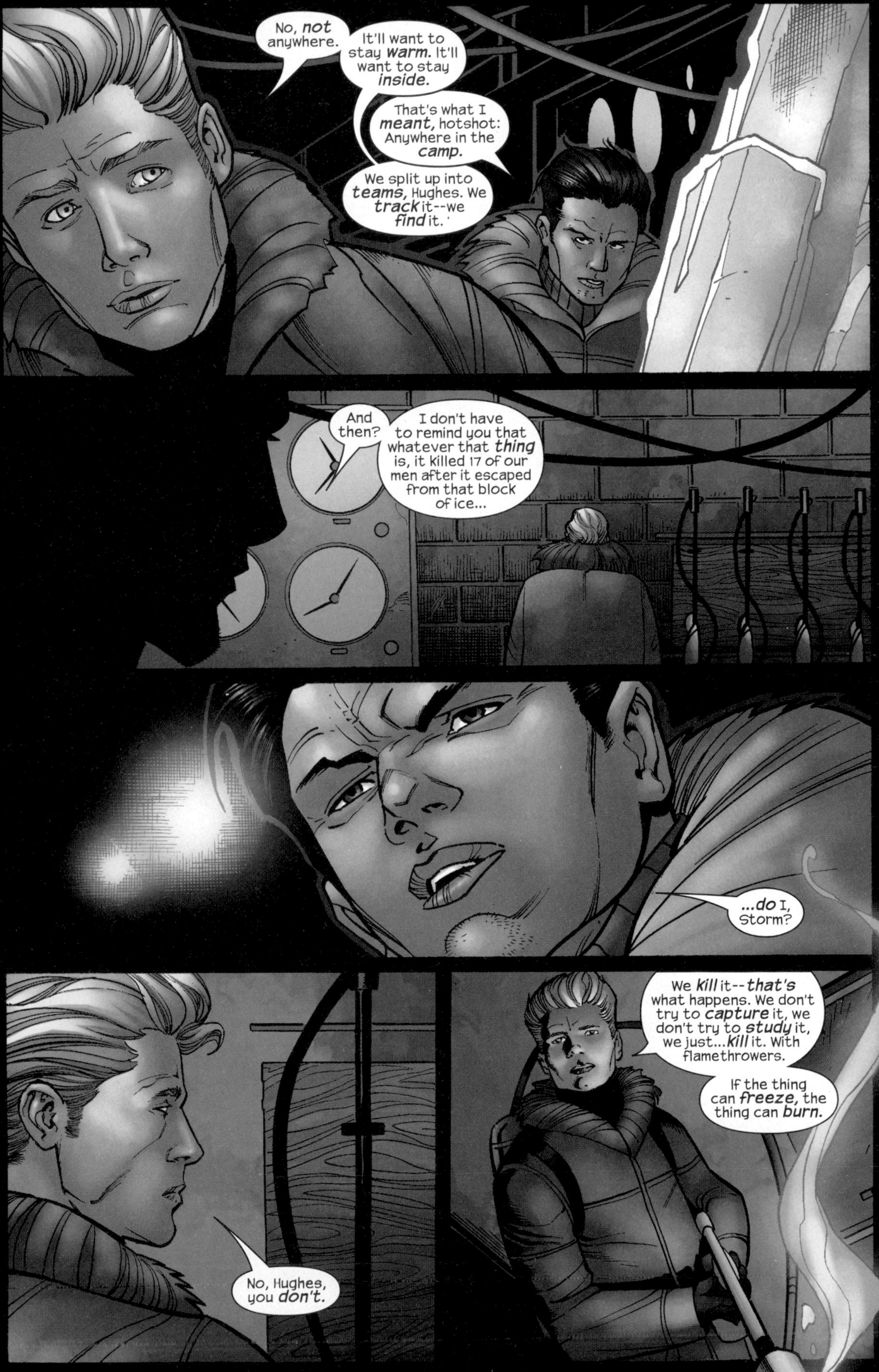
No, not anywhere.
It'll want to stay warm. It'll want to stay inside.
That's what I meant, hotshot: Anywhere in the camp.
We split up into teams, Hughes. We track it--we find it.
And then?
I don't have to remind you that whatever that thing is, it killed 17 of our men after it escaped from that block of ice...
...do I, Storm?
No, Hughes, you don't.
We kill it--that's what happens. We don't try to capture it, we don't try to study it, we just...kill it. With flamethrowers.
If the thing can freeze, the thing can burn.

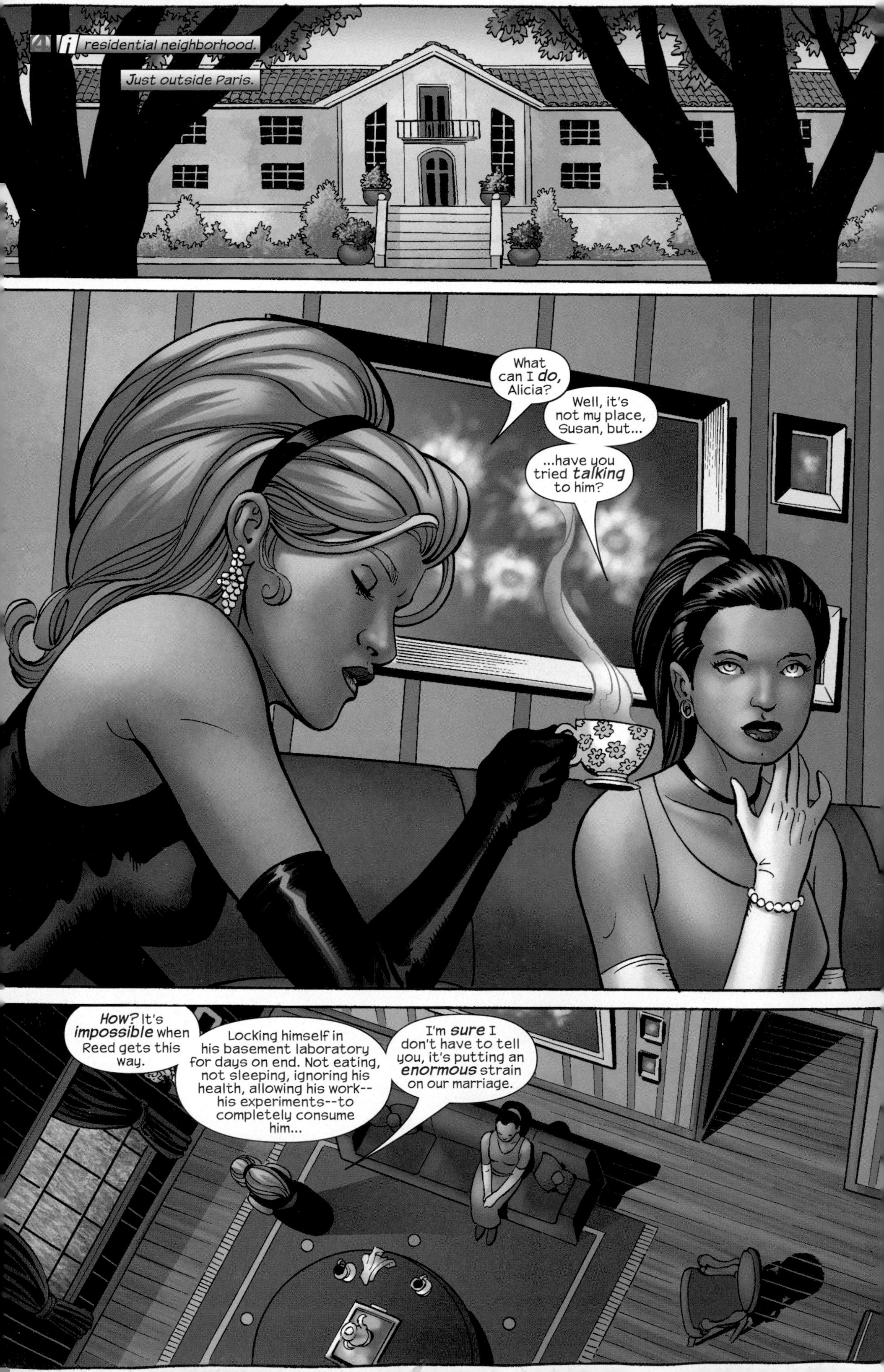

residential neighborhood.
Just outside Paris.
What can I do, Alicia?
Well, it's not my place, Susan, but...
...have you tried talking to him?
How? It's impossible when Reed gets this way.
Locking himself in his basement laboratory for days on end. Not eating, not sleeping, ignoring his health, allowing his work--his experiments--to completely consume him...
I'm sure I don't have to tell you, it's putting an enormous strain on our marriage.

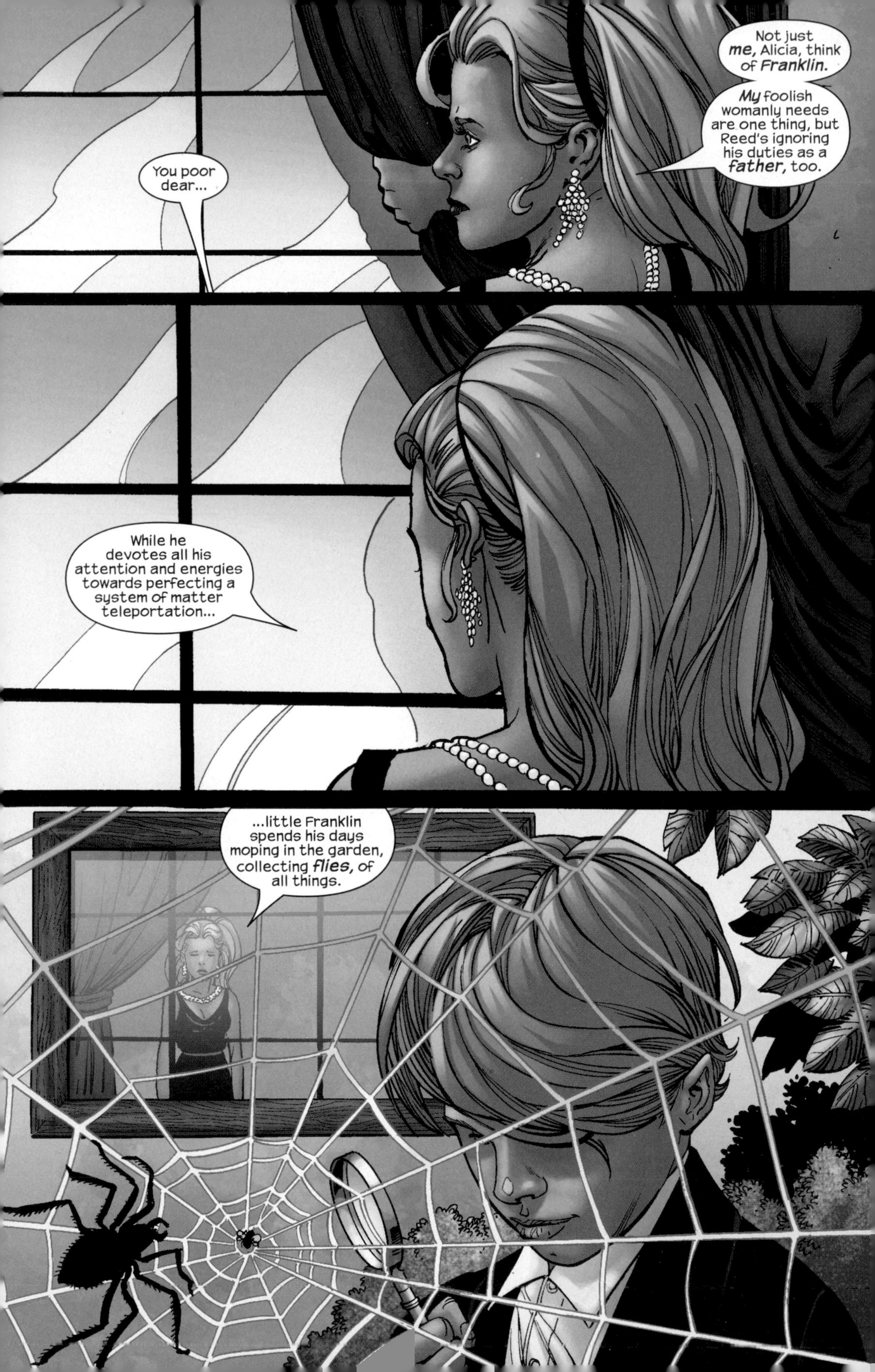
Not just *me*, Alicia, think of *Franklin*.
My foolish womanly needs are one thing, but Reed's ignoring his duties as a *father*, too.
You poor dear...
While he devotes all his attention and energies towards perfecting a system of matter teleportation...
...little Franklin spends his days moping in the garden, collecting *flies*, of all things.

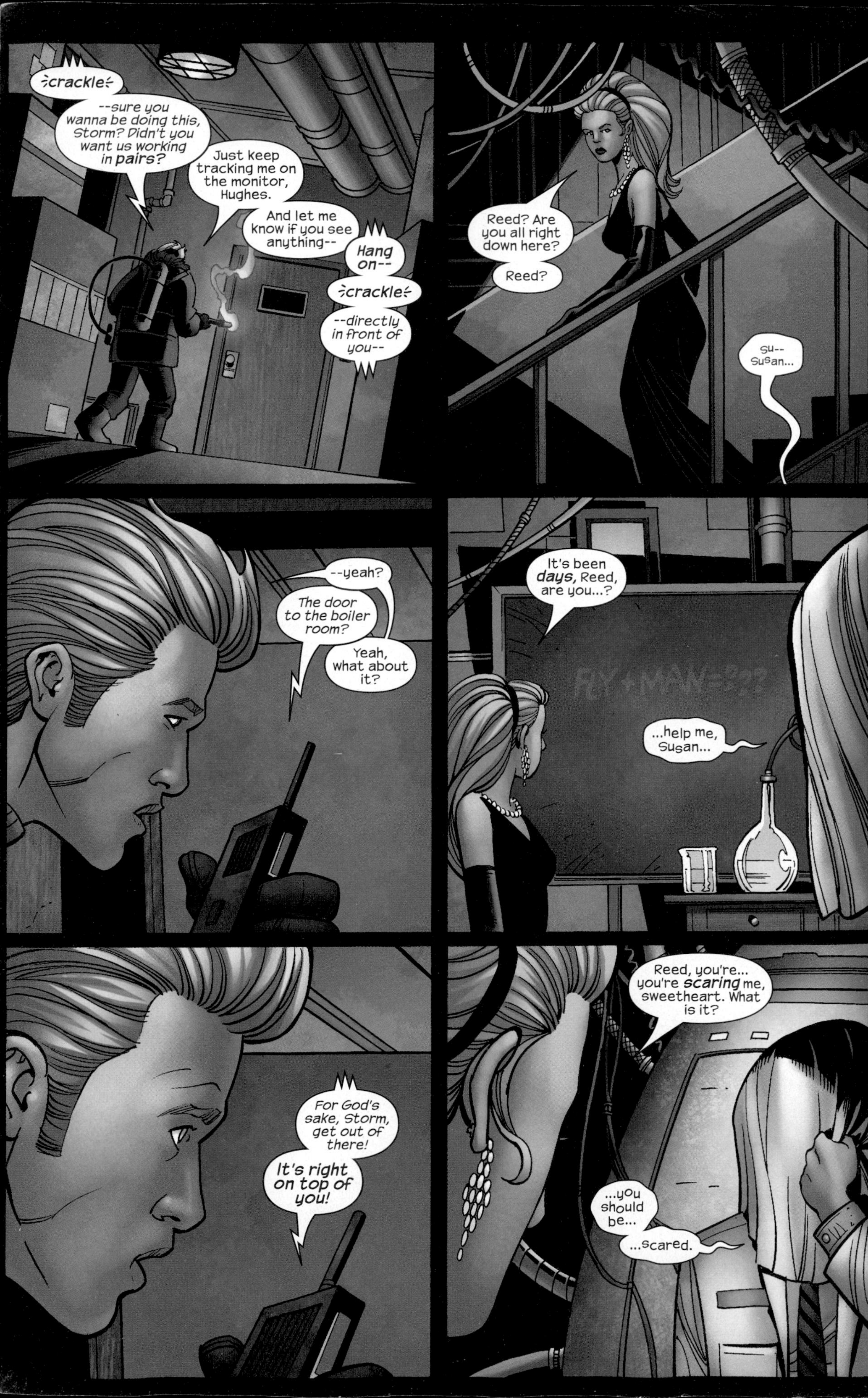

crackle
--sure you wanna be doing this, Storm? Didn't you want us working in **pairs**?
Just keep tracking me on the monitor, Hughes.
And let me know if you see anything--
Hang on--
crackle
--directly in front of you--
Reed? Are you all right down here?
Reed?
Su-- Susan...
--yeah?
The door to the boiler room?
Yeah, what about it?
It's been **days**, Reed, are you...?
...help me, Susan...
For God's sake, Storm, get out of there!
It's right on top of you!
Reed, you're... you're **scaring** me, sweetheart. What is it?
...you should be...
...scared.

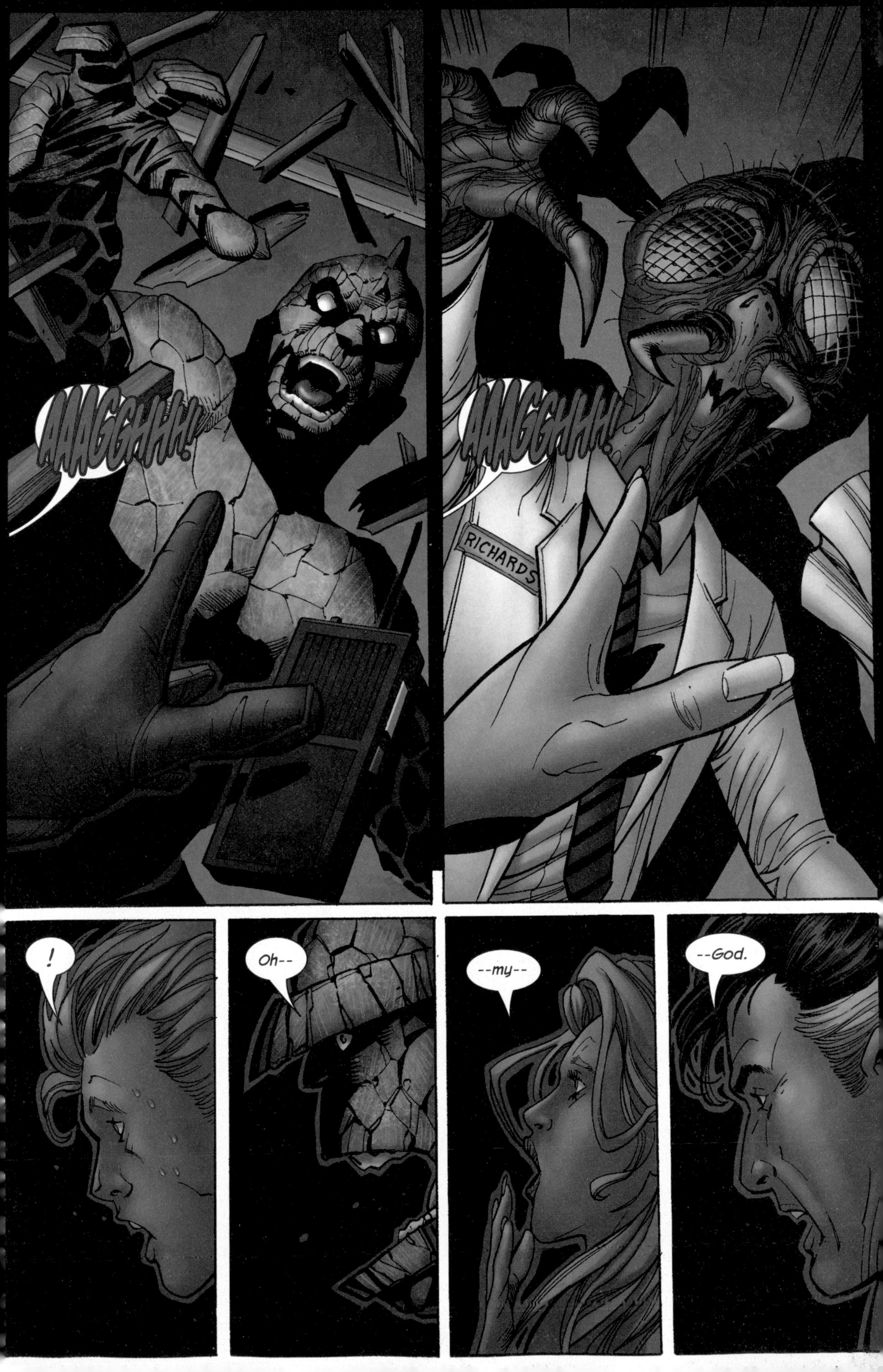
AAAGGHHH!
AAAGGHHH!
RICHARDS
!
Oh--
--my--
--God.

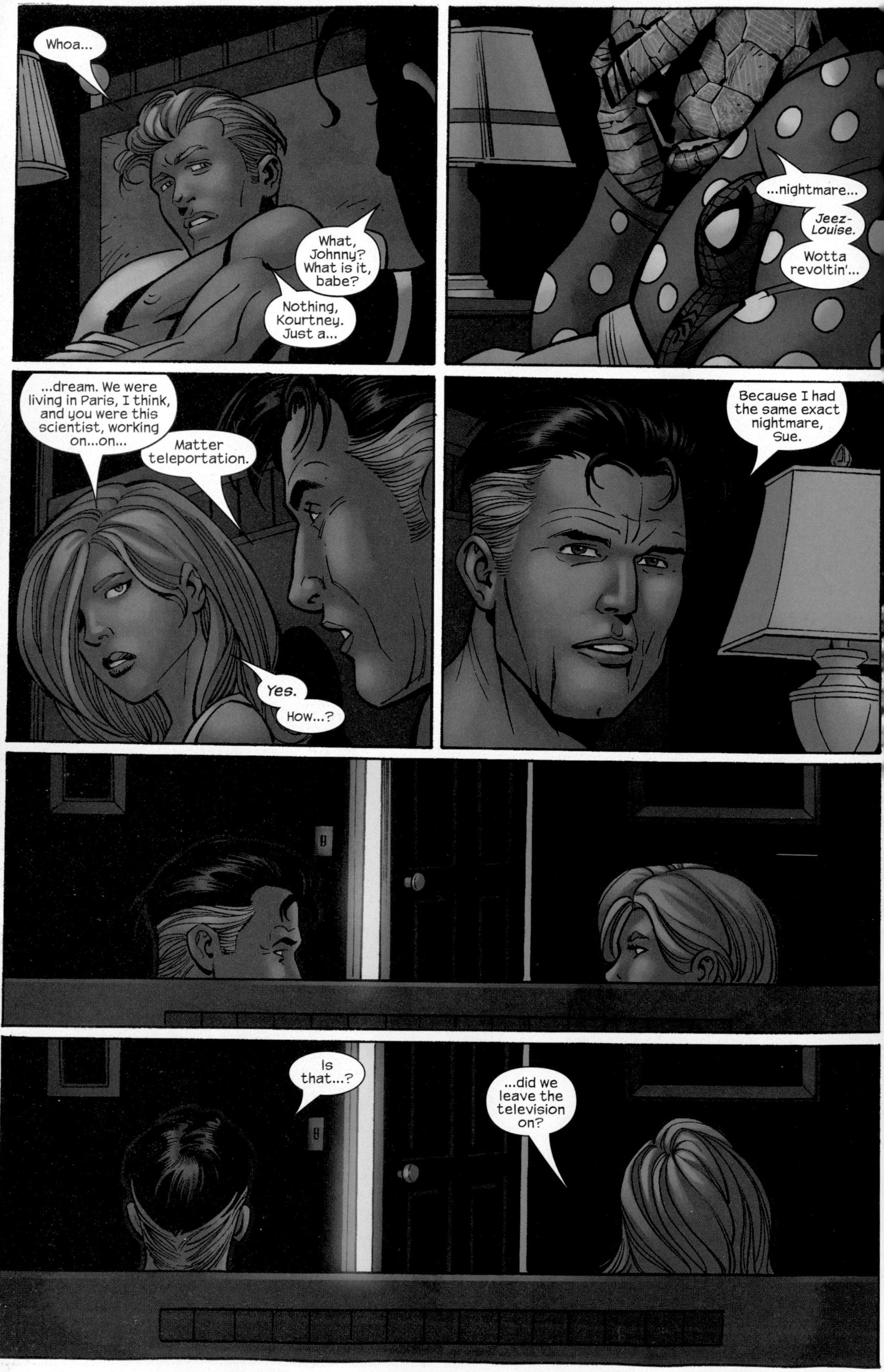
Whoa...
What, Johnny? What is it, babe?
Nothing, Kourtney. Just a...
...nightmare...
Jeez-Louise.
Wotta revoltin'...
...dream. We were living in Paris, I think, and you were this scientist, working on...on...
Matter teleportation.
Yes.
How...?
Because I had the same exact nightmare, Sue.
Is that...?
...did we leave the television on?

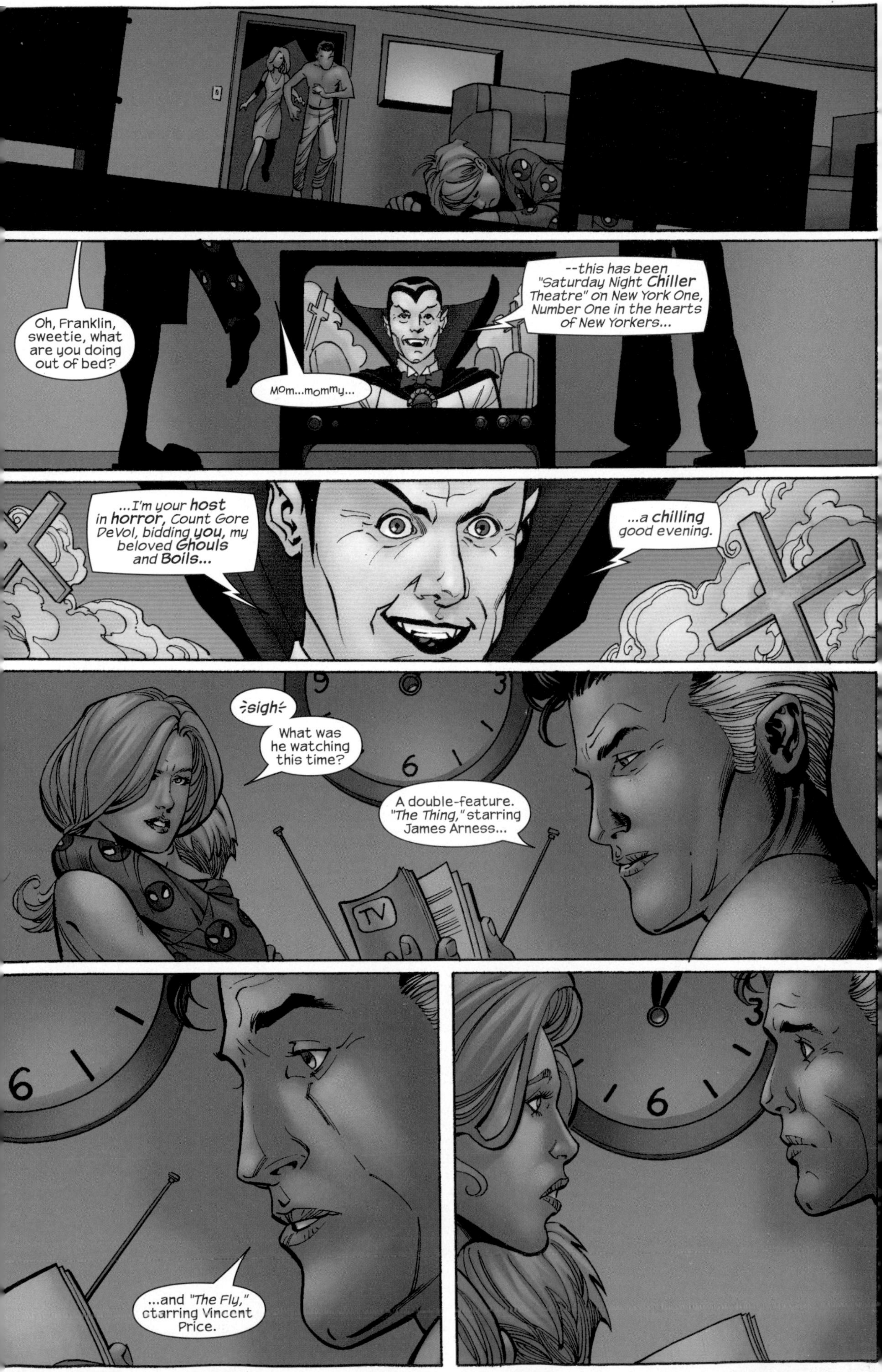
Oh, Franklin, sweetie, what are you doing out of bed?
--this has been "Saturday Night Chiller Theatre" on New York One, Number One in the hearts of New Yorkers...
Mom...mommy...
...I'm your host in horror, Count Gore DeVol, bidding you, my beloved Ghouls and Boils...
...a chilling good evening.
sigh
What was he watching this time?
A double-feature. "The Thing," starring James Arness...
TV
...and "The Fly," starring Vincent Price.

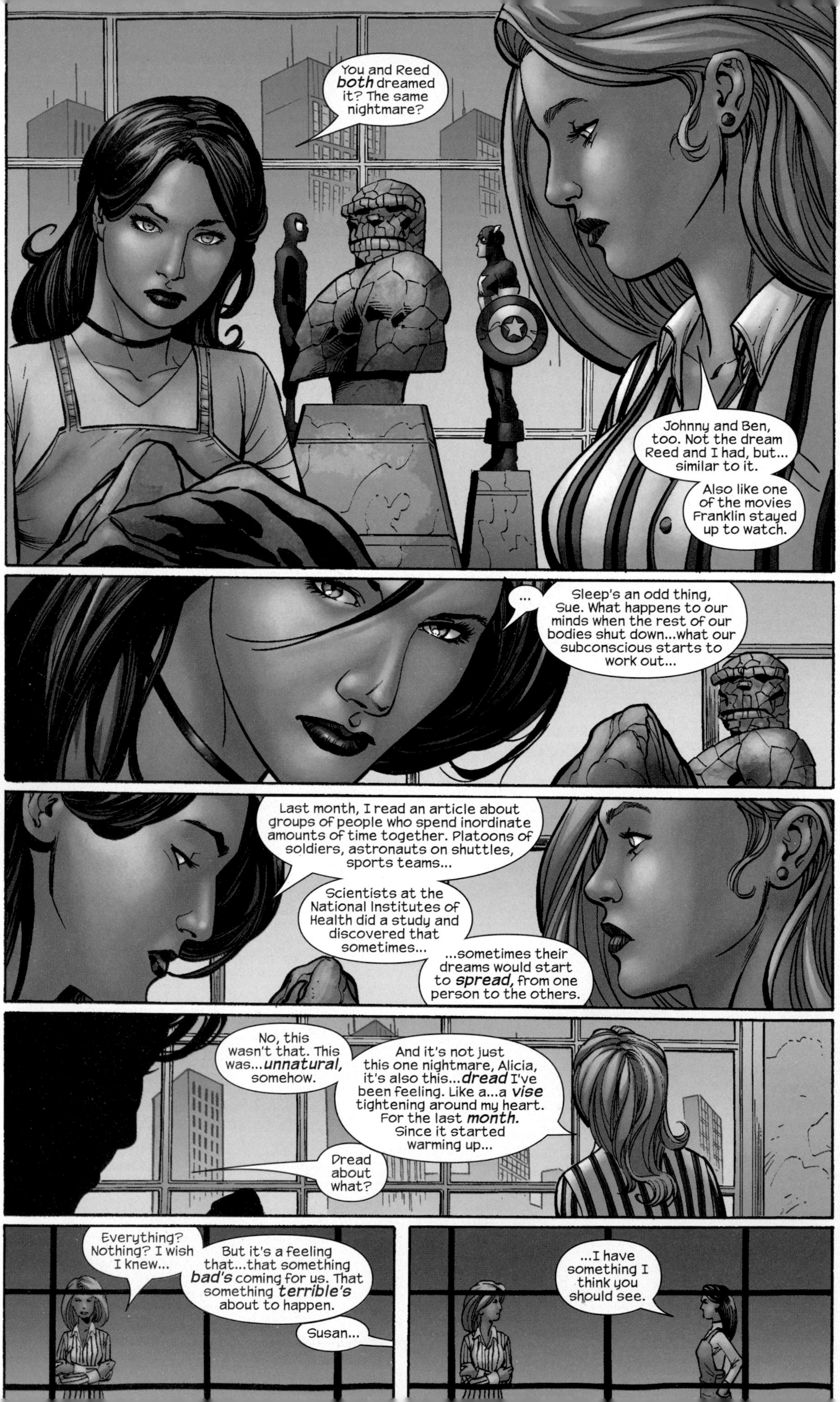
You and Reed both dreamed it? The same nightmare?
Johnny and Ben, too. Not the dream Reed and I had, but... similar to it.
Also like one of the movies Franklin stayed up to watch.
...
Sleep's an odd thing, Sue. What happens to our minds when the rest of our bodies shut down...what our subconscious starts to work out...
Last month, I read an article about groups of people who spend inordinate amounts of time together. Platoons of soldiers, astronauts on shuttles, sports teams...
Scientists at the National Institutes of Health did a study and discovered that sometimes...
...sometimes their dreams would start to spread, from one person to the others.
No, this wasn't that. This was...unnatural, somehow.
And it's not just this one nightmare, Alicia, it's also this...dread I've been feeling. Like a...a vise tightening around my heart. For the last month. Since it started warming up...
Dread about what?
Everything? Nothing? I wish I knew...
But it's a feeling that...that something bad's coming for us. That something terrible's about to happen.
Susan...
...I have something I think you should see.

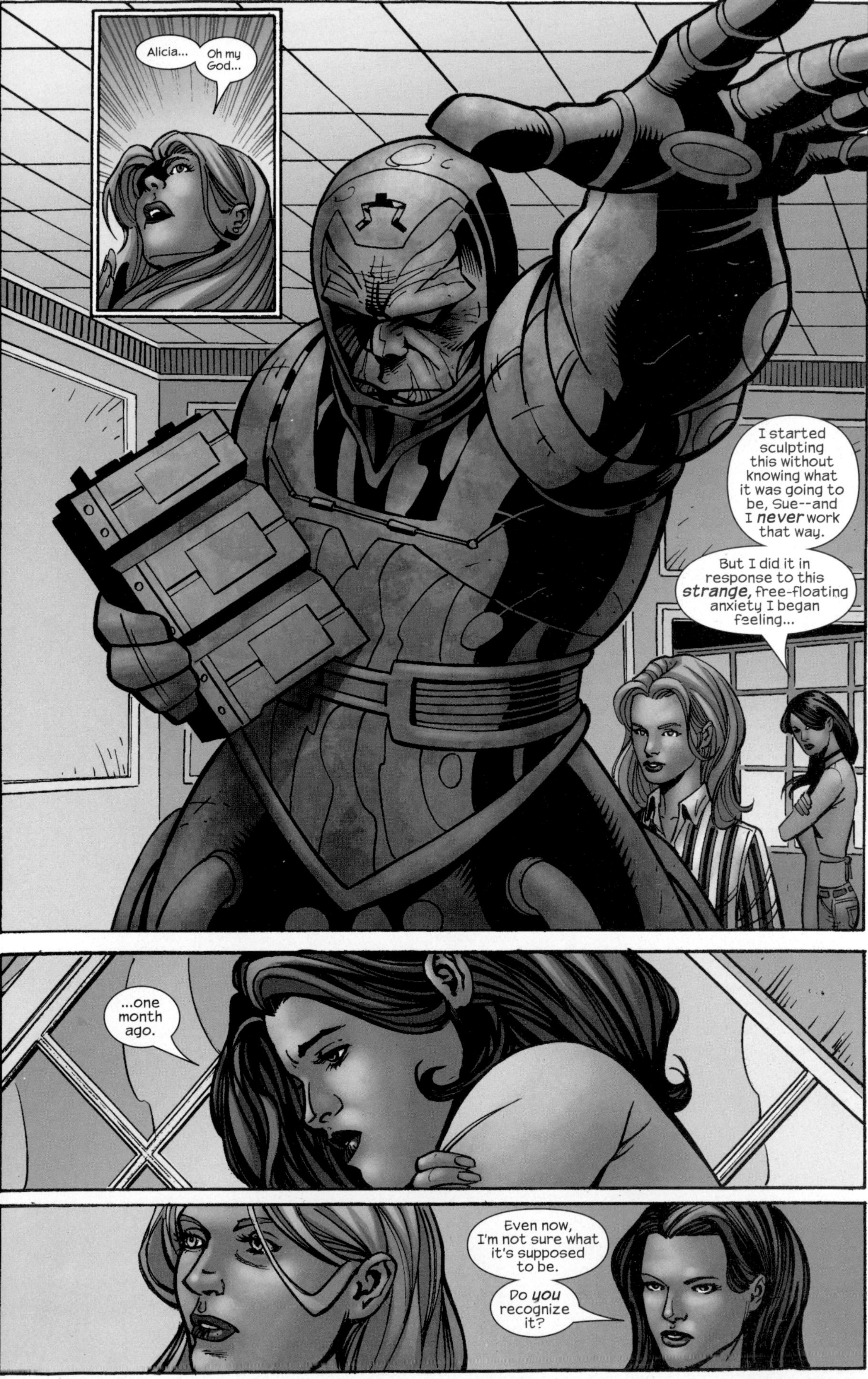
Alicia...
Oh my God...
I started sculpting this without knowing what it was going to be, Sue--and I **never** work that way.
But I did it in response to this ***strange,*** free-floating anxiety I began feeling...
...one month ago.
Even now, I'm not sure what it's supposed to be.
*Do **you** recognize it?*

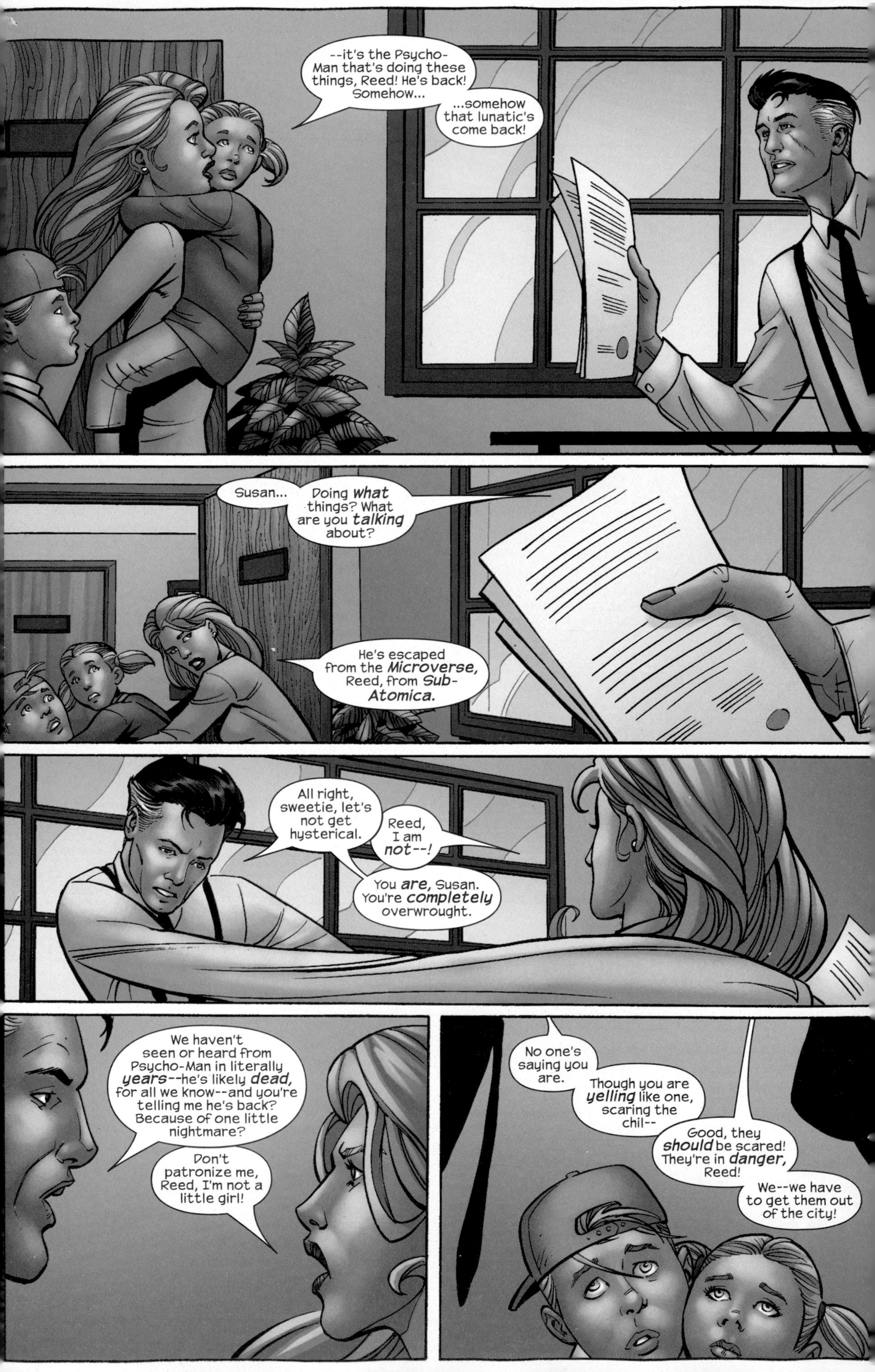
--it's the Psycho-Man that's doing these things, Reed! He's back! Somehow...
...somehow that lunatic's come back!
Susan... Doing what things? What are you talking about?
He's escaped from the Microverse, Reed, from Sub-Atomica.
All right, sweetie, let's not get hysterical.
Reed, I am not--!
You are, Susan. You're completely overwrought.
We haven't seen or heard from Psycho-Man in literally years--he's likely dead, for all we know--and you're telling me he's back? Because of one little nightmare?
Don't patronize me, Reed, I'm not a little girl!
No one's saying you are.
Though you are yelling like one, scaring the chil--
Good, they should be scared! They're in danger, Reed!
We--we have to get them out of the city!

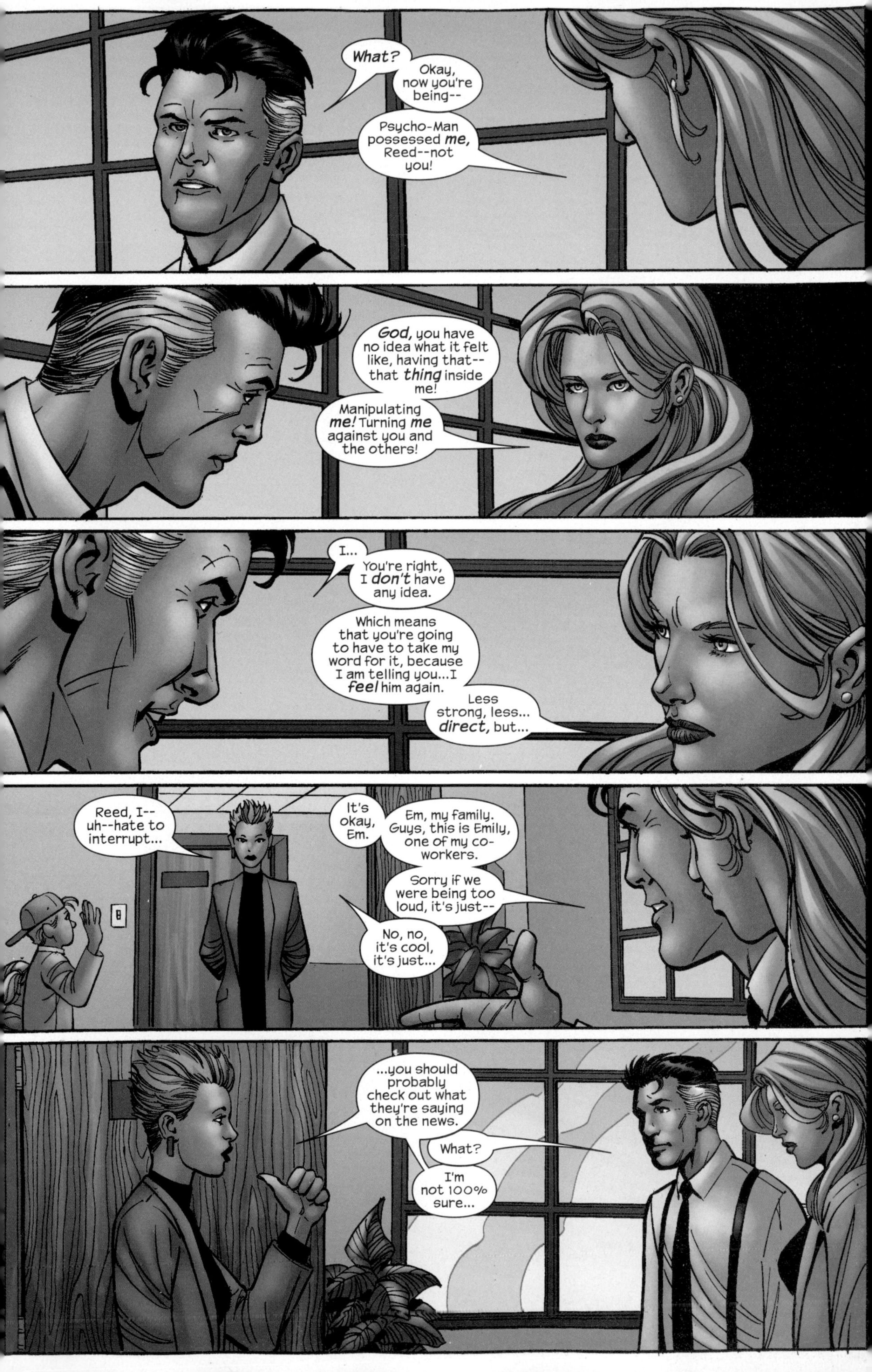
What?
Okay, now you're being--
Psycho-Man possessed me, Reed--not you!
God, you have no idea what it felt like, having that--that thing inside me!
Manipulating me! Turning me against you and the others!
I...
You're right, I don't have any idea.
Which means that you're going to have to take my word for it, because I am telling you...I feel him again.
Less strong, less... direct, but...
Reed, I--uh--hate to interrupt...
It's okay, Em.
Em, my family. Guys, this is Emily, one of my co-workers.
Sorry if we were being too loud, it's just--
No, no, it's cool, it's just...
...you should probably check out what they're saying on the news.
What?
I'm not 100% sure...

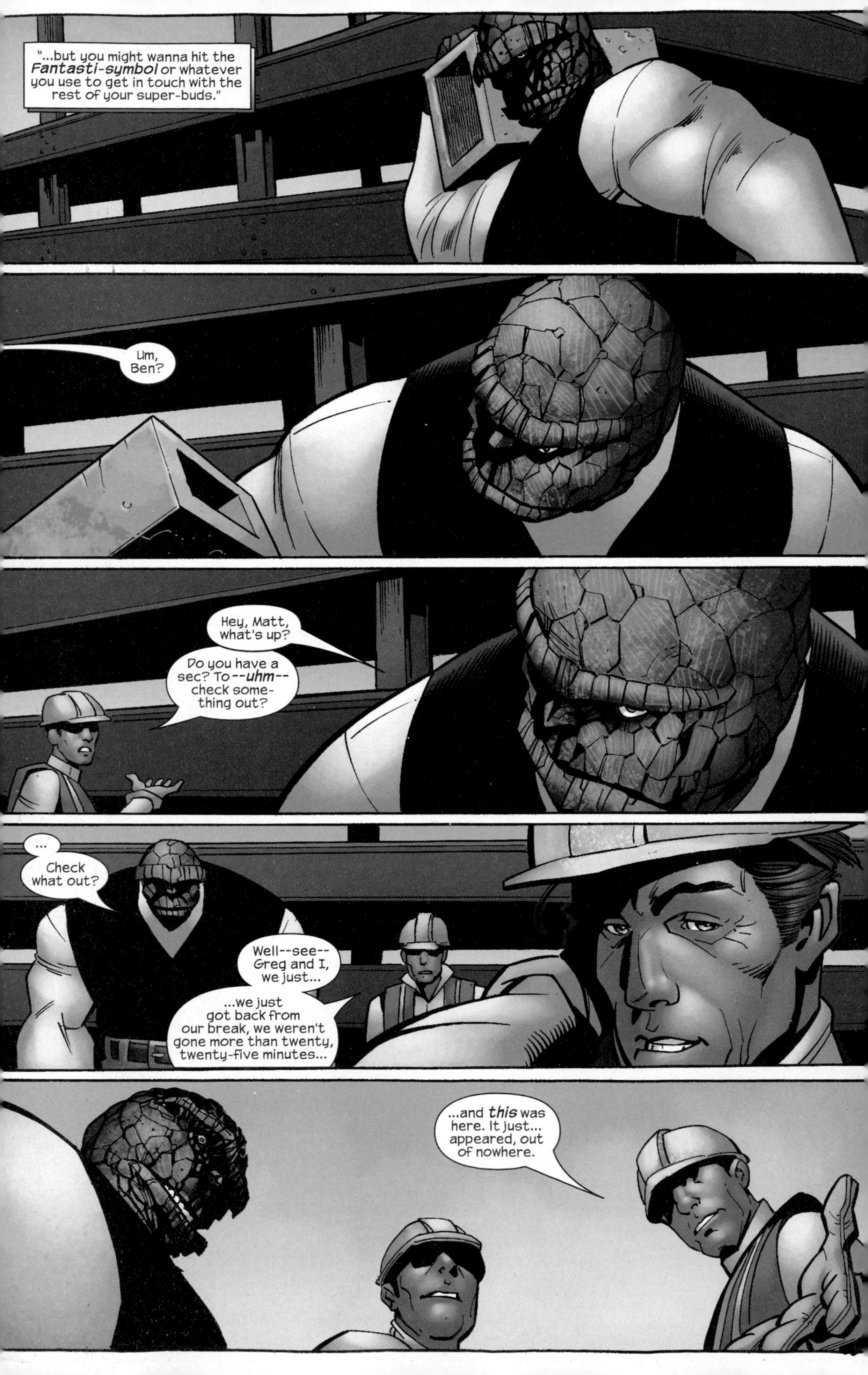
"...but you might wanna hit the Fantasti-symbol or whatever you use to get in touch with the rest of your super-buds."
Um, Ben?
Hey, Matt, what's up?
Do you have a sec? To --uhm-- check something out?
... Check what out?
Well--see-- Greg and I, we just...
...we just got back from our break, we weren't gone more than twenty, twenty-five minutes...
...and this was here. It just... appeared, out of nowhere.

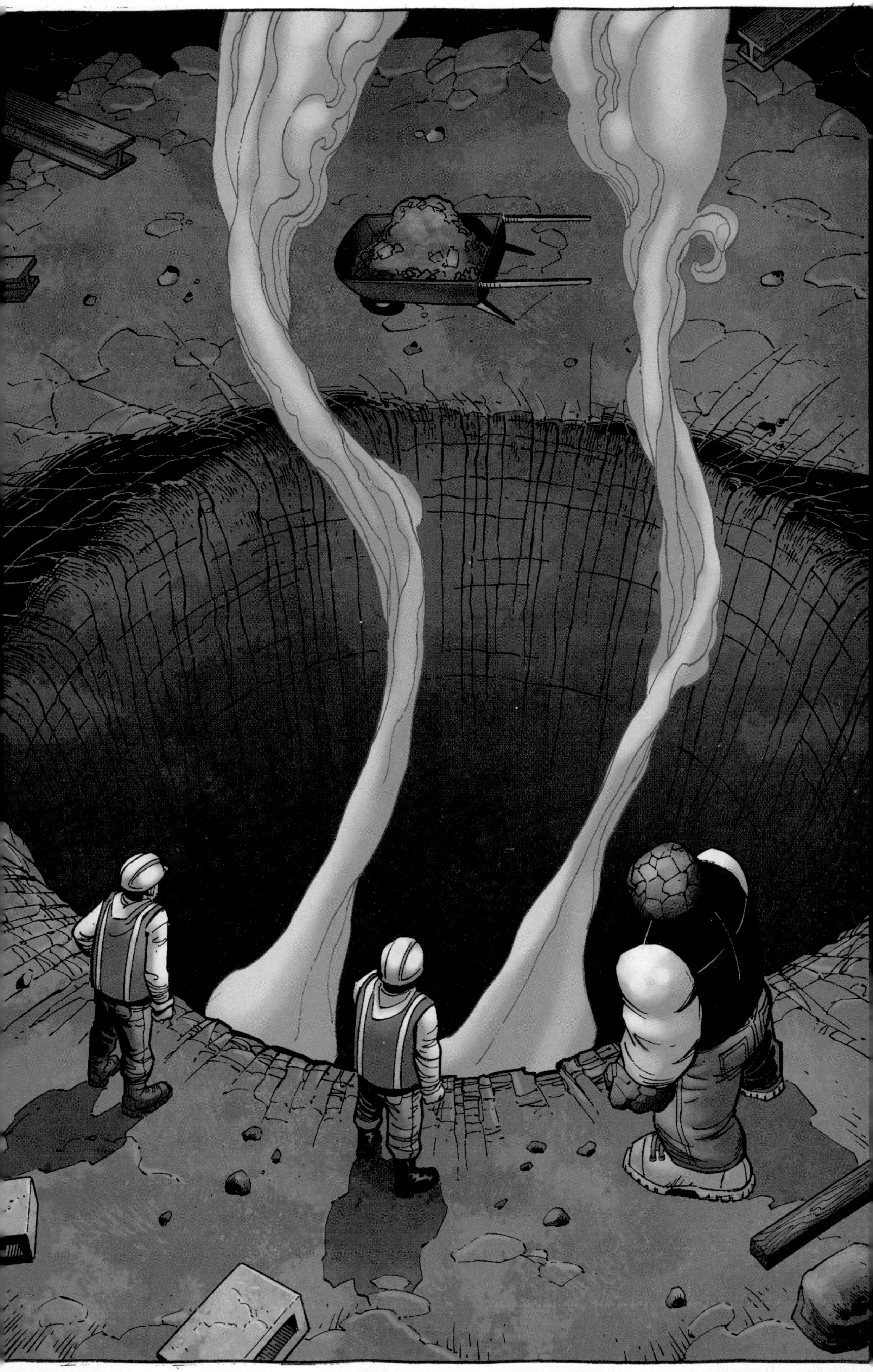

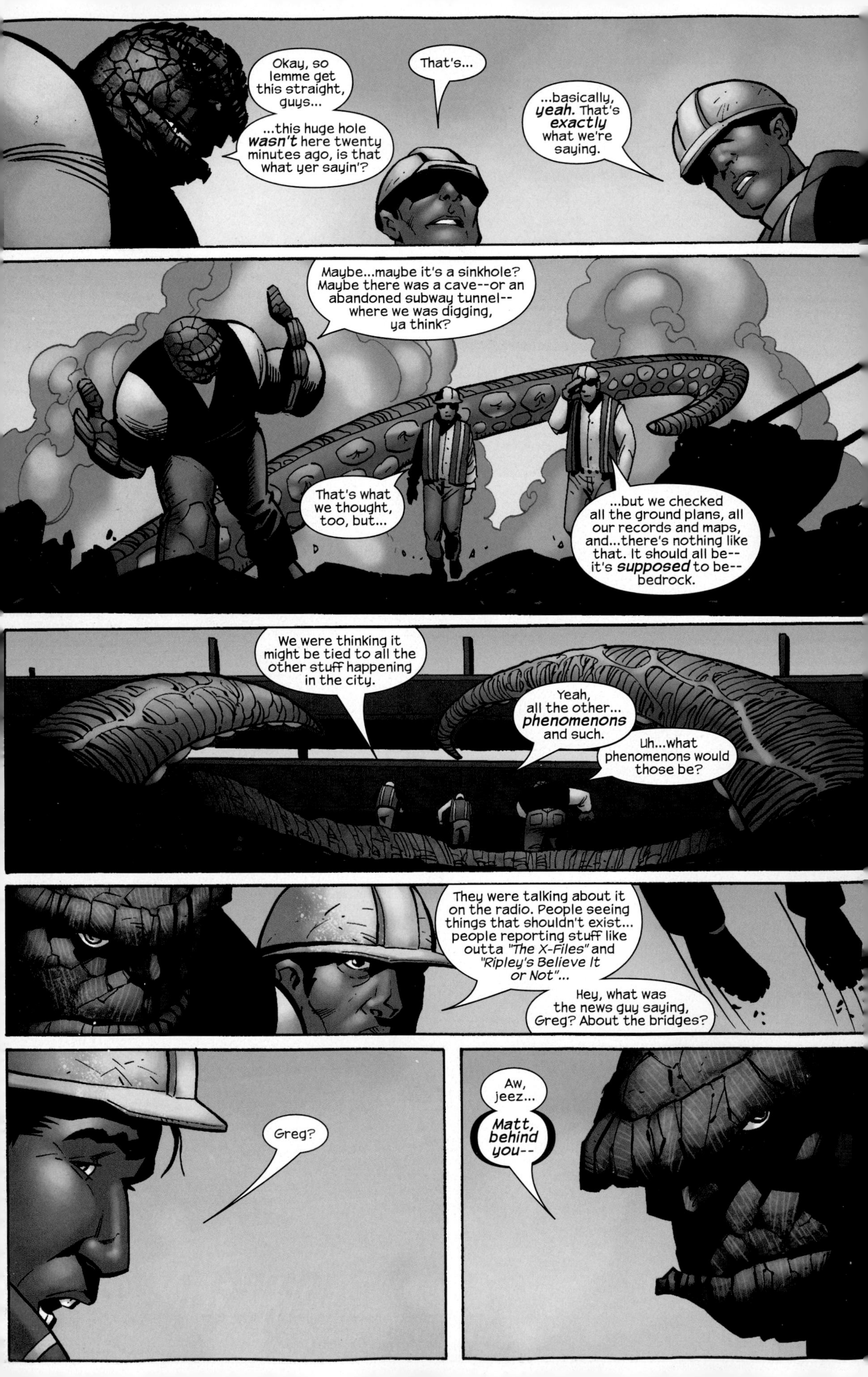
Okay, so lemme get this straight, guys...
...this huge hole *wasn't* here twenty minutes ago, is that what yer sayin'?
That's...
...basically, *yeah.* That's *exactly* what we're saying.
Maybe...maybe it's a sinkhole? Maybe there was a cave--or an abandoned subway tunnel--where we was digging, ya think?
That's what we thought, too, but...
...but we checked all the ground plans, all our records and maps, and...there's nothing like that. It should all be--it's *supposed* to be--bedrock.
We were thinking it might be tied to all the other stuff happening in the city.
Yeah, all the other... *phenomenons* and such.
Uh...what phenomenons would those be?
They were talking about it on the radio. People seeing things that shouldn't exist... people reporting stuff like outta *"The X-Files"* and *"Ripley's Believe It or Not"*...
Hey, what was the news guy saying, Greg? About the bridges?
Greg?
Aw, jeez...
Matt, behind you--

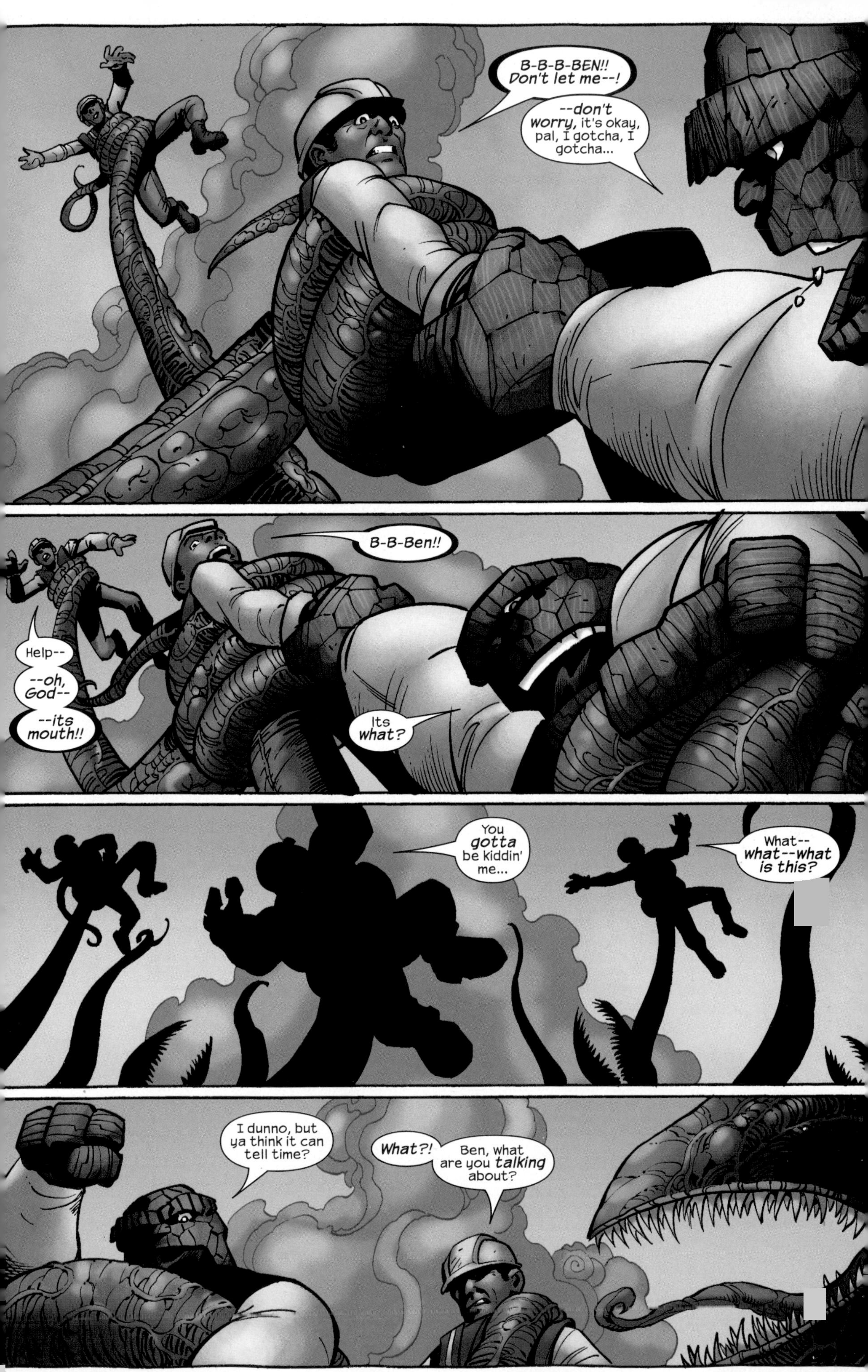
B-B-B-BEN!! Don't let me--!
--don't worry, it's okay, pal, I gotcha, I gotcha...
B-B-Ben!!
Help--
--oh, God--
--its mouth!!
Its what?
You gotta be kiddin' me...
What--what--what is this?
I dunno, but ya think it can tell time?
What?!
Ben, what are you talking about?

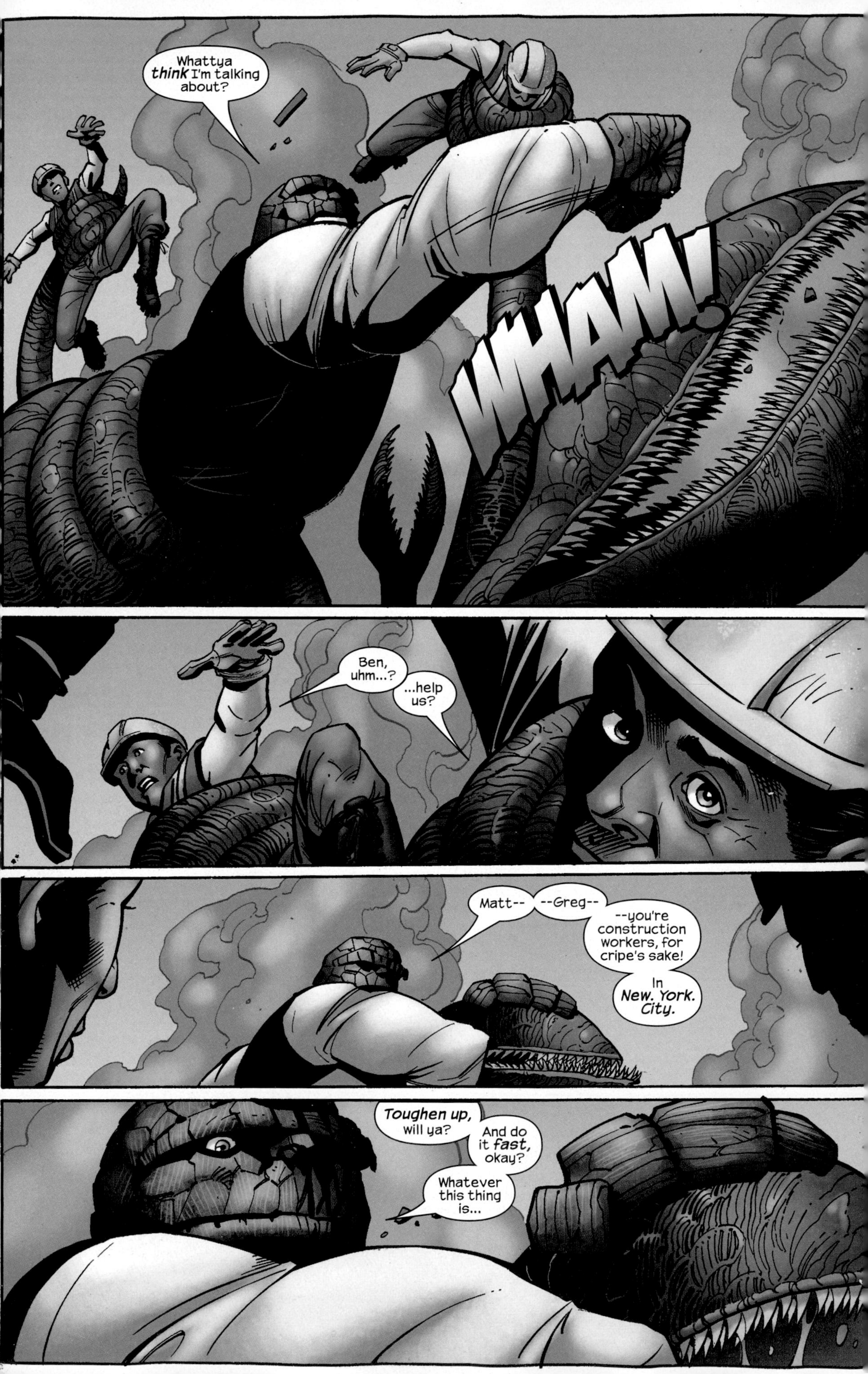
Whattya think I'm talking about?
WHAM!
Ben, uhm...?
...help us?
Matt--
--Greg--
--you're construction workers, for cripe's sake!
In New. York. City.
Toughen up, will ya?
And do it fast, okay?
Whatever this thing is...

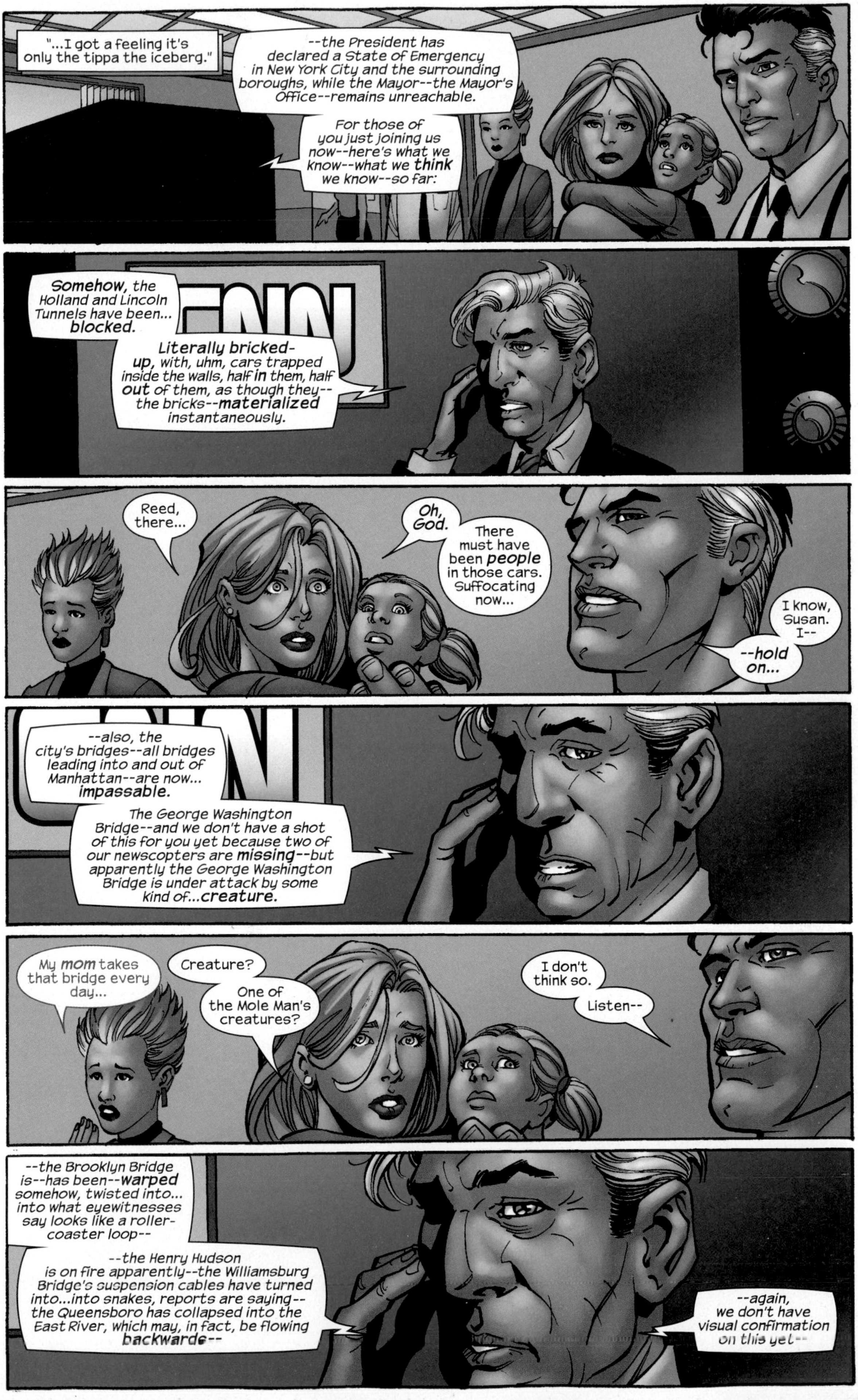
"...I got a feeling it's only the tippa the iceberg."
--the President has declared a State of Emergency in New York City and the surrounding boroughs, while the Mayor--the Mayor's Office--remains unreachable.
For those of you just joining us now--here's what we know--what we think we know--so far:
Somehow, the Holland and Lincoln Tunnels have been... blocked.
Literally bricked-up, with, uhm, cars trapped inside the walls, half in them, half out of them, as though they--the bricks--materialized instantaneously.
Reed, there...
Oh, God.
There must have been people in those cars. Suffocating now...
I know, Susan. I--
--hold on...
--also, the city's bridges--all bridges leading into and out of Manhattan--are now... impassable.
The George Washington Bridge--and we don't have a shot of this for you yet because two of our newscopters are missing--but apparently the George Washington Bridge is under attack by some kind of...creature.
My mom takes that bridge every day...
Creature?
One of the Mole Man's creatures?
I don't think so.
Listen--
--the Brooklyn Bridge is--has been--warped somehow, twisted into... into what eyewitnesses say looks like a roller-coaster loop--
--the Henry Hudson is on fire apparently--the Williamsburg Bridge's suspension cables have turned into...into snakes, reports are saying--the Queensboro has collapsed into the East River, which may, in fact, be flowing backwards--
--again, we don't have visual confirmation on this yet--

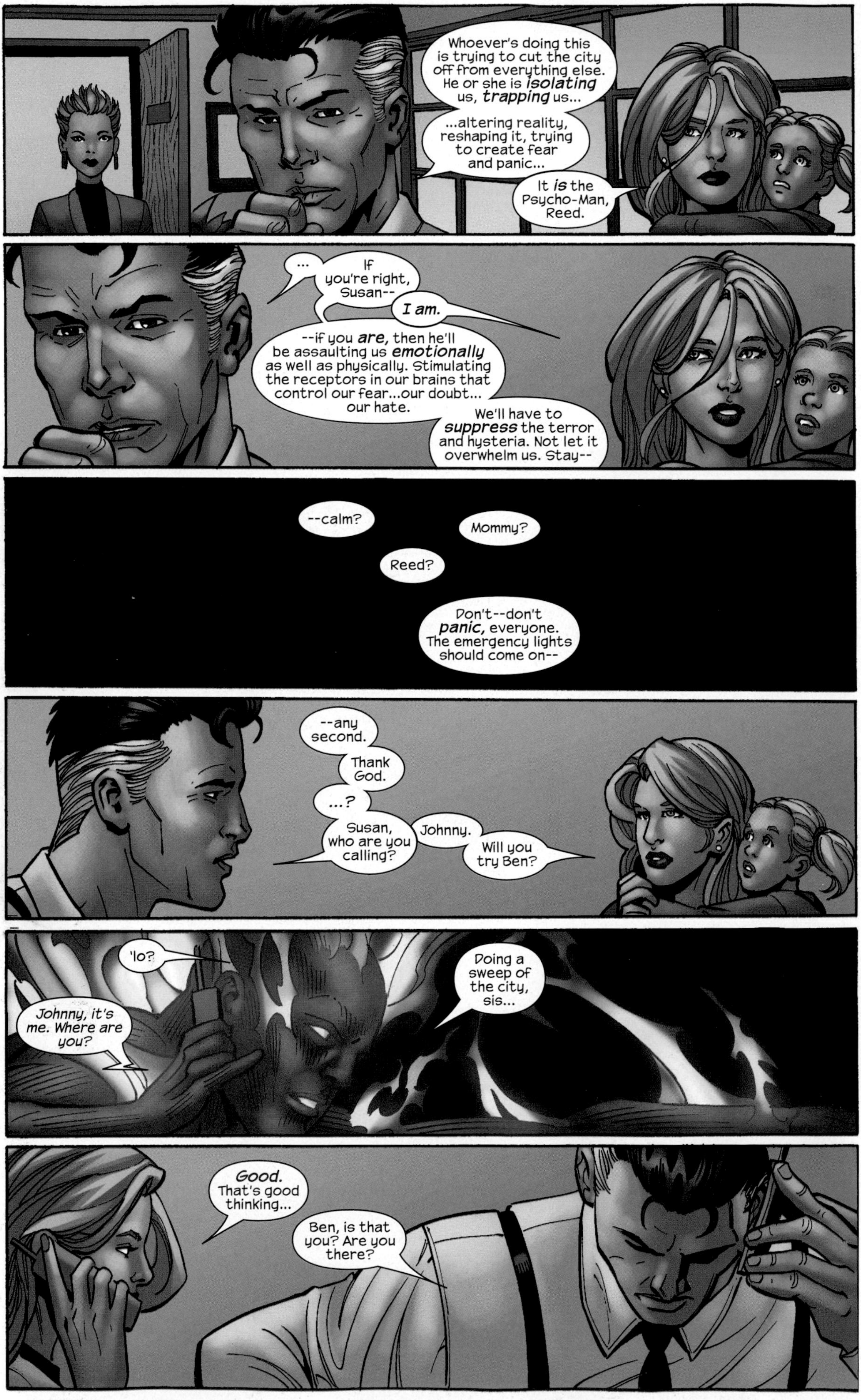
Whoever's doing this is trying to cut the city off from everything else. He or she is *isolating* us, *trapping* us...
...altering reality, reshaping it, trying to create fear and panic...
It *is* the Psycho-Man, Reed.
...
If you're right, Susan--
I am.
--if you *are*, then he'll be assaulting us *emotionally* as well as physically. Stimulating the receptors in our brains that control our fear...our doubt... our hate.
We'll have to *suppress* the terror and hysteria. Not let it overwhelm us. Stay--
--calm?
Mommy?
Reed?
Don't--don't *panic*, everyone. The emergency lights should come on--
--any second.
Thank God.
...?
Susan, who are you calling?
Johnny.
Will you try Ben?
'lo?
Johnny, it's me. Where are you?
Doing a sweep of the city, sis...
Good. That's good thinking...
Ben, is that you? Are you there?

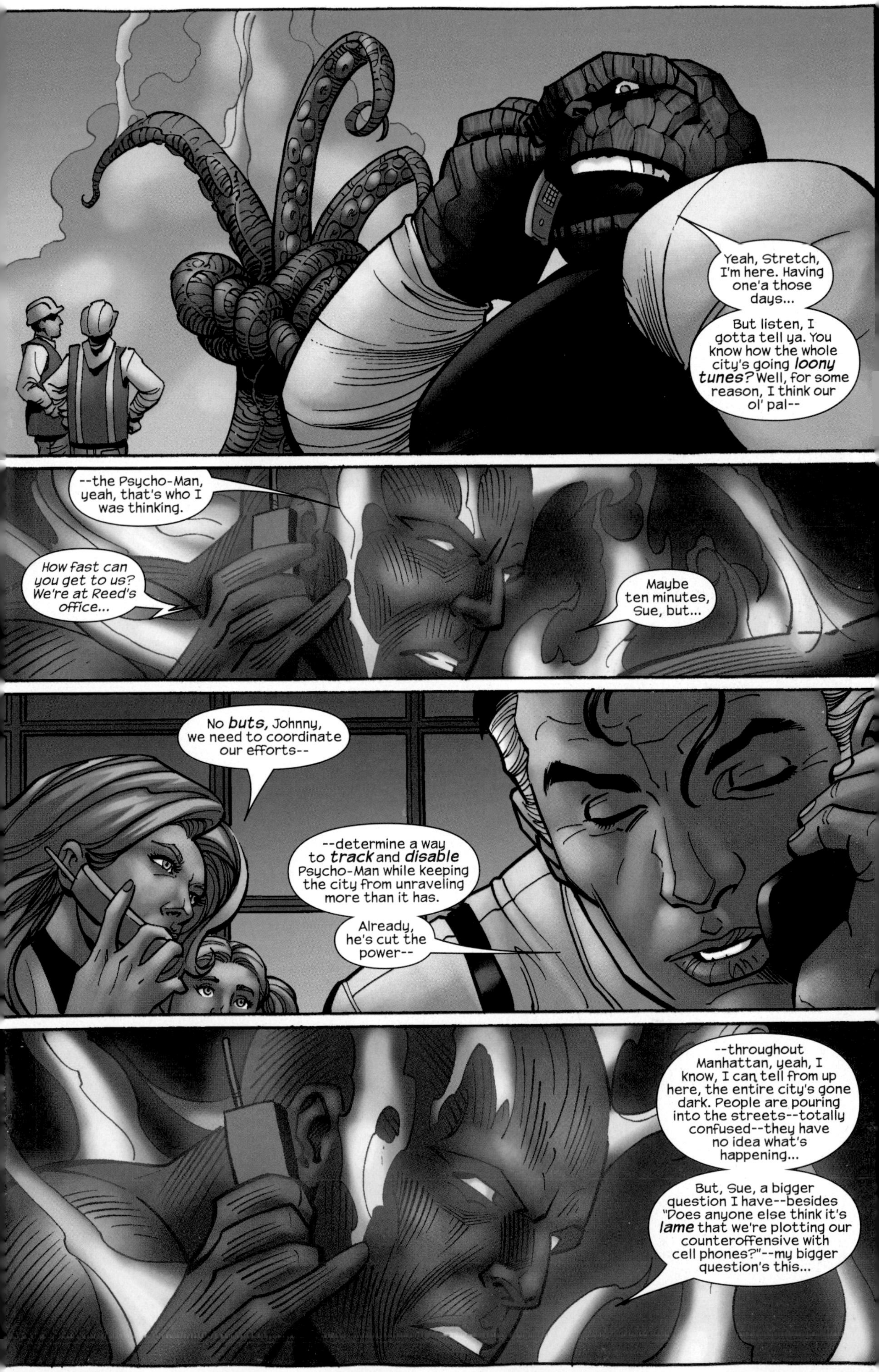
Yeah, Stretch, I'm here. Having one'a those days...
But listen, I gotta tell ya. You know how the whole city's going *loony tunes?* Well, for some reason, I think our ol' pal--
--the Psycho-Man, yeah, that's who I was thinking.
How fast can you get to us? We're at Reed's office...
Maybe ten minutes, Sue, but...
No *buts,* Johnny, we need to coordinate our efforts--
--determine a way to *track* and *disable* Psycho-Man while keeping the city from unraveling more than it has.
Already, he's cut the power--
--throughout Manhattan, yeah, I know, I can tell from up here, the entire city's gone dark. People are pouring into the streets--totally confused--they have no idea what's happening...
But, Sue, a bigger question I have--besides "Does anyone else think it's *lame* that we're plotting our counteroffensive with cell phones?"--my bigger question's this...

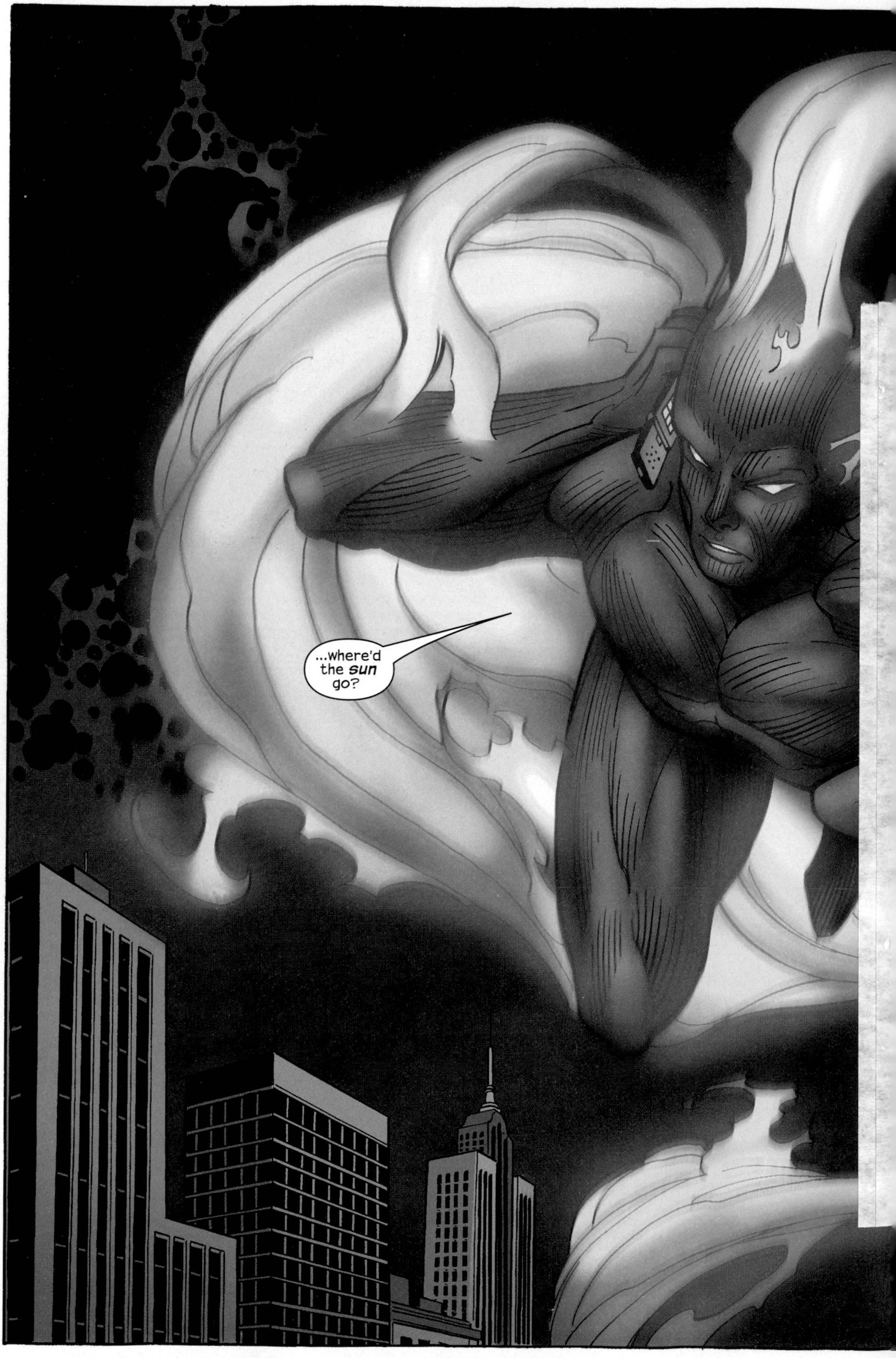
...where'd the *sun* go?

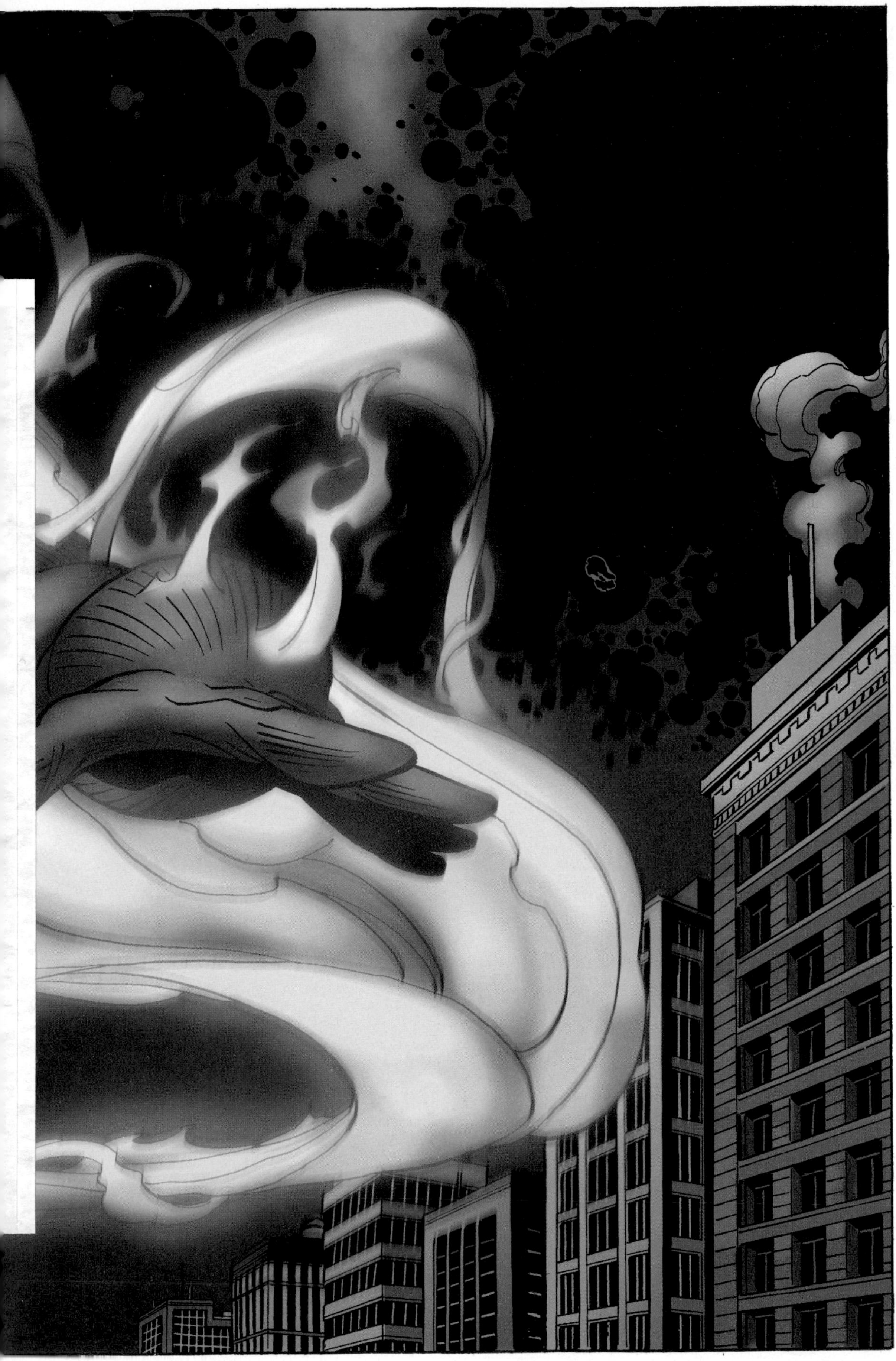

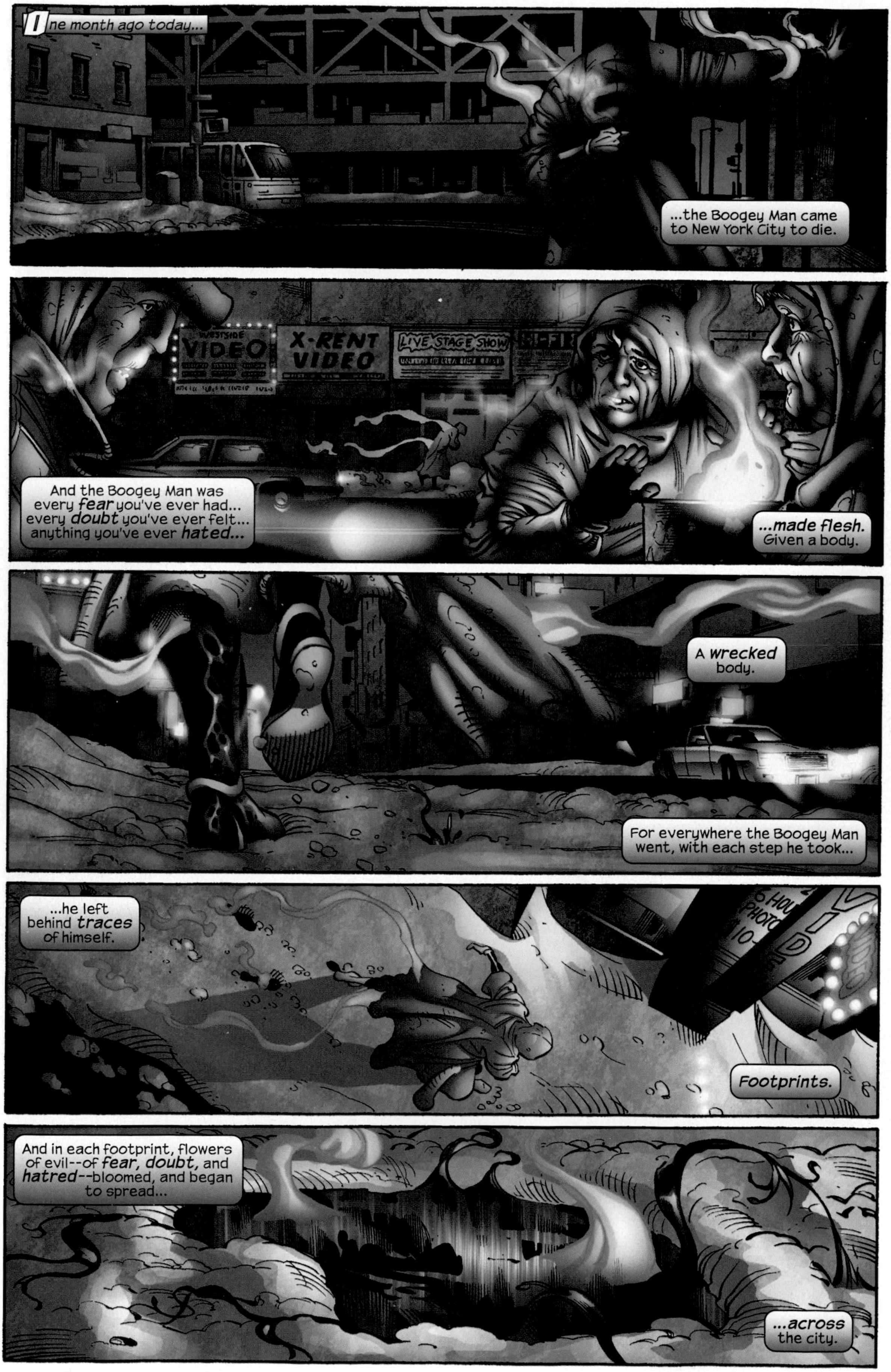
One month ago today...
...the Boogey Man came to New York City to die.
VIDEO
X-RENT VIDEO
LIVE STAGE SHOW
And the Boogey Man was every fear you've ever had... every doubt you've ever felt... anything you've ever hated...
...made flesh. Given a body.
A wrecked body.
For everywhere the Boogey Man went, with each step he took...
...he left behind traces of himself.
Footprints.
And in each footprint, flowers of evil--of fear, doubt, and hatred--bloomed, and began to spread...
...across the city.

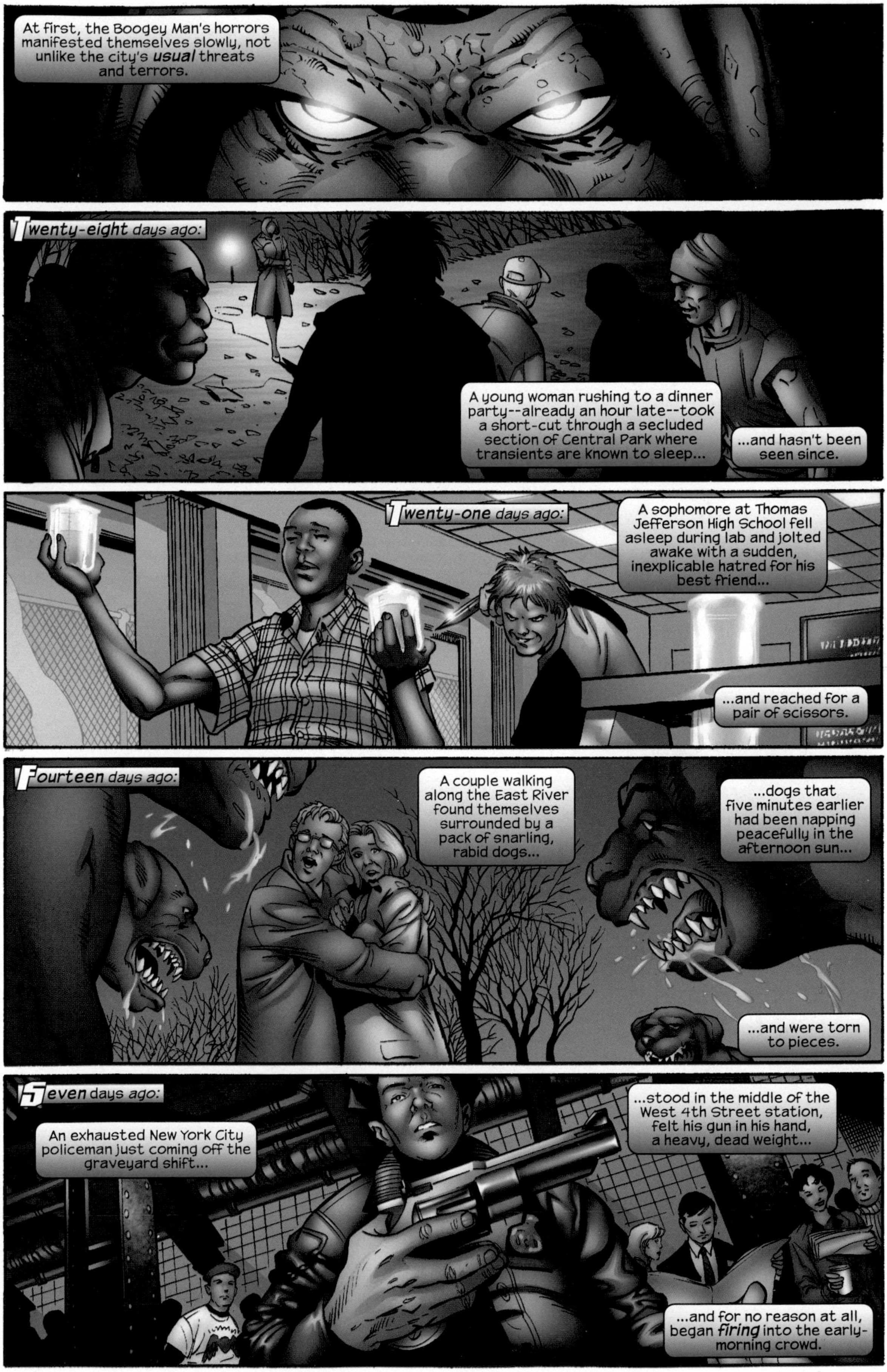
At first, the Boogey Man's horrors manifested themselves slowly, not unlike the city's *usual* threats and terrors.
Twenty-eight days ago:
A young woman rushing to a dinner party--already an hour late--took a short-cut through a secluded section of Central Park where transients are known to sleep...
...and hasn't been seen since.
Twenty-one days ago:
A sophomore at Thomas Jefferson High School fell asleep during lab and jolted awake with a sudden, inexplicable hatred for his best friend...
...and reached for a pair of scissors.
Fourteen days ago:
A couple walking along the East River found themselves surrounded by a pack of snarling, rabid dogs...
...dogs that five minutes earlier had been napping peacefully in the afternoon sun...
...and were torn to pieces.
Seven days ago:
An exhausted New York City policeman just coming off the graveyard shift...
...stood in the middle of the West 4th Street station, felt his gun in his hand, a heavy, dead weight...
...and for no reason at all, began *firing* into the early-morning crowd.

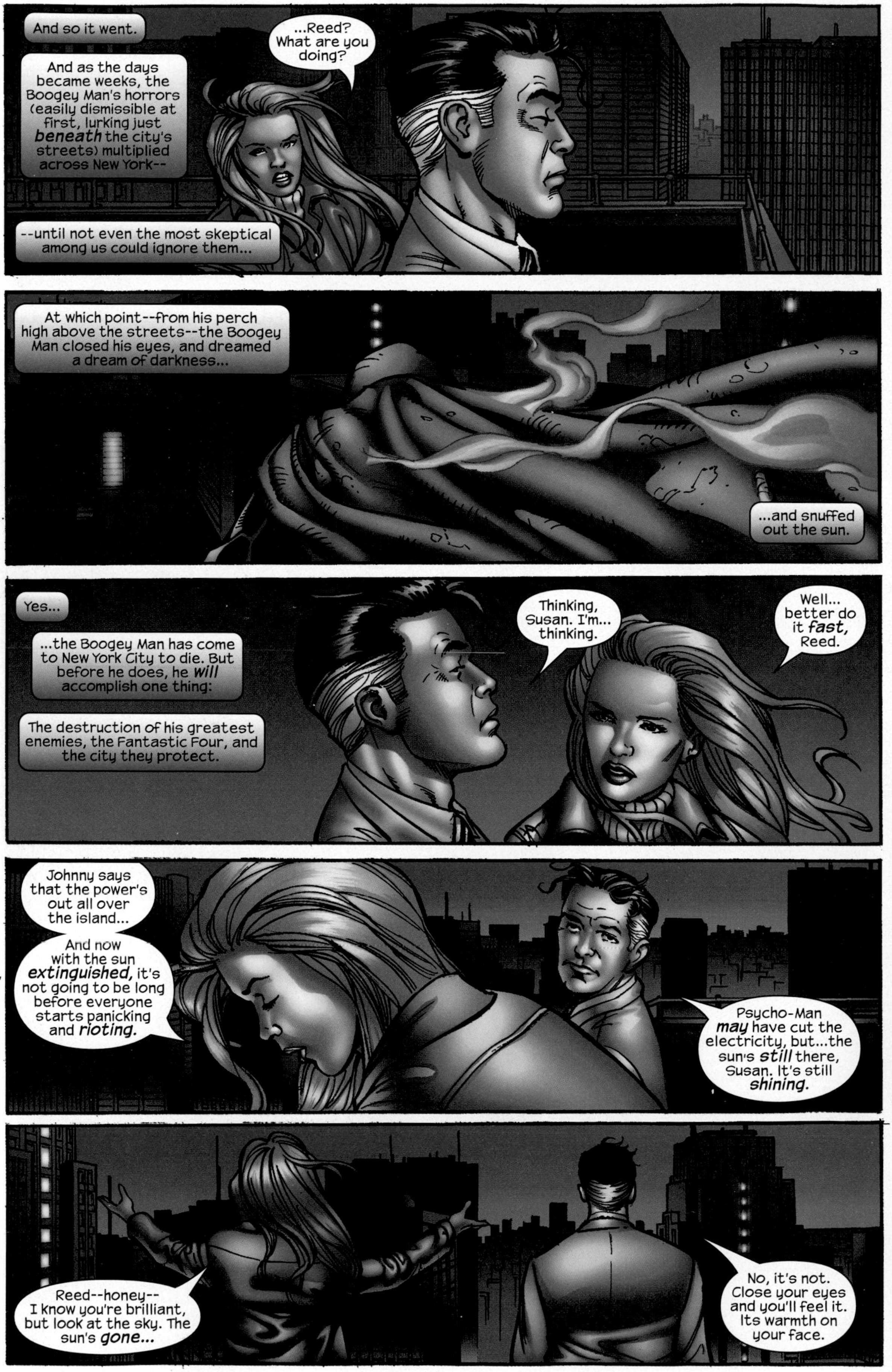
And so it went.
And as the days became weeks, the Boogey Man's horrors (easily dismissible at first, lurking just *beneath* the city's streets) multiplied across New York--
...Reed? What are you doing?
--until not even the most skeptical among us could ignore them...
At which point--from his perch high above the streets--the Boogey Man closed his eyes, and dreamed a dream of darkness...
...and snuffed out the sun.
Yes...
...the Boogey Man has come to New York City to die. But before he does, he *will* accomplish one thing:
The destruction of his greatest enemies, the Fantastic Four, and the city they protect.
Thinking, Susan. I'm... thinking.
Well... better do it *fast,* Reed.
Johnny says that the power's out all over the island...
And now with the sun *extinguished,* it's not going to be long before everyone starts panicking and *rioting.*
Psycho-Man *may* have cut the electricity, but...the sun's *still* there, Susan. It's still *shining.*
Reed--honey-- I know you're brilliant, but look at the sky. The sun's *gone...*
No, it's not. Close your eyes and you'll feel it. Its warmth on your face.

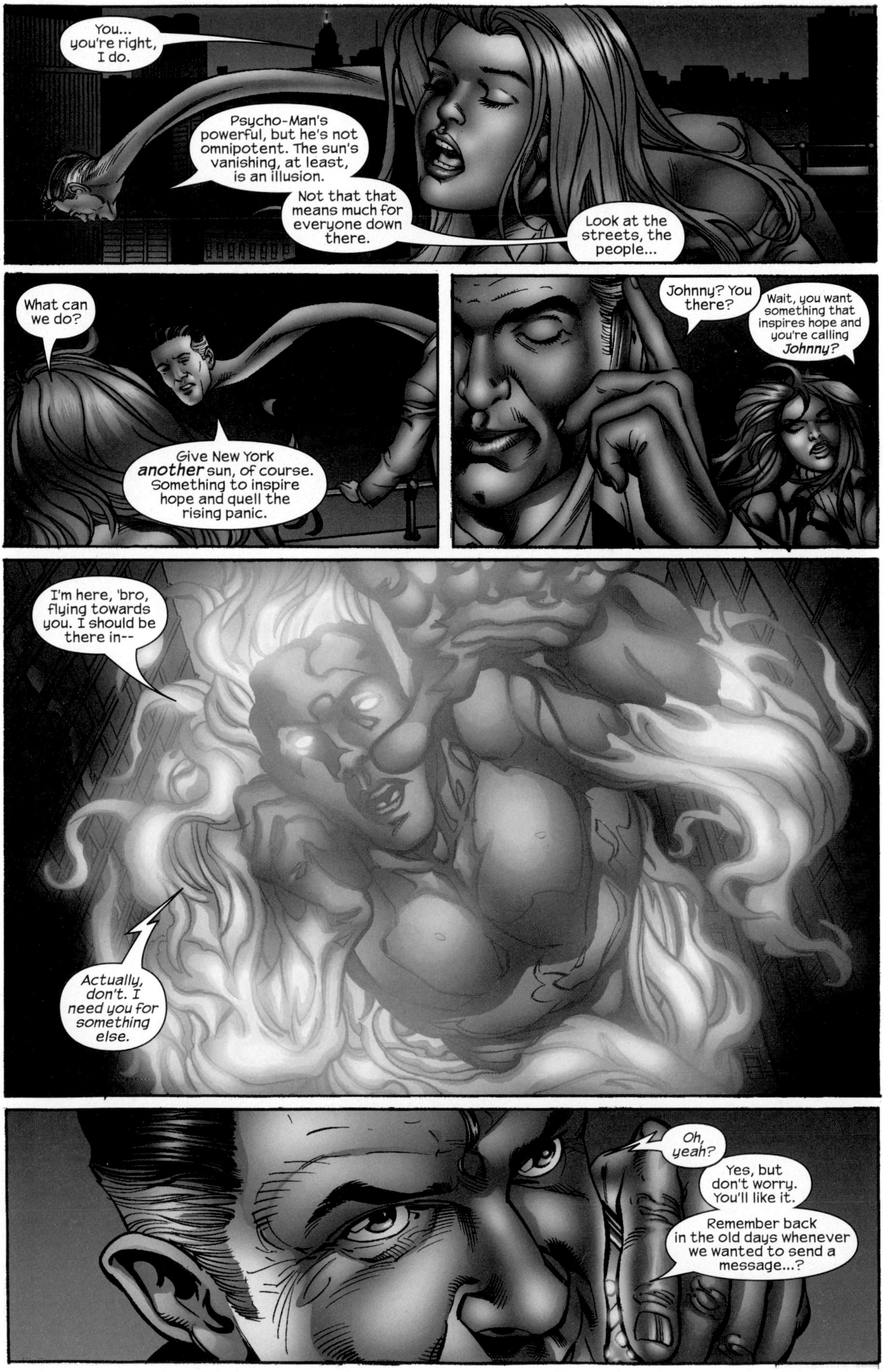
You... you're right, I do.
Psycho-Man's powerful, but he's not omnipotent. The sun's vanishing, at least, is an illusion.
Not that that means much for everyone down there.
Look at the streets, the people...
What can we do?
Give New York *another* sun, of course. Something to inspire hope and quell the rising panic.
Johnny? You there?
Wait, you want something that inspires hope and you're calling *Johnny?*
I'm here, 'bro, flying towards you. I should be there in--
Actually, don't. I need you for something else.
Oh, yeah?
Yes, but don't worry. You'll like it.
Remember back in the old days whenever we wanted to send a message...?

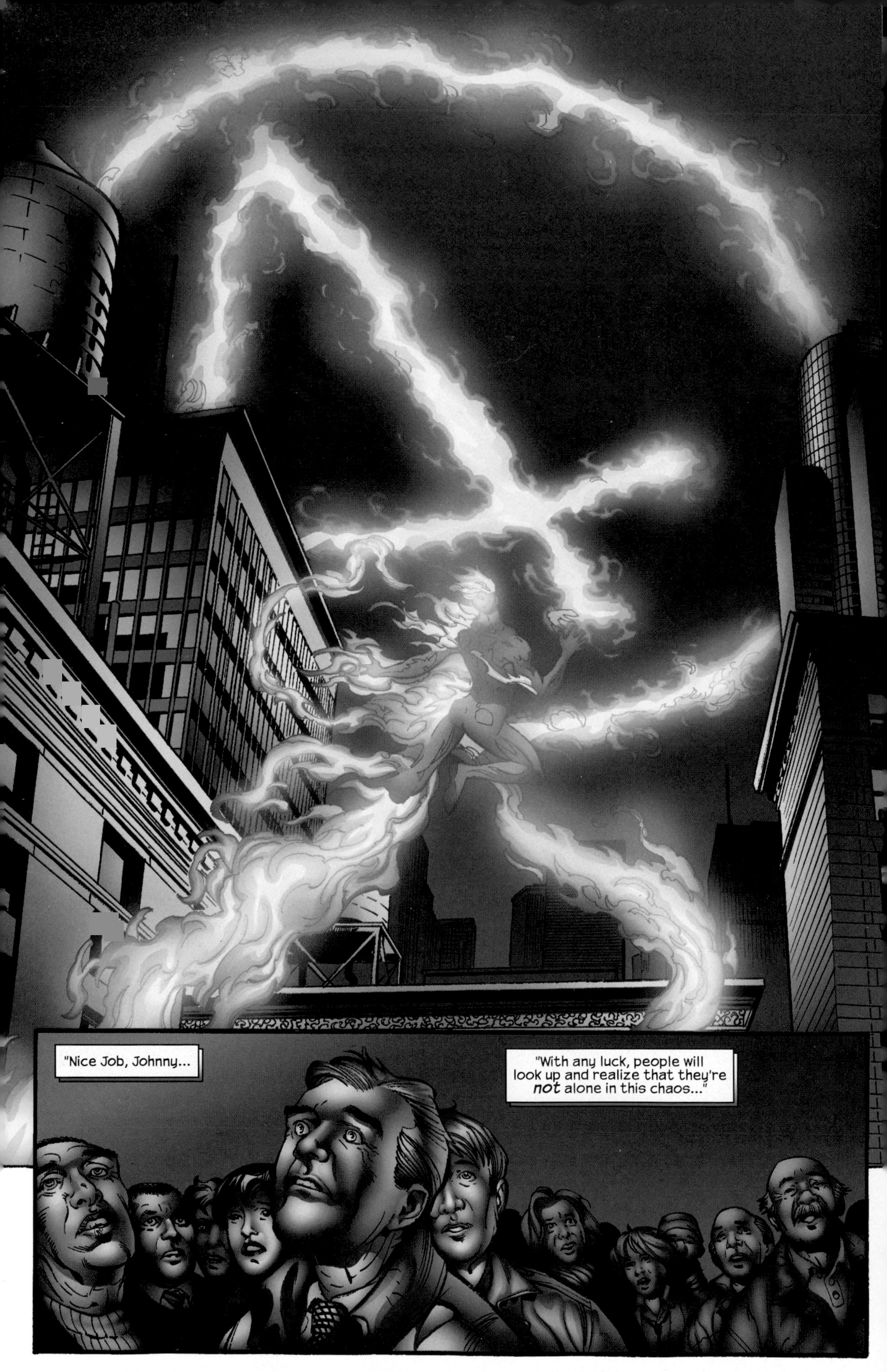
"Nice Job, Johnny...
"With any luck, people will look up and realize that they're *not* alone in this chaos..."

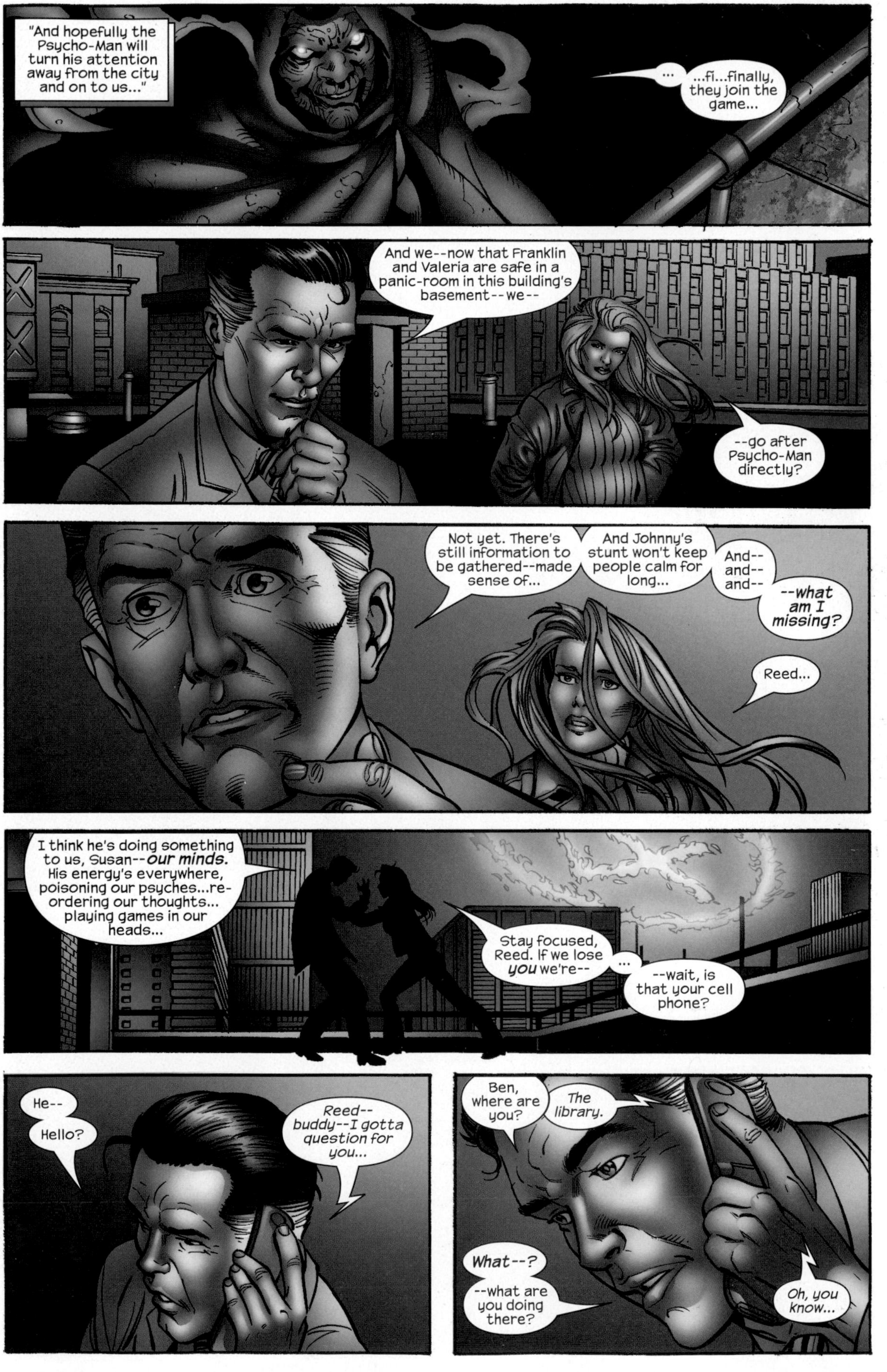
"And hopefully the Psycho-Man will turn his attention away from the city and on to us..."
...
...fi...finally, they join the game...
And we--now that Franklin and Valeria are safe in a panic-room in this building's basement--we--
--go after Psycho-Man directly?
Not yet. There's still information to be gathered--made sense of...
And Johnny's stunt won't keep people calm for long...
And--and--and--
--what am I missing?
Reed...
I think he's doing something to us, Susan--our minds. His energy's everywhere, poisoning our psyches...re-ordering our thoughts... playing games in our heads...
Stay focused, Reed. If we lose you we're--
...
--wait, is that your cell phone?
He--
Hello?
Reed--buddy--I gotta question for you...
Ben, where are you?
The library.
What--?
--what are you doing there?
Oh, you know...

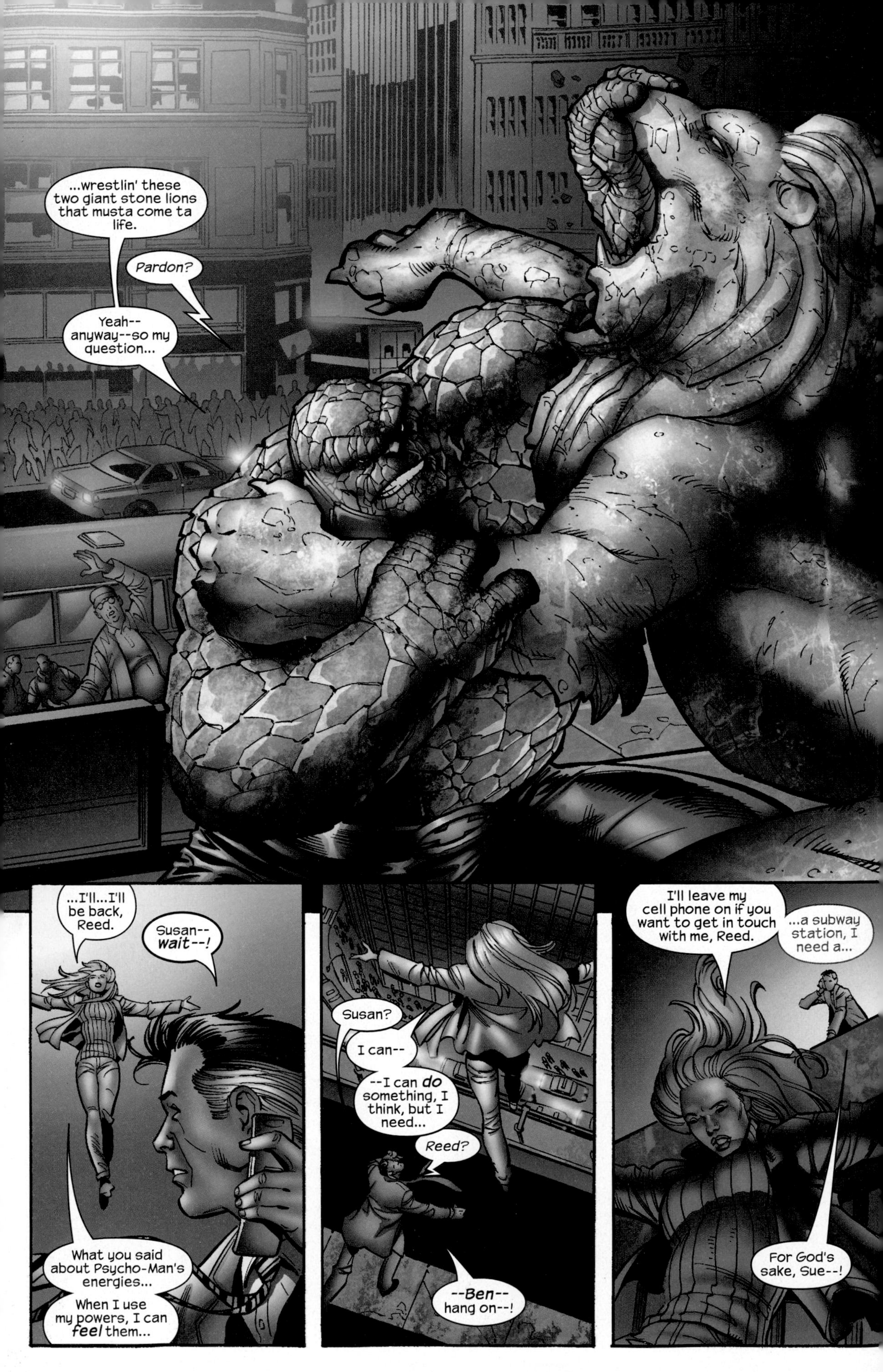
...wrestlin' these two giant stone lions that musta come ta life.
Pardon?
Yeah-- anyway--so my question...
...I'll...I'll be back, Reed.
Susan-- wait--!
What you said about Psycho-Man's energies...
When I use my powers, I can feel them...
Susan?
I can--
--I can do something, I think, but I need...
Reed?
--Ben-- hang on--!
I'll leave my cell phone on if you want to get in touch with me, Reed.
...a subway station, I need a...
For God's sake, Sue--!

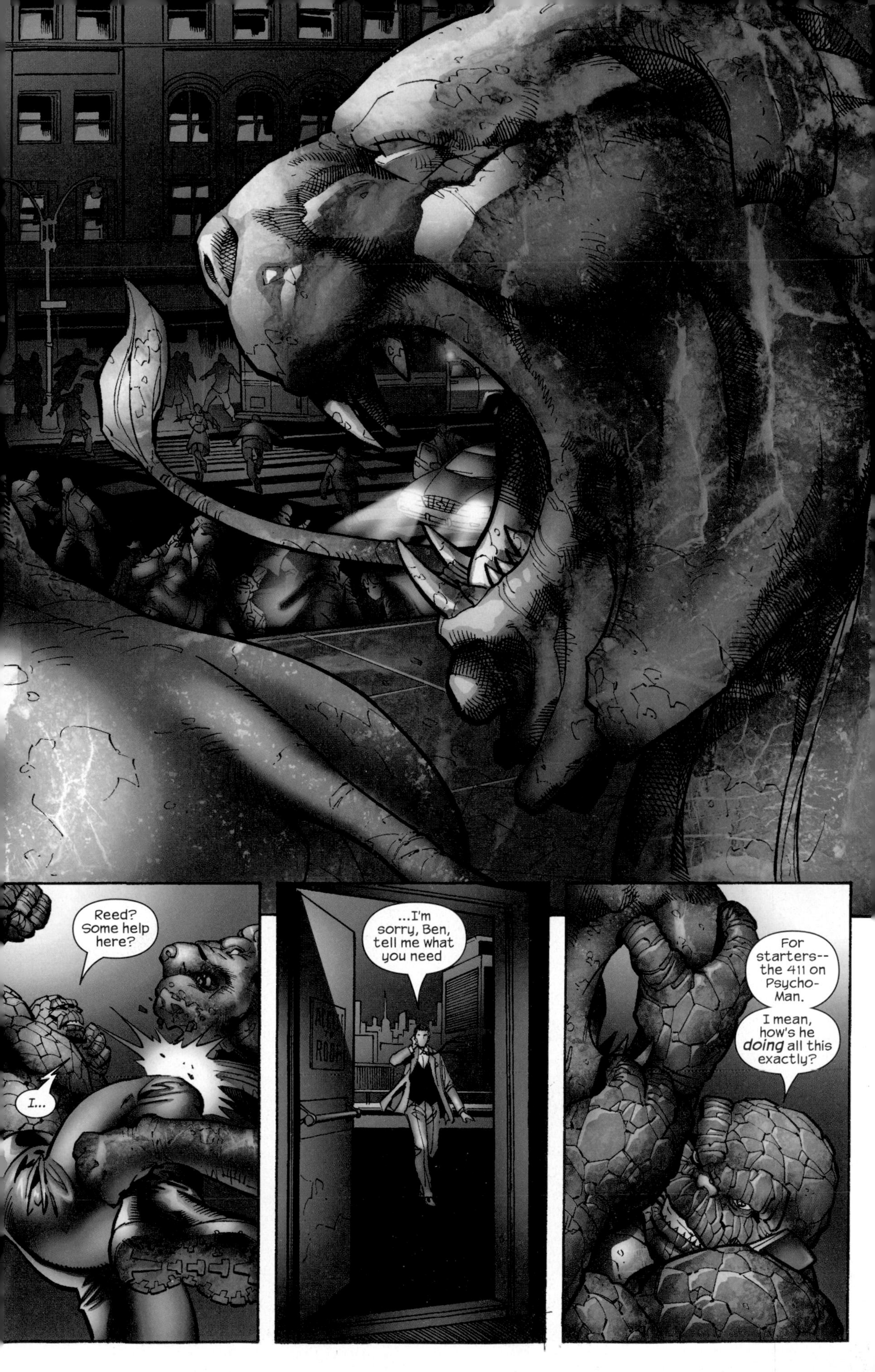

Reed? Some help here?
I...
...I'm sorry, Ben, tell me what you need
For starters-- the 411 on Psycho-Man.
I mean, how's he *doing* all this exactly?

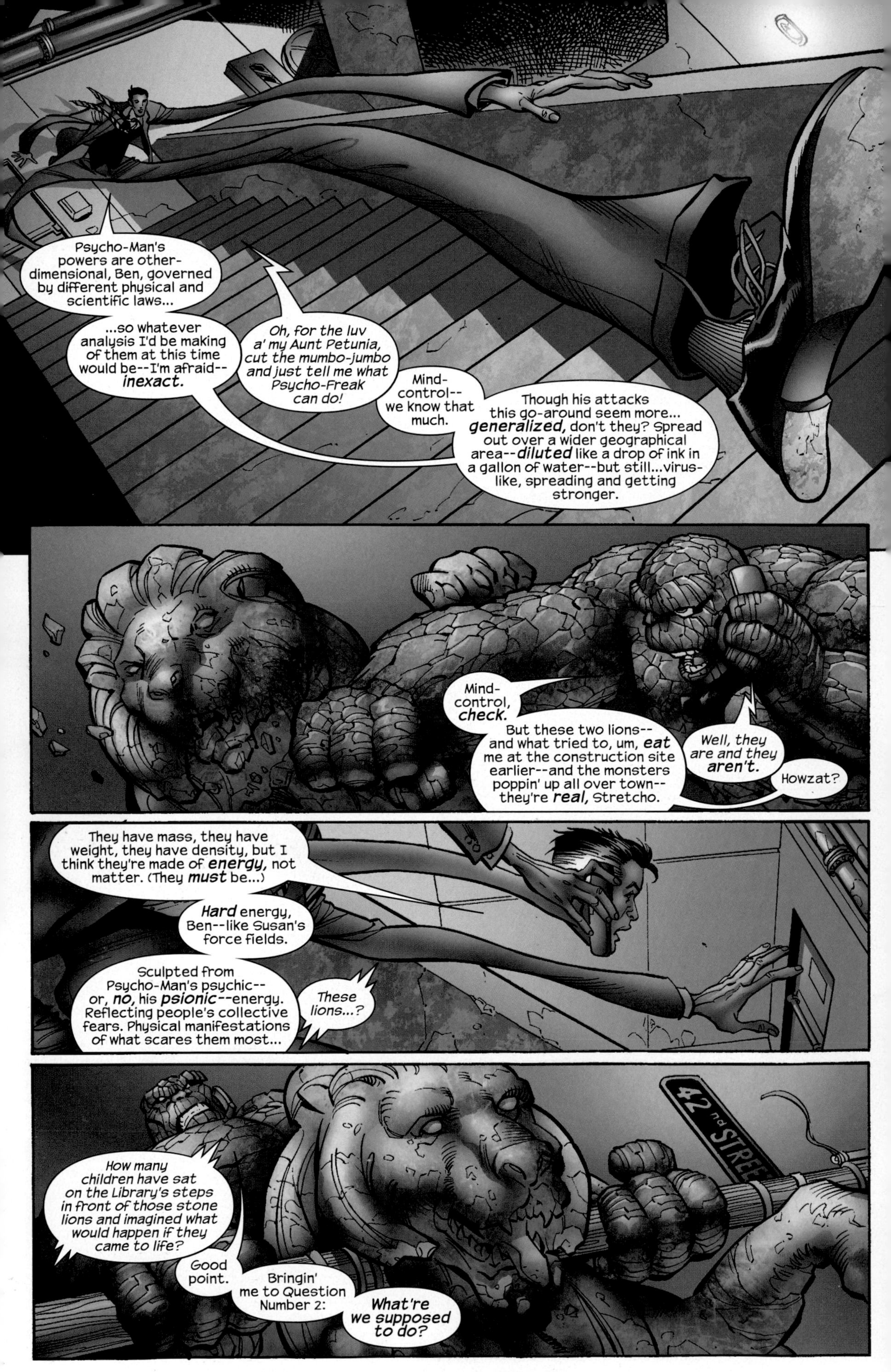

Psycho-Man's powers are other-dimensional, Ben, governed by different physical and scientific laws...
...so whatever analysis I'd be making of them at this time would be--I'm afraid--*inexact.*
Oh, for the luv a' my Aunt Petunia, cut the mumbo-jumbo and just tell me what Psycho-Freak can do!
Mind-control--we know that much.
Though his attacks this go-around seem more... ***generalized,*** don't they? Spread out over a wider geographical area--***diluted*** like a drop of ink in a gallon of water--but still...virus-like, spreading and getting stronger.
Mind-control, ***check.***
But these two lions--and what tried to, um, ***eat*** me at the construction site earlier--and the monsters poppin' up all over town--they're ***real,*** Stretcho.
Well, they are and they ***aren't.***
Howzat?
They have mass, they have weight, they have density, but I think they're made of ***energy,*** not matter. (They ***must*** be...)
Hard energy, Ben--like Susan's force fields.
Sculpted from Psycho-Man's psychic--or, ***no,*** his ***psionic***--energy. Reflecting people's collective fears. Physical manifestations of what scares them most...
These lions...?
42nd STREE
How many children have sat on the Library's steps in front of those stone lions and imagined what would happen if they came to life?
Good point.
Bringin' me to Question Number 2:
What're we supposed to do?

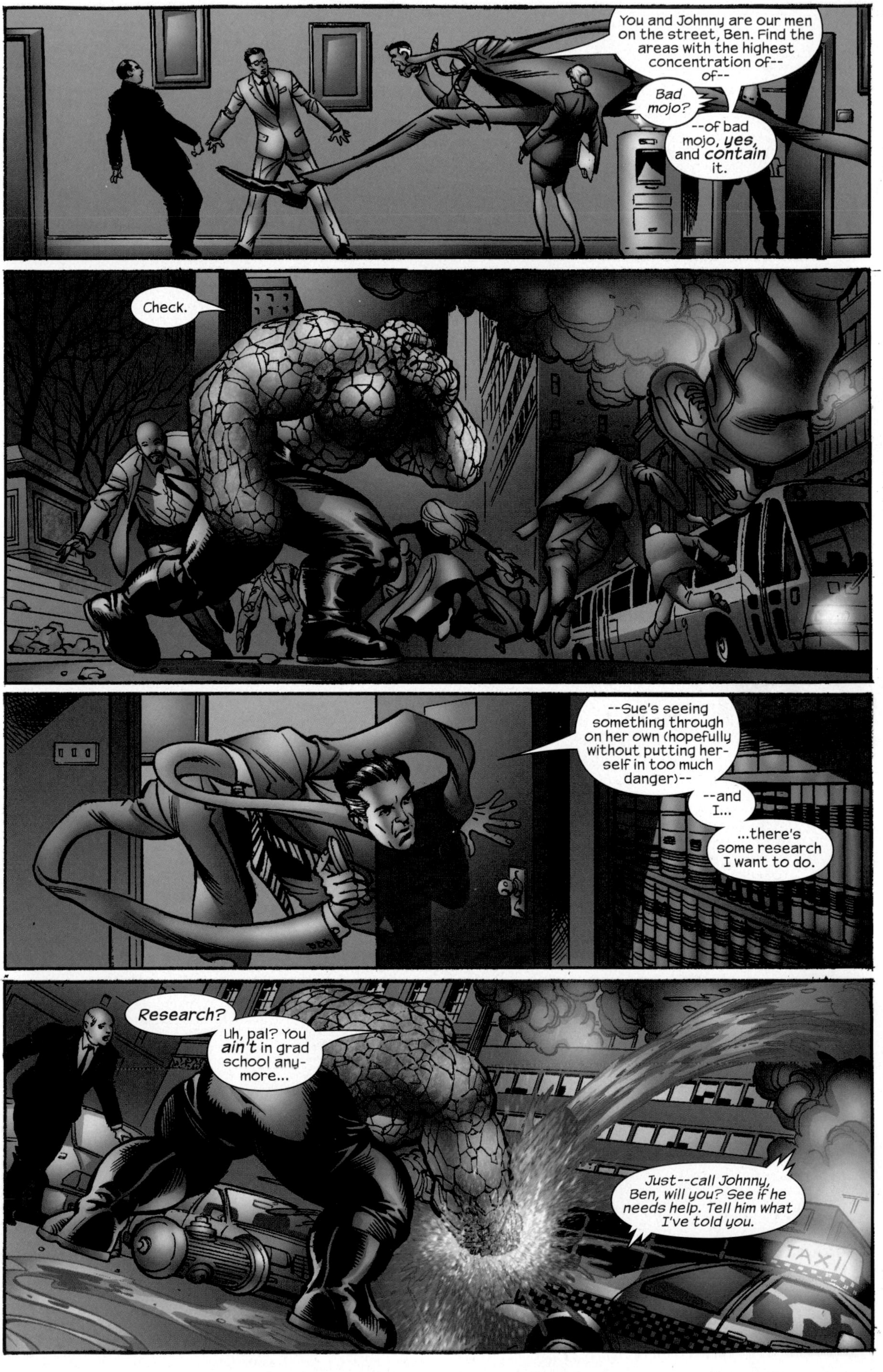
You and Johnny are our men on the street, Ben. Find the areas with the highest concentration of-- of--
Bad mojo?
--of bad mojo, yes, and contain it.
Check.
--Sue's seeing something through on her own (hopefully without putting herself in too much danger)--
--and I...
...there's some research I want to do.
Research?
Uh, pal? You ain't in grad school anymore...
Just--call Johnny, Ben, will you? See if he needs help. Tell him what I've told you.
TAXI

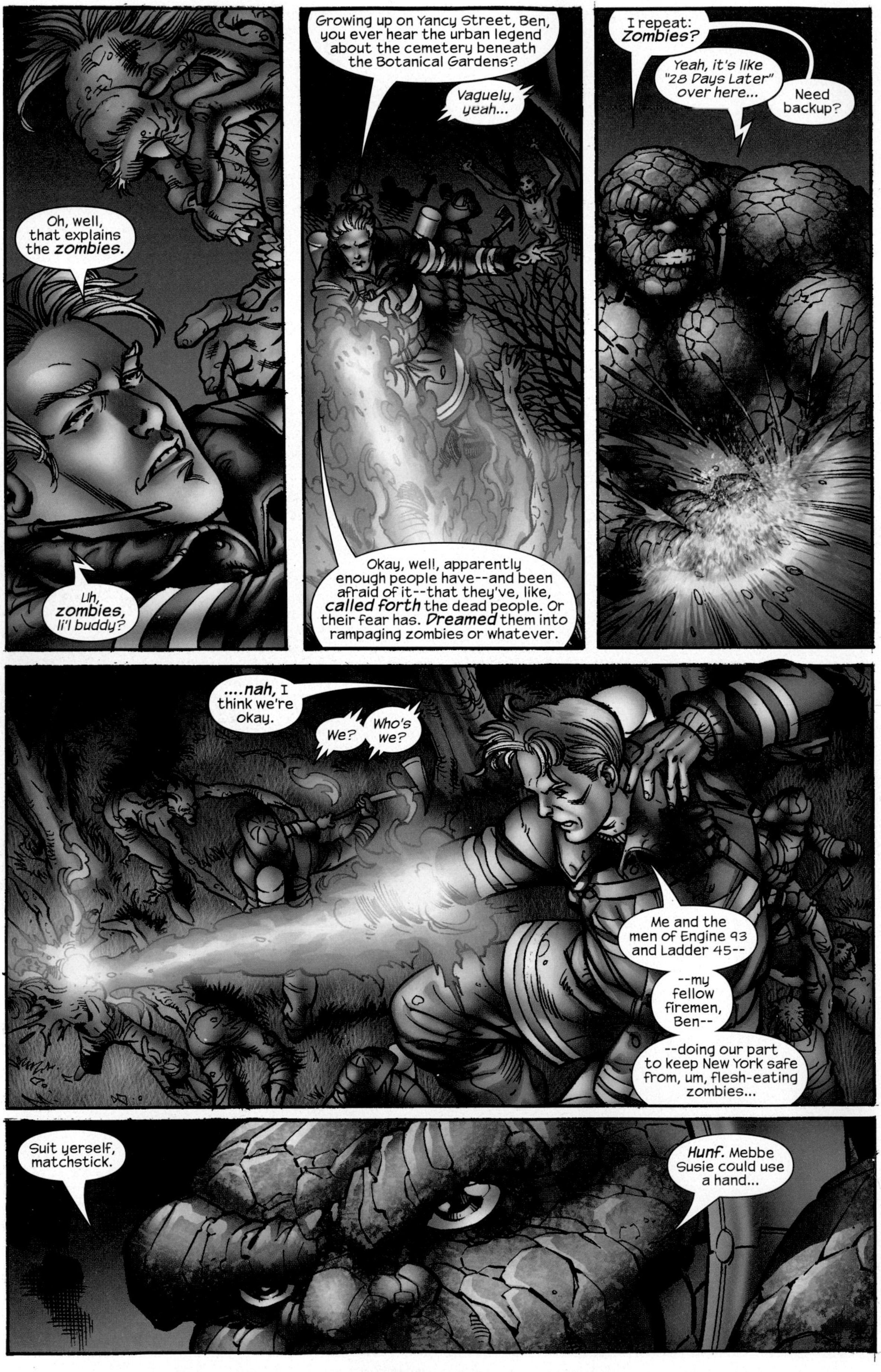
Oh, well, that explains the *zombies.*
Uh, *zombies,* li'l buddy?
Growing up on Yancy Street, Ben, you ever hear the urban legend about the cemetery beneath the Botanical Gardens?
Vaguely, yeah...
Okay, well, apparently enough people have--and been afraid of it--that they've, like, ***called forth*** the dead people. Or their fear has. ***Dreamed*** them into rampaging zombies or whatever.
I repeat: ***Zombies?***
Yeah, it's like "28 Days Later" over here...
Need backup?
....nah, I think we're okay.
We?
Who's we?
Me and the men of Engine 93 and Ladder 45--
--my fellow firemen, Ben--
--doing our part to keep New York safe from, um, flesh-eating zombies...
Suit yourself, matchstick.
Hunf. Mebbe Susie could use a hand...

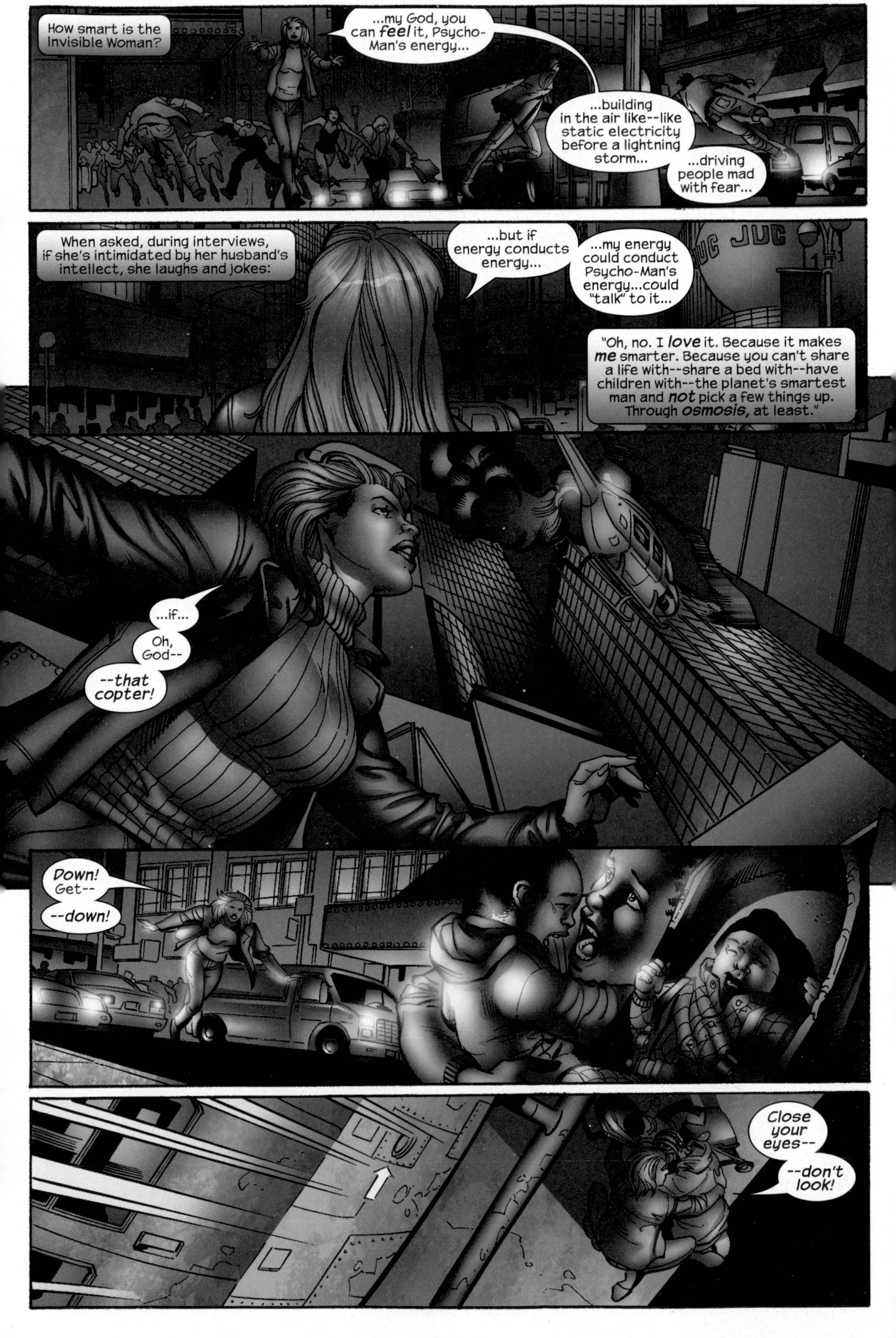
How smart is the Invisible Woman?
...my God, you can feel it, Psycho-Man's energy...
...building in the air like--like static electricity before a lightning storm...
...driving people mad with fear...
When asked, during interviews, if she's intimidated by her husband's intellect, she laughs and jokes:
...but if energy conducts energy...
...my energy could conduct Psycho-Man's energy...could "talk" to it...
"Oh, no. I love it. Because it makes me smarter. Because you can't share a life with--share a bed with--have children with--the planet's smartest man and not pick a few things up. Through osmosis, at least."
...if...
Oh, God--
--that copter!
Down! Get--
--down!
Close your eyes--
--don't look!

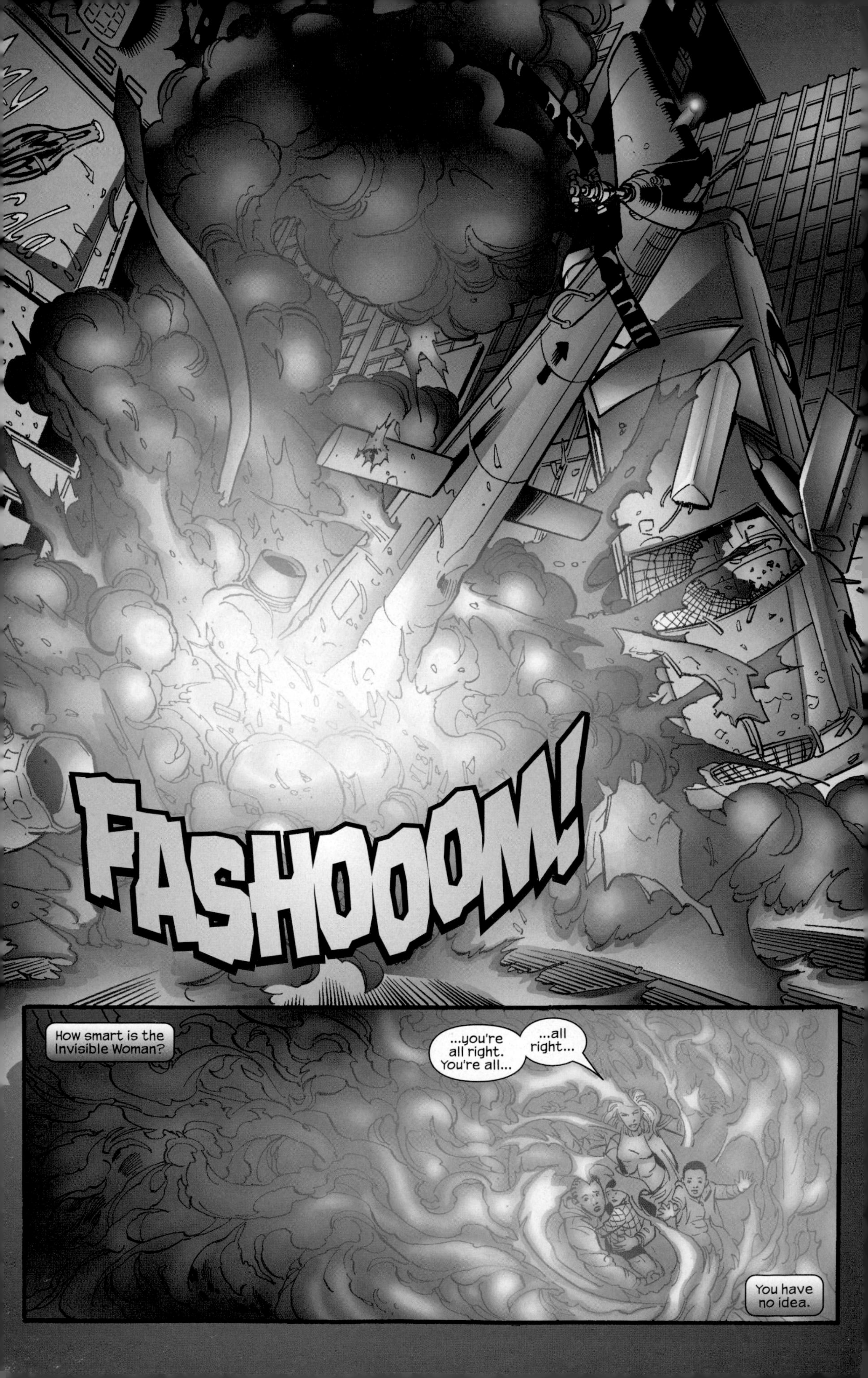
FASHOOOM!
How smart is the Invisible Woman?
...you're all right. You're all...
...all right...
You have no idea.

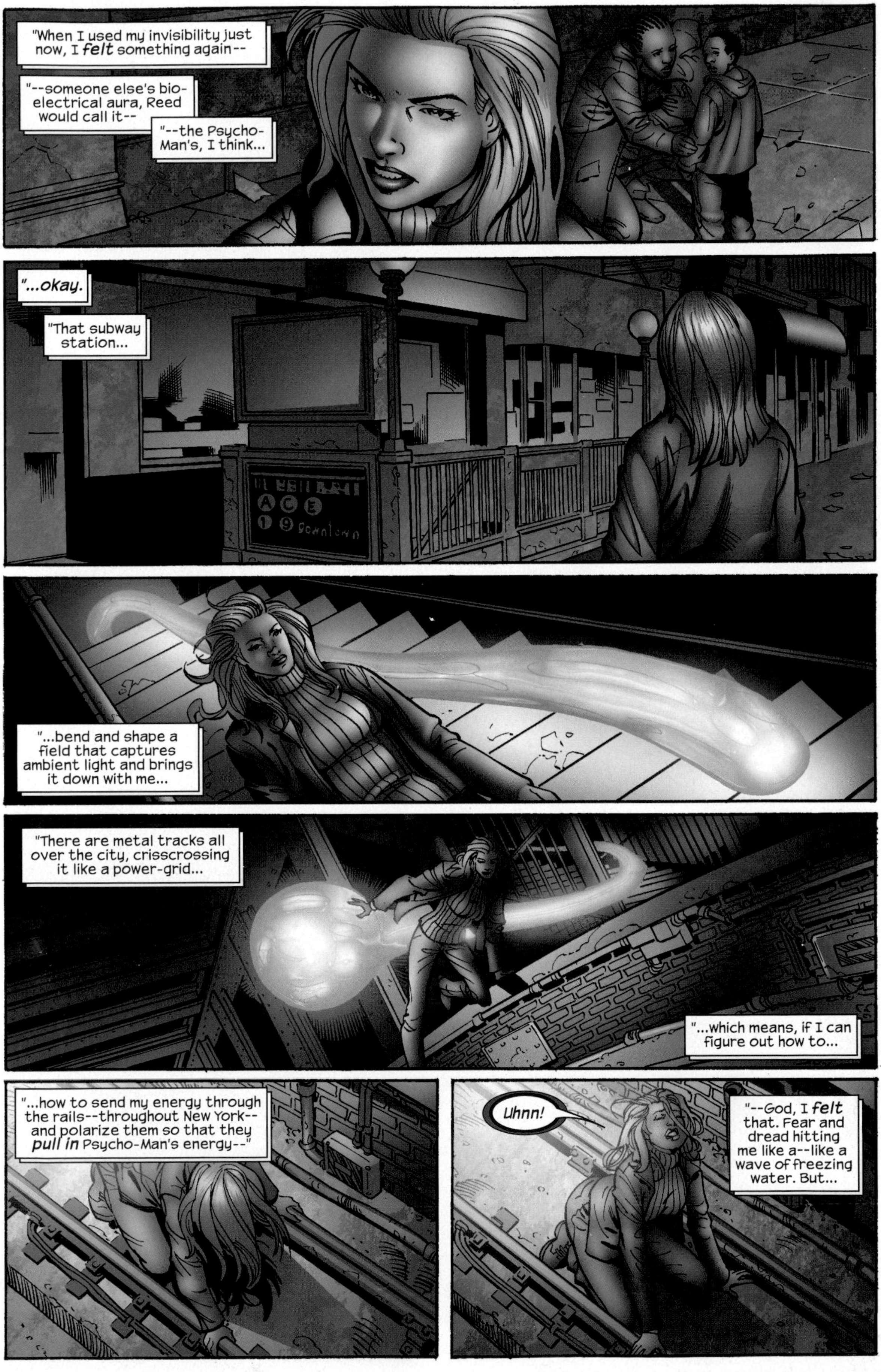
"When I used my invisibility just now, I *felt* something again--
"--someone else's bio-electrical aura, Reed would call it--
"--the Psycho-Man's, I think...
"...okay.
"That subway station...
A C E
1 9 Downtown
"...bend and shape a field that captures ambient light and brings it down with me...
"There are metal tracks all over the city, crisscrossing it like a power-grid...
"...which means, if I can figure out how to...
"...how to send my energy through the rails--throughout New York--and polarize them so that they *pull in* Psycho-Man's energy--"
Uhnn!
"--God, I *felt* that. Fear and dread hitting me like a--like a wave of freezing water. But...

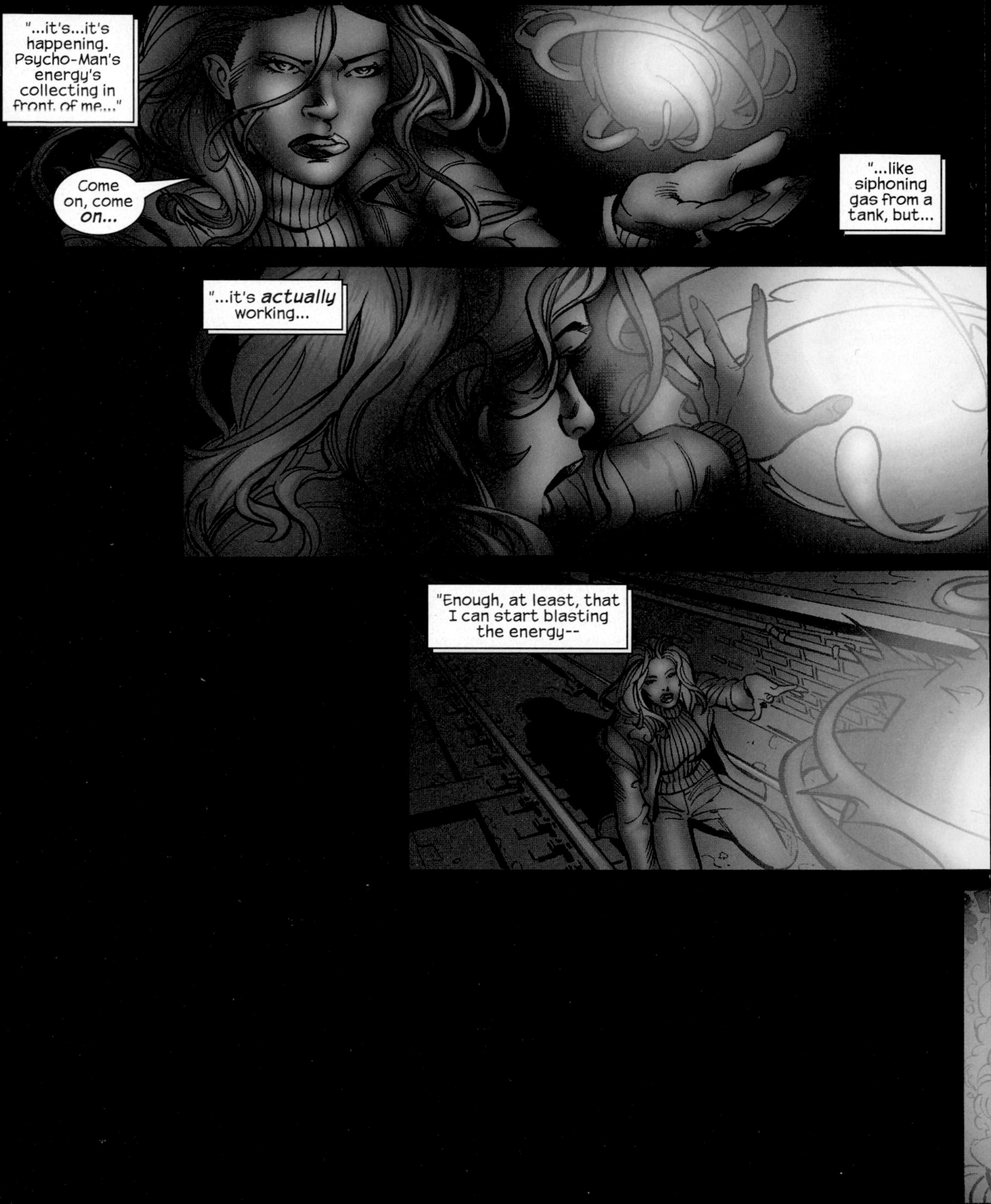
"...it's...it's happening. Psycho-Man's energy's collecting in front of me..."
Come on, come on...
"...like siphoning gas from a tank, but...
"...it's actually working...
"Enough, at least, that I can start blasting the energy--

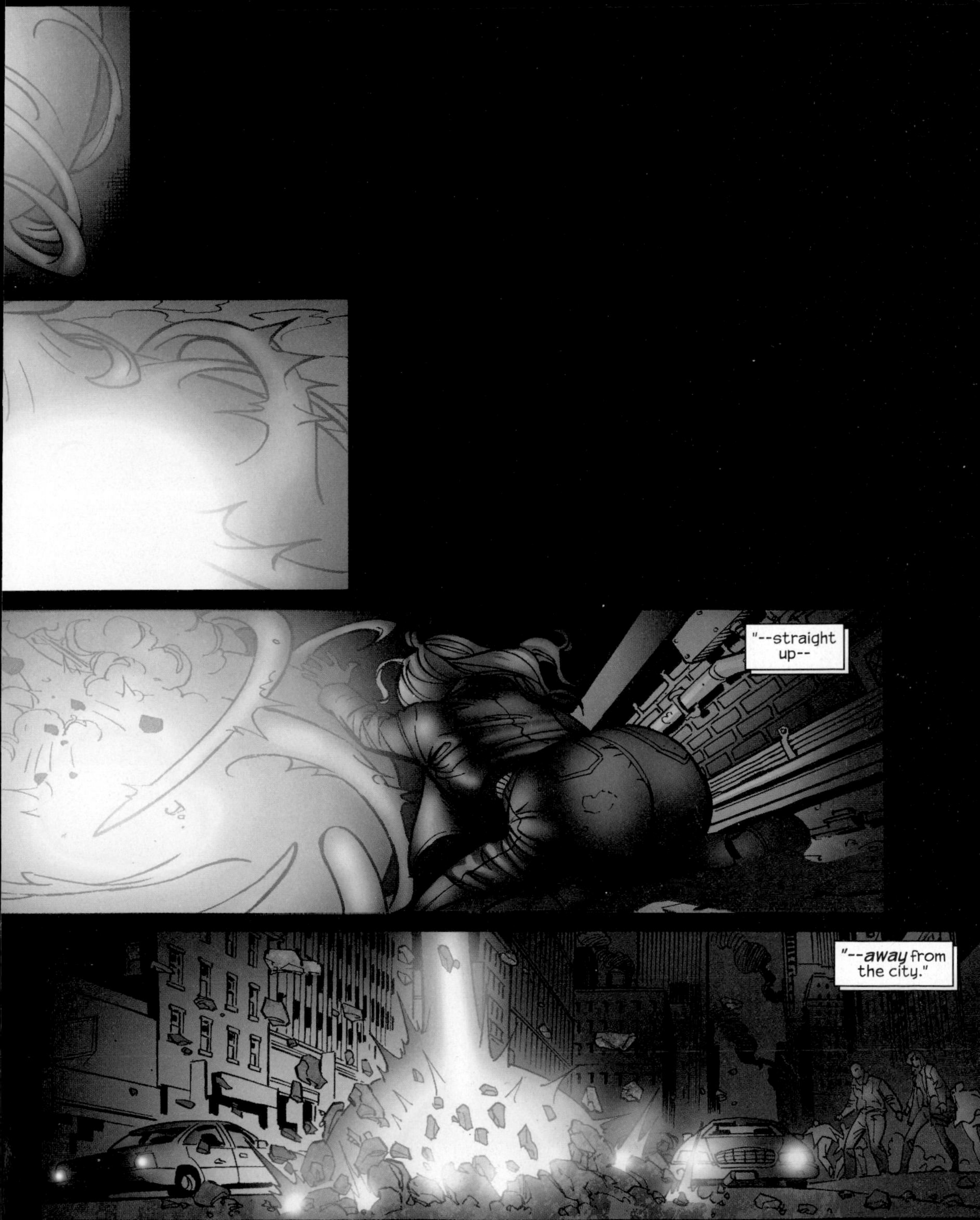
"--straight up--
"--*away* from the city."

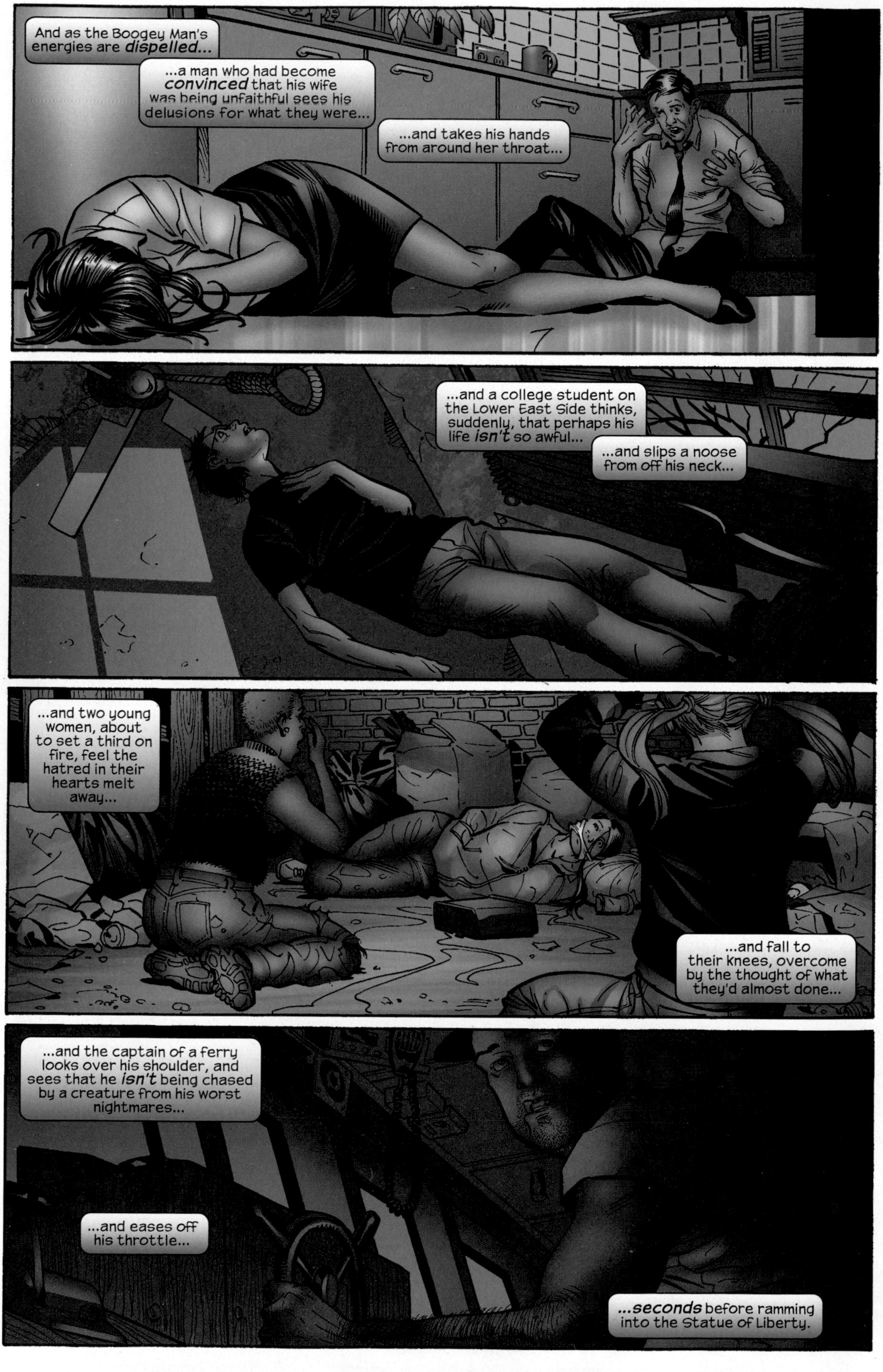
And as the Boogey Man's energies are *dispelled...*
...a man who had become *convinced* that his wife was being unfaithful sees his delusions for what they were...
...and takes his hands from around her throat...
...and a college student on the Lower East Side thinks, suddenly, that perhaps his life *isn't* so awful...
...and slips a noose from off his neck...
...and two young women, about to set a third on fire, feel the hatred in their hearts melt away...
...and fall to their knees, overcome by the thought of what they'd almost done...
...and the captain of a ferry looks over his shoulder, and sees that he *isn't* being chased by a creature from his worst nightmares...
...and eases off his throttle...
...seconds before ramming into the Statue of Liberty.

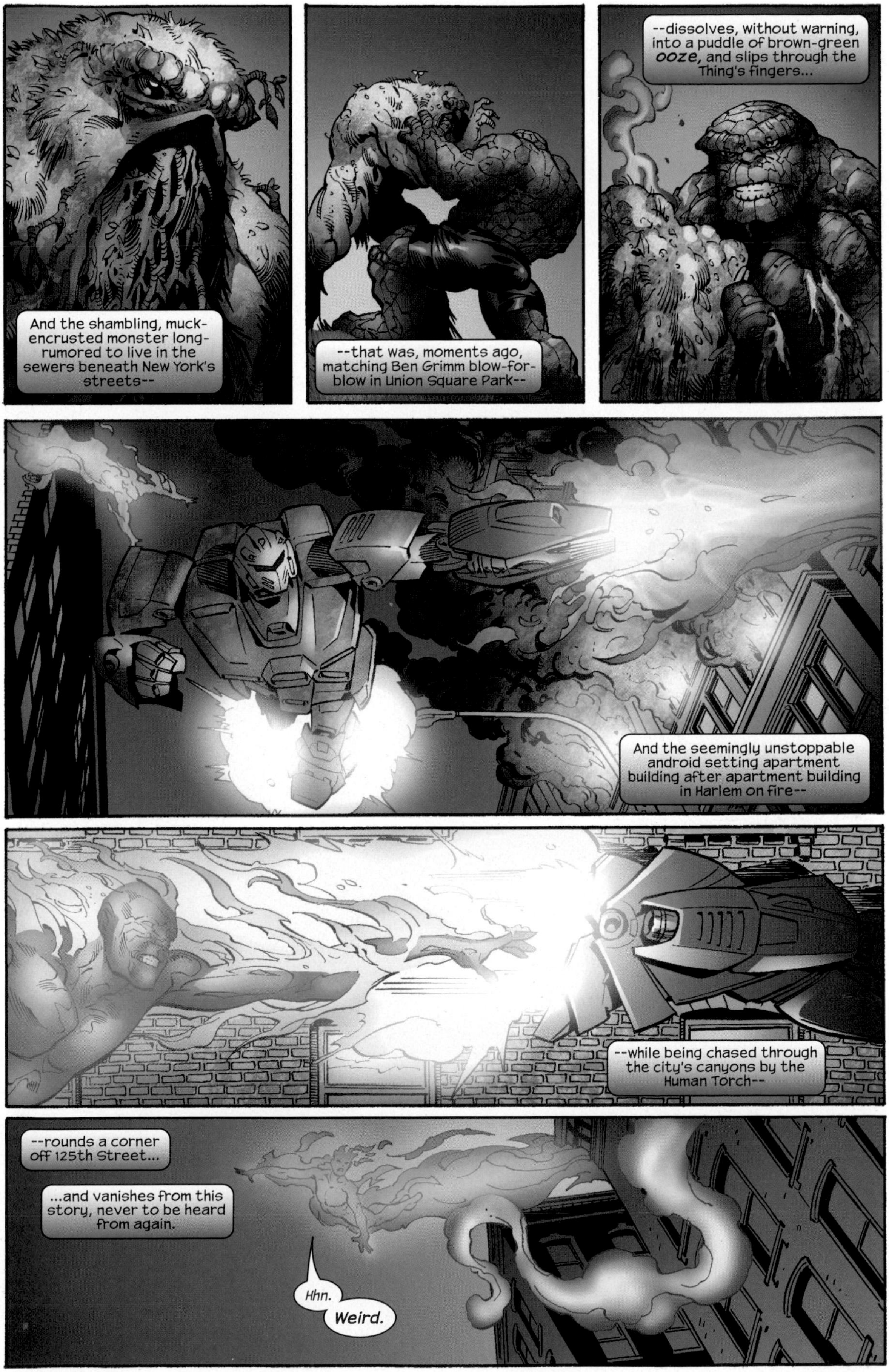
And the shambling, muck-encrusted monster long-rumored to live in the sewers beneath New York's streets--
--that was, moments ago, matching Ben Grimm blow-for-blow in Union Square Park--
--dissolves, without warning, into a puddle of brown-green ooze, and slips through the Thing's fingers...
And the seemingly unstoppable android setting apartment building after apartment building in Harlem on fire--
--while being chased through the city's canyons by the Human Torch--
--rounds a corner off 125th Street...
...and vanishes from this story, never to be heard from again.
Hhn.
Weird.

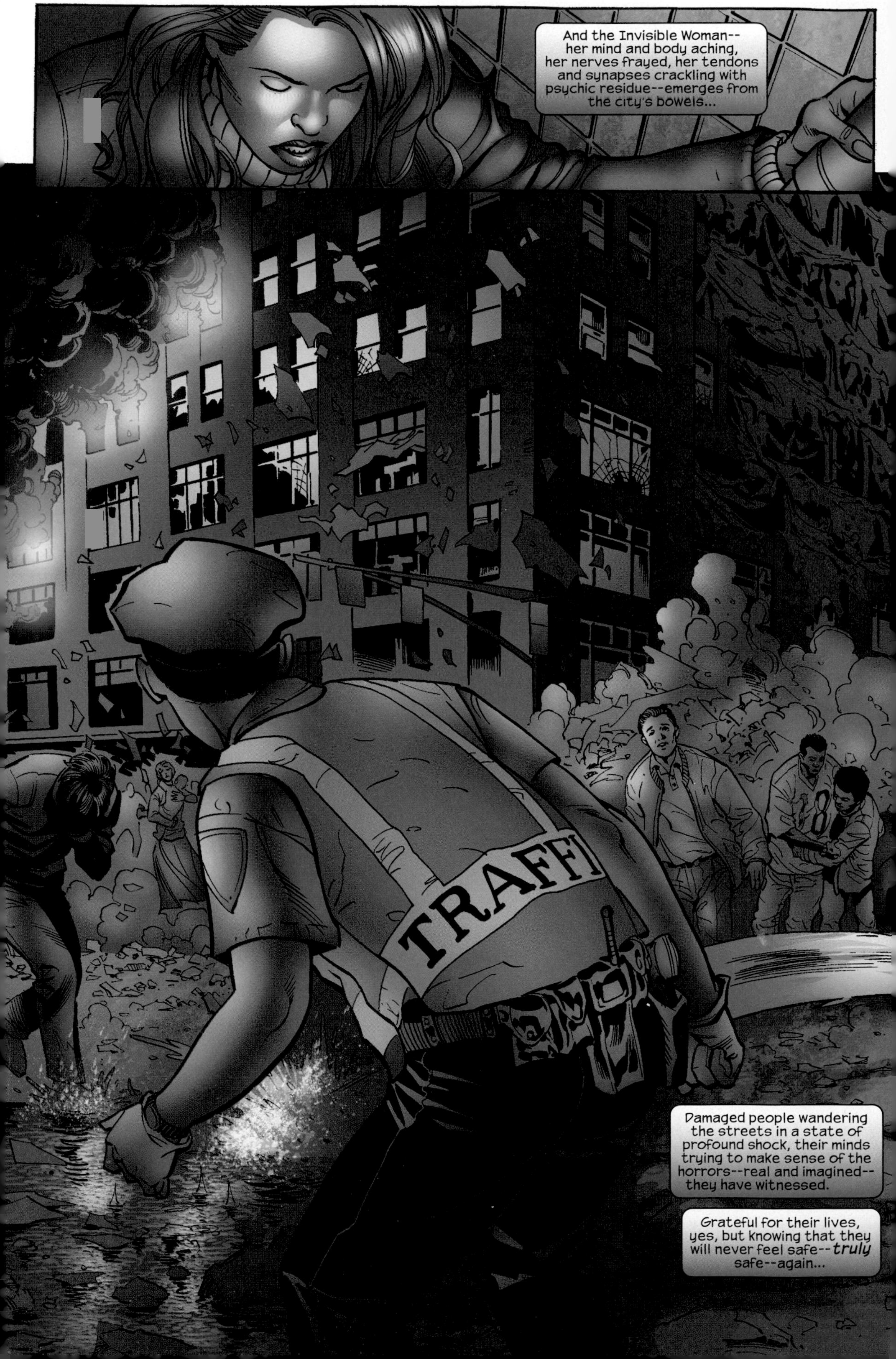
And the Invisible Woman--her mind and body aching, her nerves frayed, her tendons and synapses crackling with psychic residue--emerges from the city's bowels...
TRAFFI
Damaged people wandering the streets in a state of profound shock, their minds trying to make sense of the horrors--real and imagined--they have witnessed.
Grateful for their lives, yes, but knowing that they will never feel safe--*truly* safe--again...

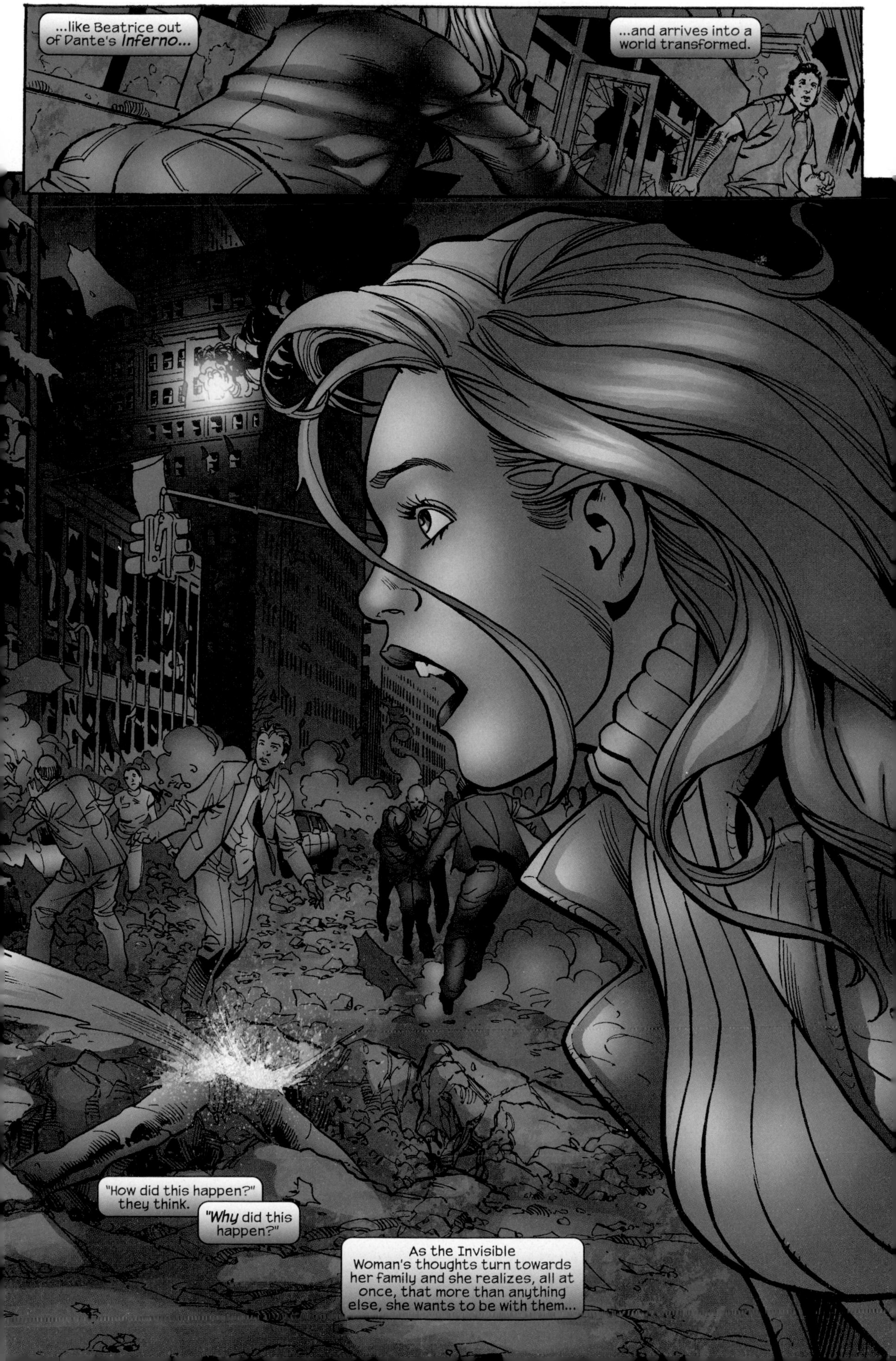
...like Beatrice out of Dante's *Inferno*...
...and arrives into a world transformed.
"How did this happen?" they think.
"*Why* did this happen?"
As the Invisible Woman's thoughts turn towards her family and she realizes, all at once, that more than anything else, she wants to be with them...

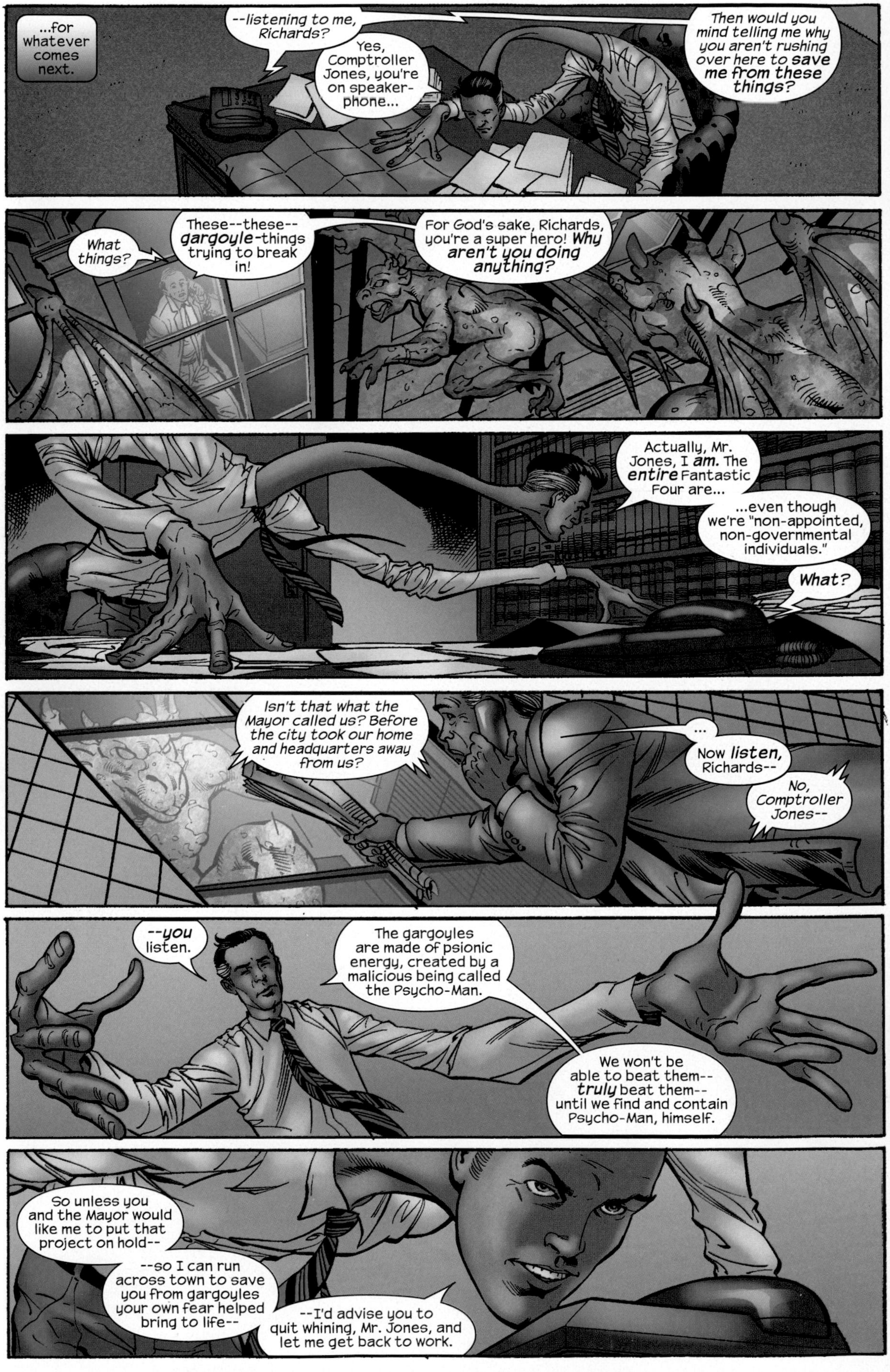
...for whatever comes next.
--listening to me, Richards?
Yes, Comptroller Jones, you're on speaker-phone...
Then would you mind telling me why you aren't rushing over here to save me from these things?
What things?
These--these--gargoyle-things trying to break in!
For God's sake, Richards, you're a super hero! Why aren't you doing anything?
Actually, Mr. Jones, I am. The entire Fantastic Four are...
...even though we're "non-appointed, non-governmental individuals."
What?
Isn't that what the Mayor called us? Before the city took our home and headquarters away from us?
...
Now listen, Richards--
No, Comptroller Jones--
--you listen.
The gargoyles are made of psionic energy, created by a malicious being called the Psycho-Man.
We won't be able to beat them--truly beat them--until we find and contain Psycho-Man, himself.
So unless you and the Mayor would like me to put that project on hold--
--so I can run across town to save you from gargoyles your own fear helped bring to life--
--I'd advise you to quit whining, Mr. Jones, and let me get back to work.

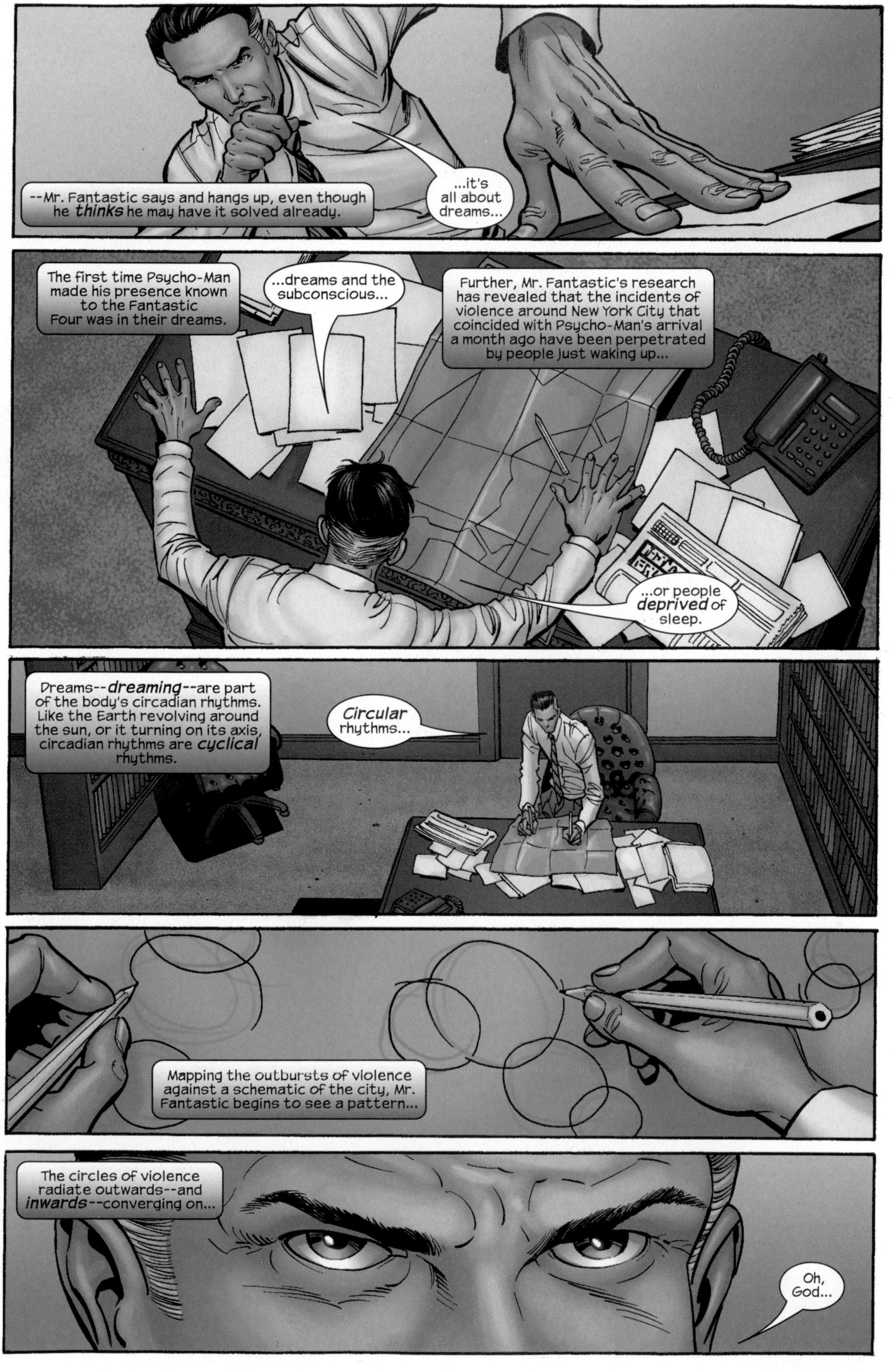
--Mr. Fantastic says and hangs up, even though he *thinks* he may have it solved already.
...it's all about dreams...
The first time Psycho-Man made his presence known to the Fantastic Four was in their dreams.
...dreams and the subconscious...
Further, Mr. Fantastic's research has revealed that the incidents of violence around New York City that coincided with Psycho-Man's arrival a month ago have been perpetrated by people just waking up...
...or people *deprived* of sleep.
Dreams--*dreaming*--are part of the body's circadian rhythms. Like the Earth revolving around the sun, or it turning on its axis, circadian rhythms are *cyclical* rhythms.
Circular rhythms...
Mapping the outbursts of violence against a schematic of the city, Mr. Fantastic begins to see a pattern...
The circles of violence radiate outwards--and *inwards*--converging on...
Oh, God...

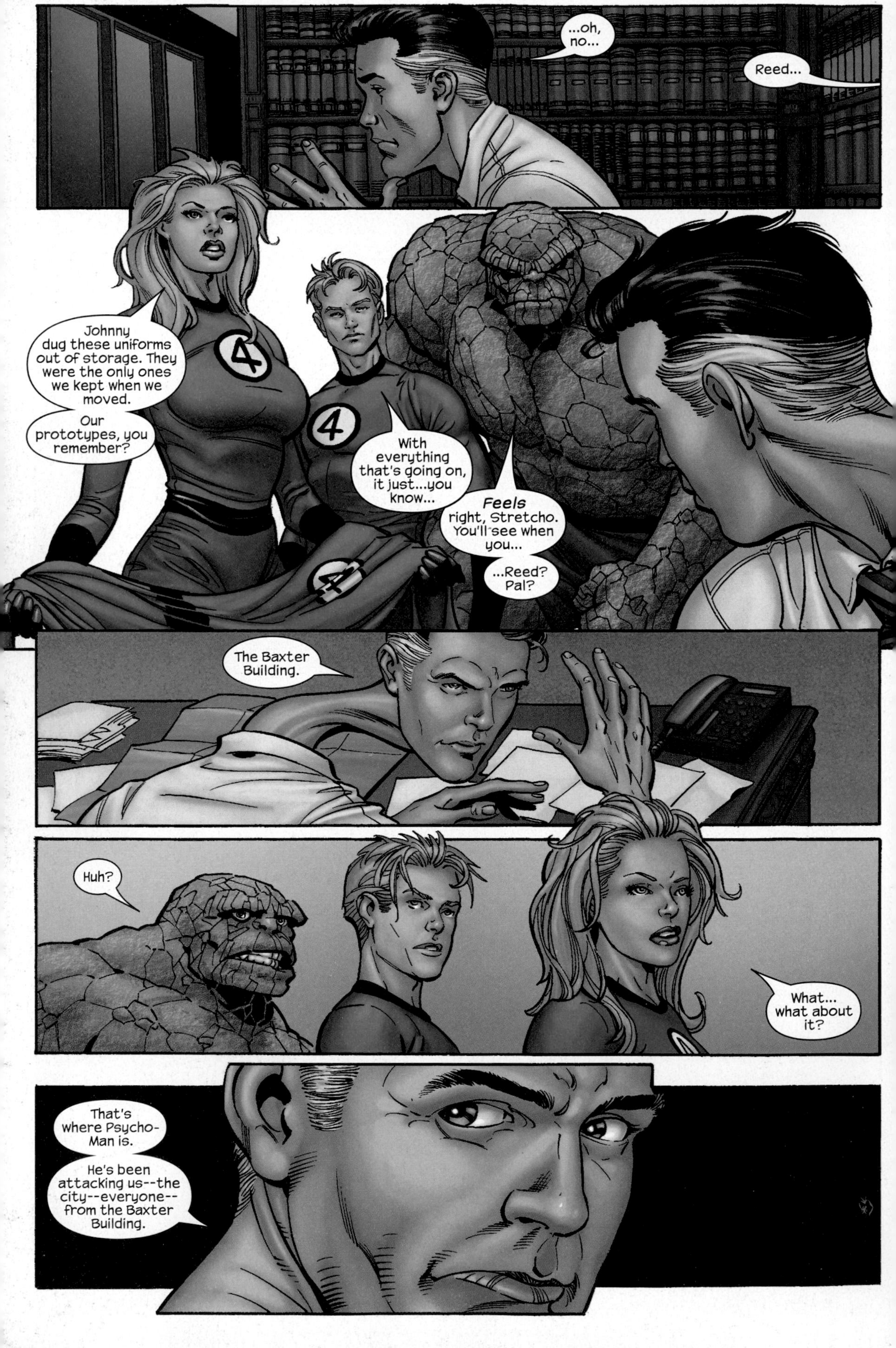
...oh, no...
Reed...
Johnny dug these uniforms out of storage. They were the only ones we kept when we moved.
Our prototypes, you remember?
With everything that's going on, it just...you know...
Feels right, Stretcho. You'll see when you...
...Reed? Pal?
The Baxter Building.
Huh?
What... what about it?
That's where Psycho-Man is.
He's been attacking us--the city--everyone--from the Baxter Building.

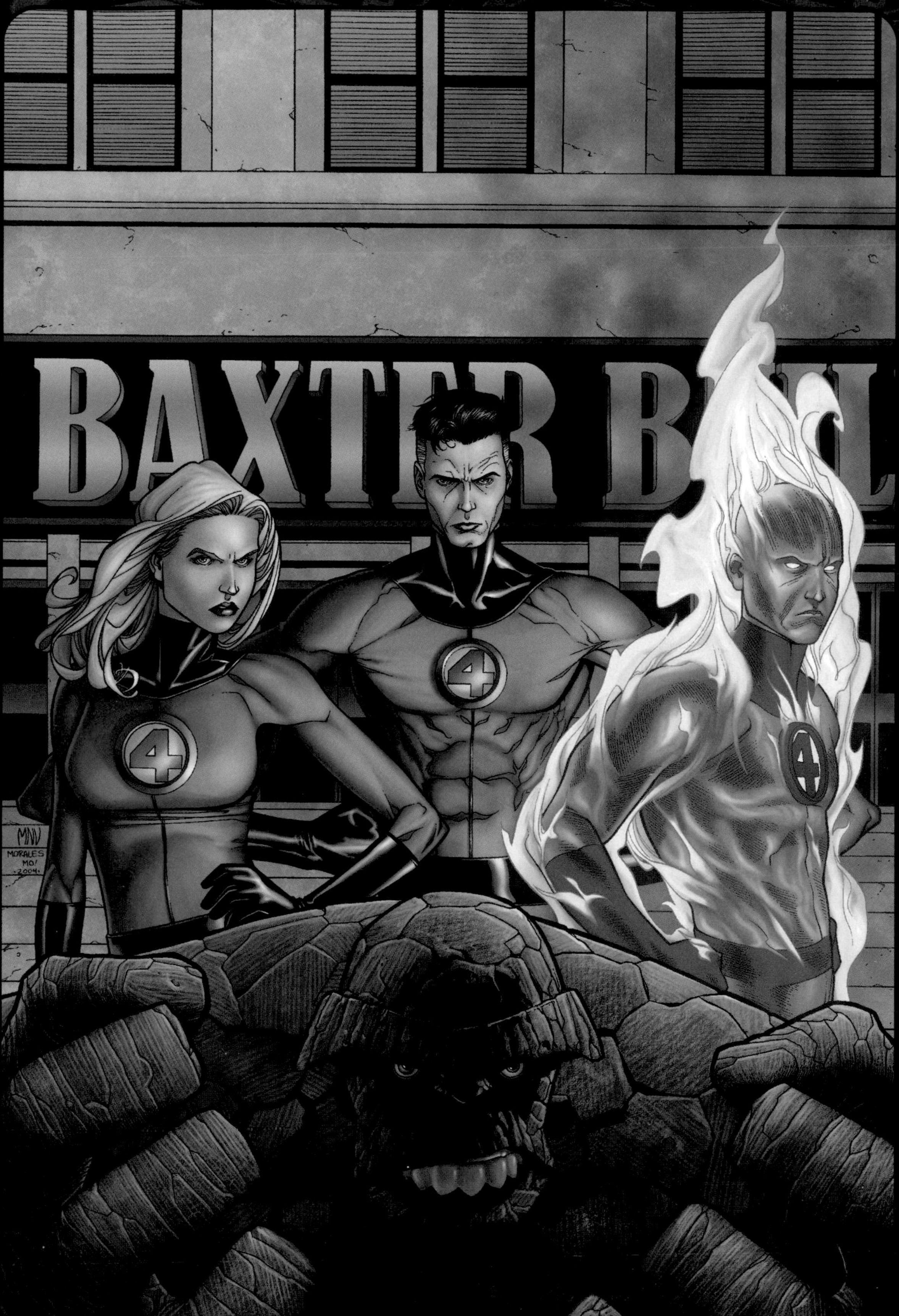
BAXTER BUIL
MORALES
MO!
2004

#12

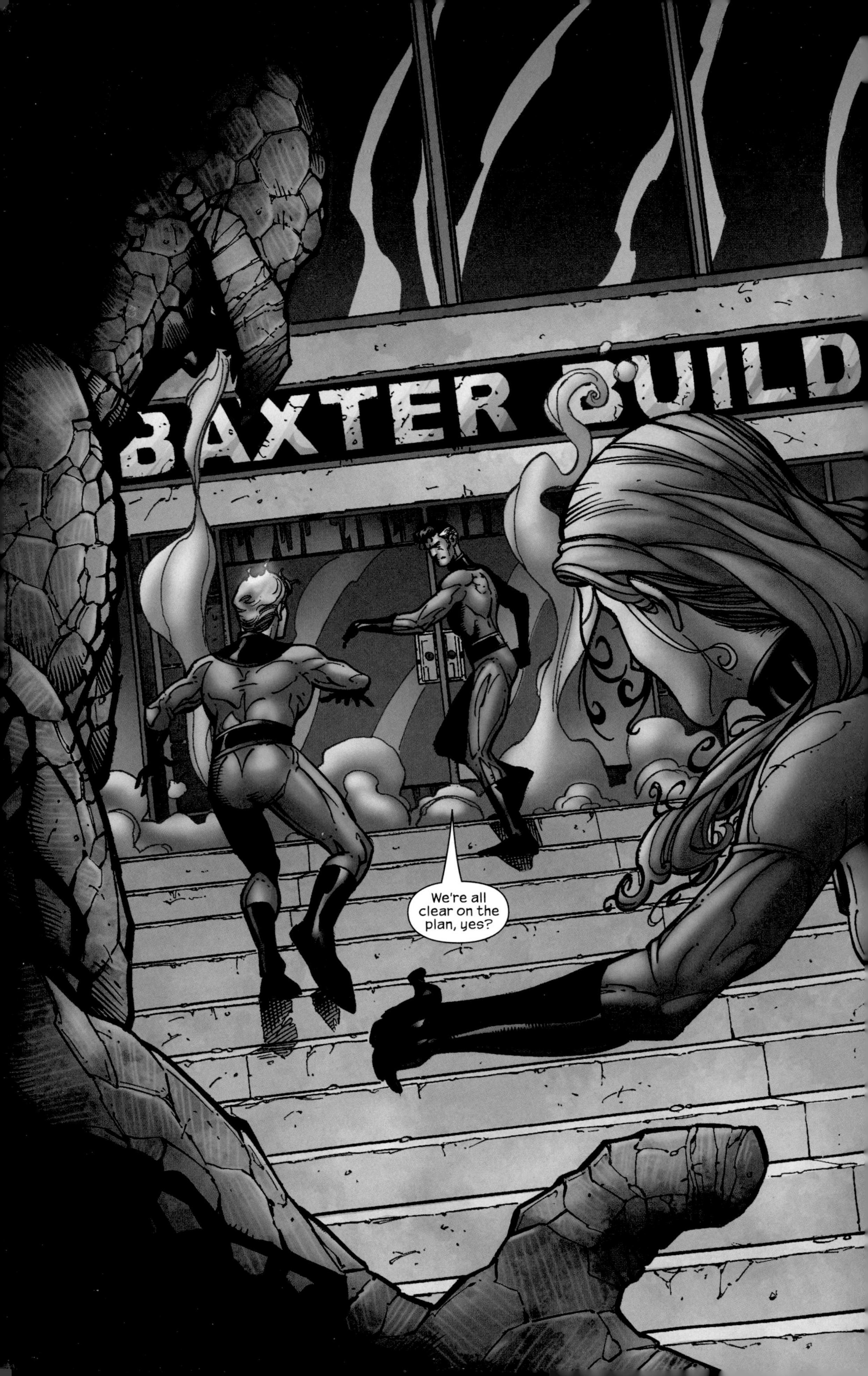
BAXTER BUILD
We're all clear on the plan, yes?

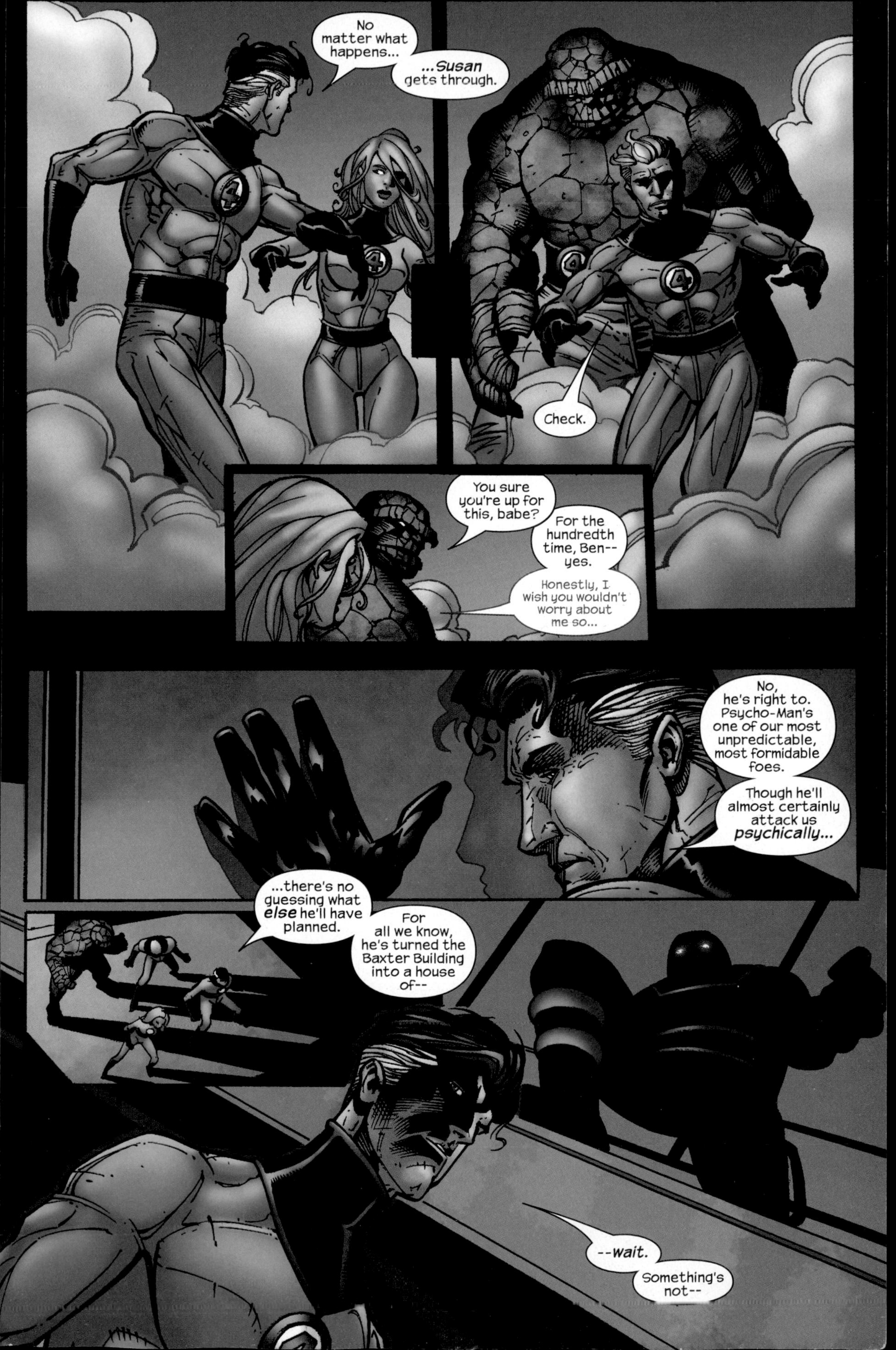
No matter what happens...
...Susan gets through.
Check.
You sure you're up for this, babe?
For the hundredth time, Ben-- yes.
Honestly, I wish you wouldn't worry about me so...
No, he's right to. Psycho-Man's one of our most unpredictable, most formidable foes.
Though he'll almost certainly attack us psychically...
...there's no guessing what else he'll have planned.
For all we know, he's turned the Baxter Building into a house of--
--wait.
Something's not--

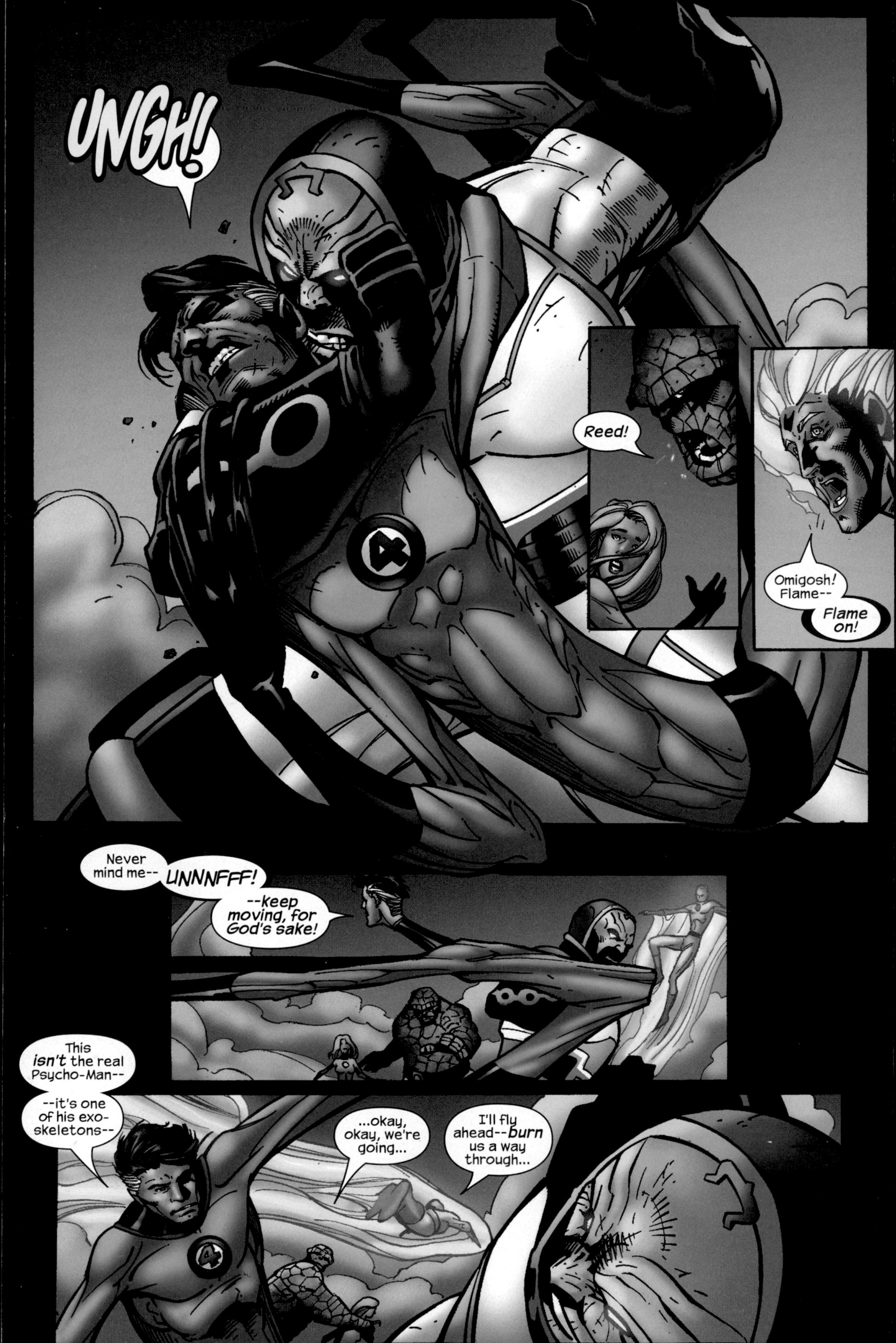
UNGH!
Reed!
Omigosh! Flame--
Flame on!
Never mind me--
UNNNFFF!
--keep moving, for God's sake!
This isn't the real Psycho-Man--
--it's one of his exo-skeletons--
...okay, okay, we're going...
I'll fly ahead--burn us a way through...

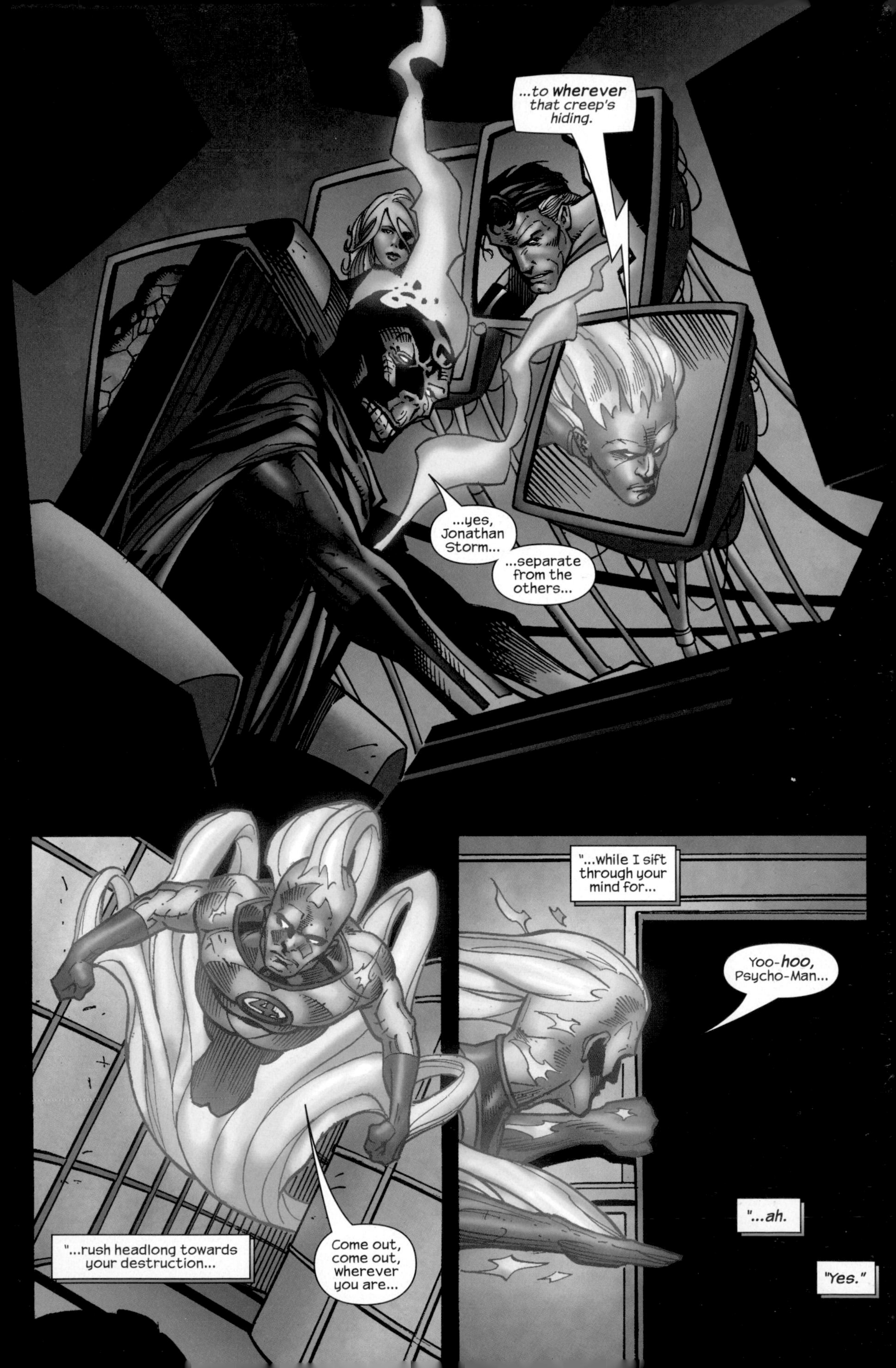
...to wherever that creep's hiding.
...yes, Jonathan Storm...
...separate from the others...
"...while I sift through your mind for...
"...rush headlong towards your destruction...
Come out, come out, wherever you are...
Yoo-hoo, Psycho-Man...
"...ah.
"Yes."

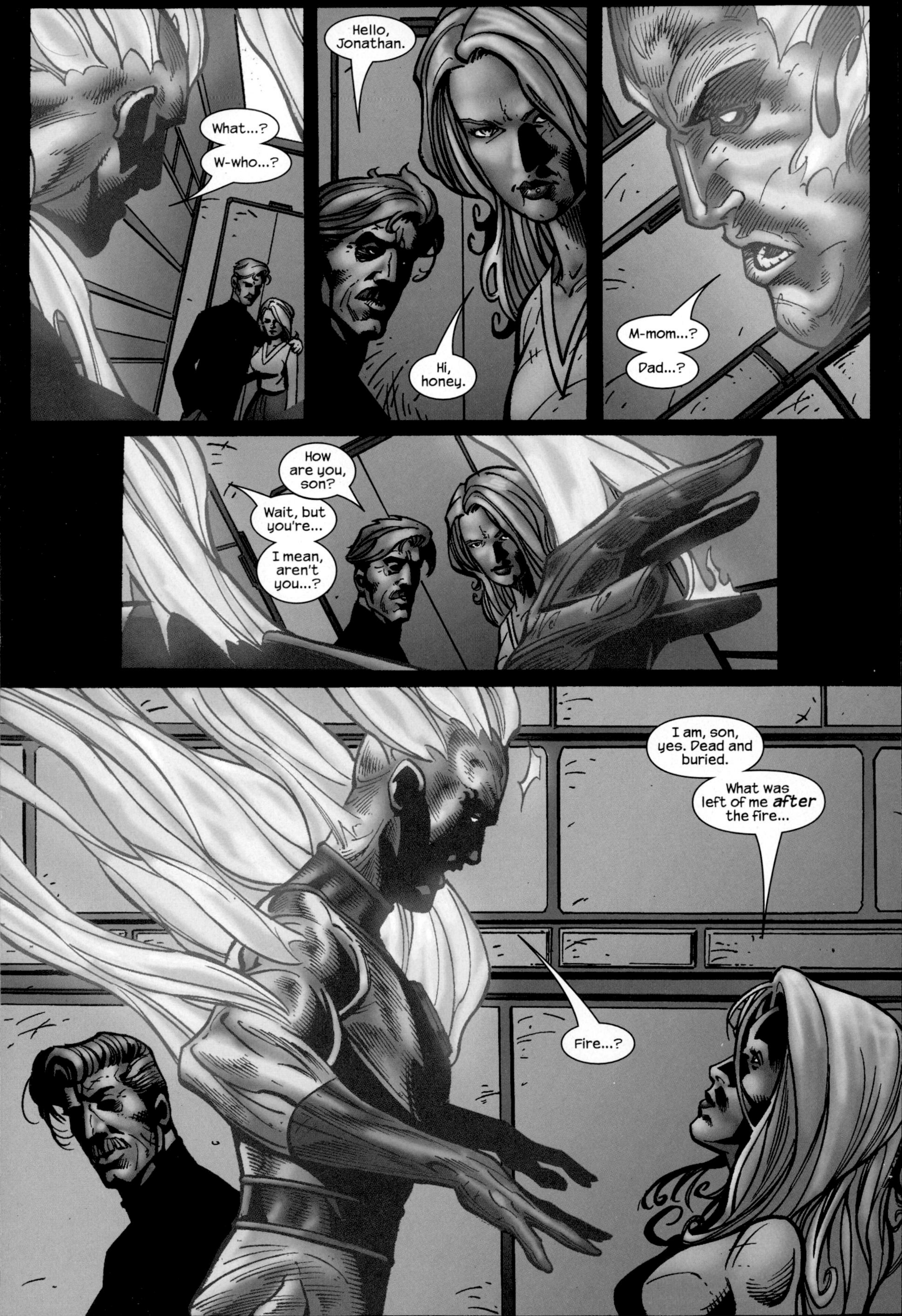

What...?
W-who...?
Hello, Jonathan.
Hi, honey.
M-mom...?
Dad...?
How are you, son?
Wait, but you're...
I mean, aren't you...?
I am, son, yes. Dead and buried.
What was left of me *after* the fire...
Fire...?

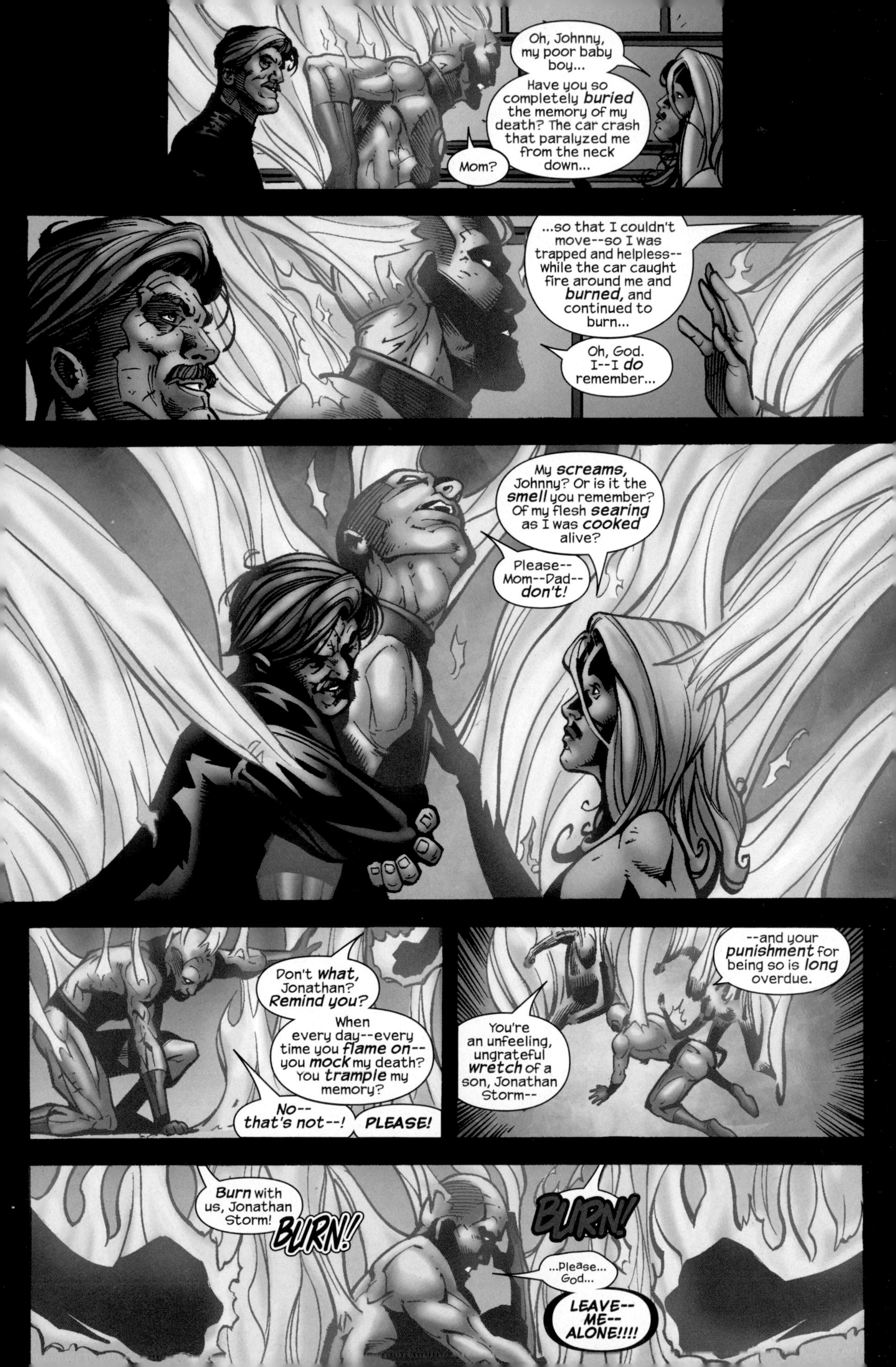

Oh, Johnny, my poor baby boy...
Have you so completely buried the memory of my death? The car crash that paralyzed me from the neck down...
Mom?
...so that I couldn't move--so I was trapped and helpless--while the car caught fire around me and burned, and continued to burn...
Oh, God. I--I do remember...
My screams, Johnny? Or is it the smell you remember? Of my flesh searing as I was cooked alive?
Please--Mom--Dad--don't!
Don't what, Jonathan? Remind you?
When every day--every time you flame on--you mock my death? You trample my memory?
No--that's not--!
PLEASE!
You're an unfeeling, ungrateful wretch of a son, Jonathan Storm--
--and your punishment for being so is long overdue.
Burn with us, Jonathan Storm!
BURN!
BURN!
...Please... God...
LEAVE--ME--ALONE!!!!

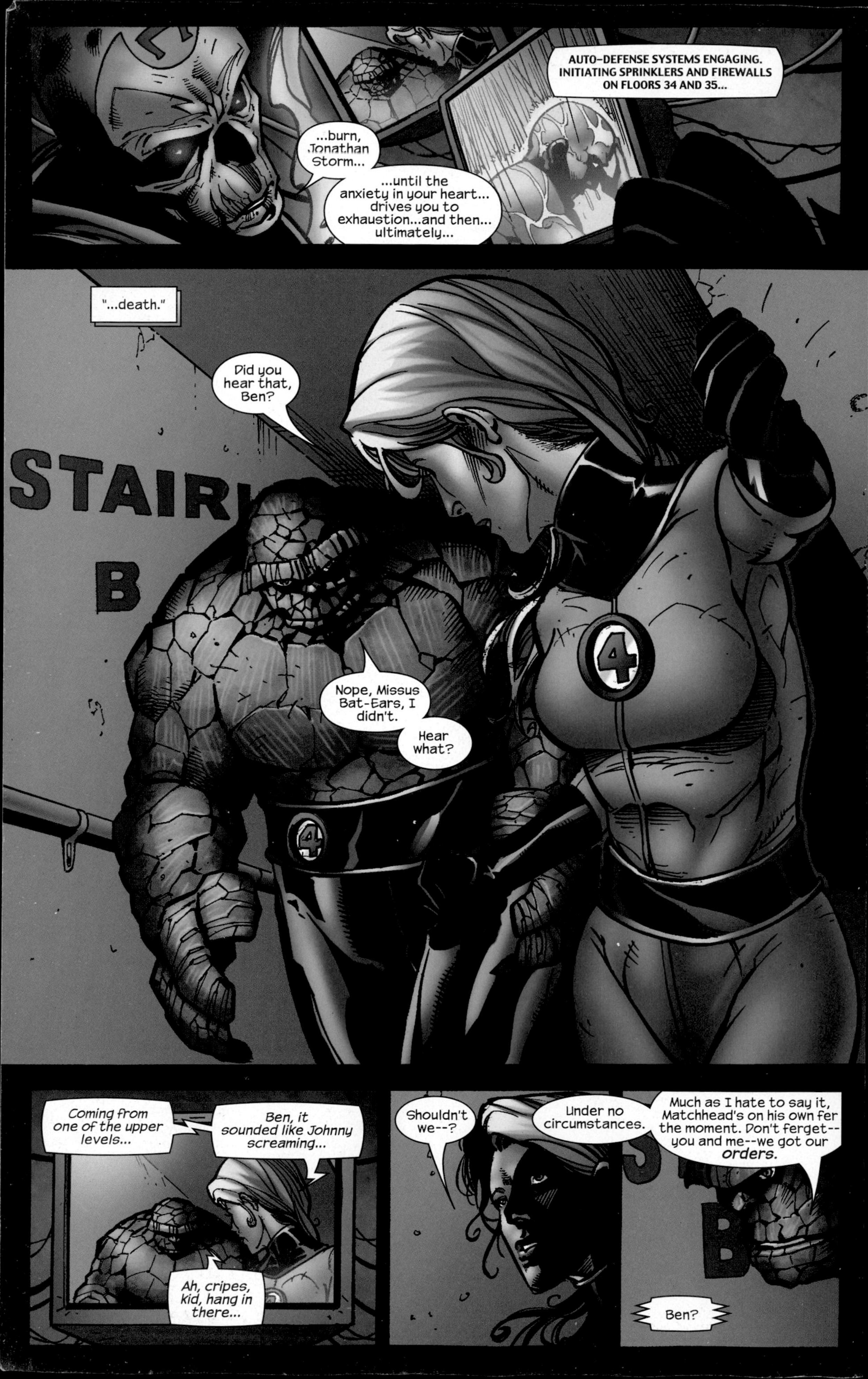
AUTO-DEFENSE SYSTEMS ENGAGING. INITIATING SPRINKLERS AND FIREWALLS ON FLOORS 34 AND 35...
...burn, Jonathan Storm...
...until the anxiety in your heart... drives you to exhaustion...and then... ultimately...
"...death."
Did you hear that, Ben?
STAIR
B
Nope, Missus Bat-Ears, I didn't.
Hear what?
Coming from one of the upper levels...
Ben, it sounded like Johnny screaming...
Ah, cripes, kid, hang in there...
Shouldn't we--?
Under no circumstances.
Much as I hate to say it, Matchhead's on his own fer the moment. Don't ferget-- you and me--we got our orders.
Ben?

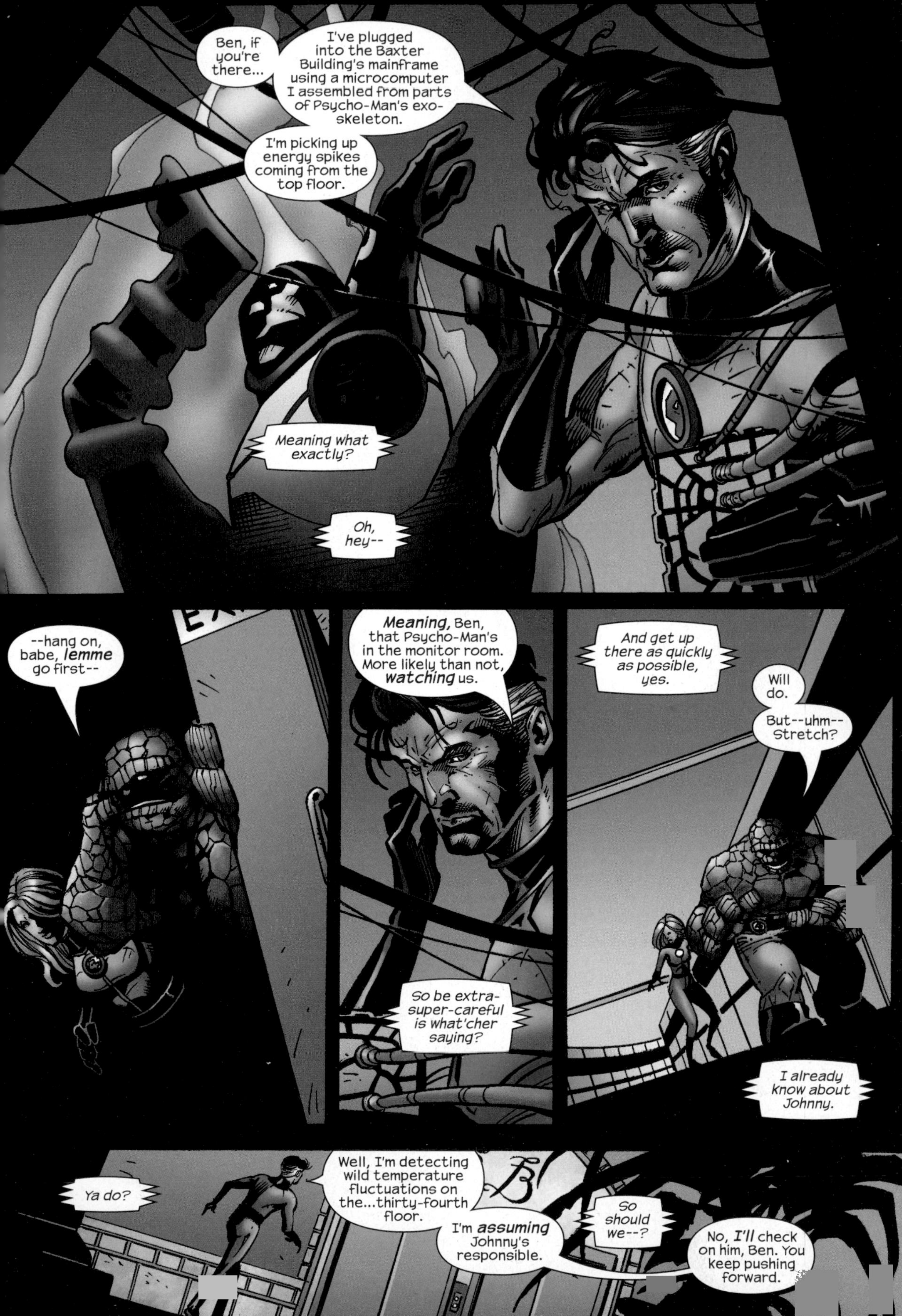
Ben, if you're there...
I've plugged into the Baxter Building's mainframe using a microcomputer I assembled from parts of Psycho-Man's exo-skeleton.
I'm picking up energy spikes coming from the top floor.
Meaning what exactly?
Oh, hey--
--hang on, babe, **lemme** go first--
Meaning, Ben, that Psycho-Man's in the monitor room. More likely than not, **watching** us.
So be extra-super-careful is what'cher saying?
And get up there as quickly as possible, yes.
Will do.
But--uhm--Stretch?
I already know about Johnny.
Ya do?
Well, I'm detecting wild temperature fluctuations on the...thirty-fourth floor.
I'm **assuming** Johnny's responsible.
So should we--?
No, **I'll** check on him, Ben. You keep pushing forward.

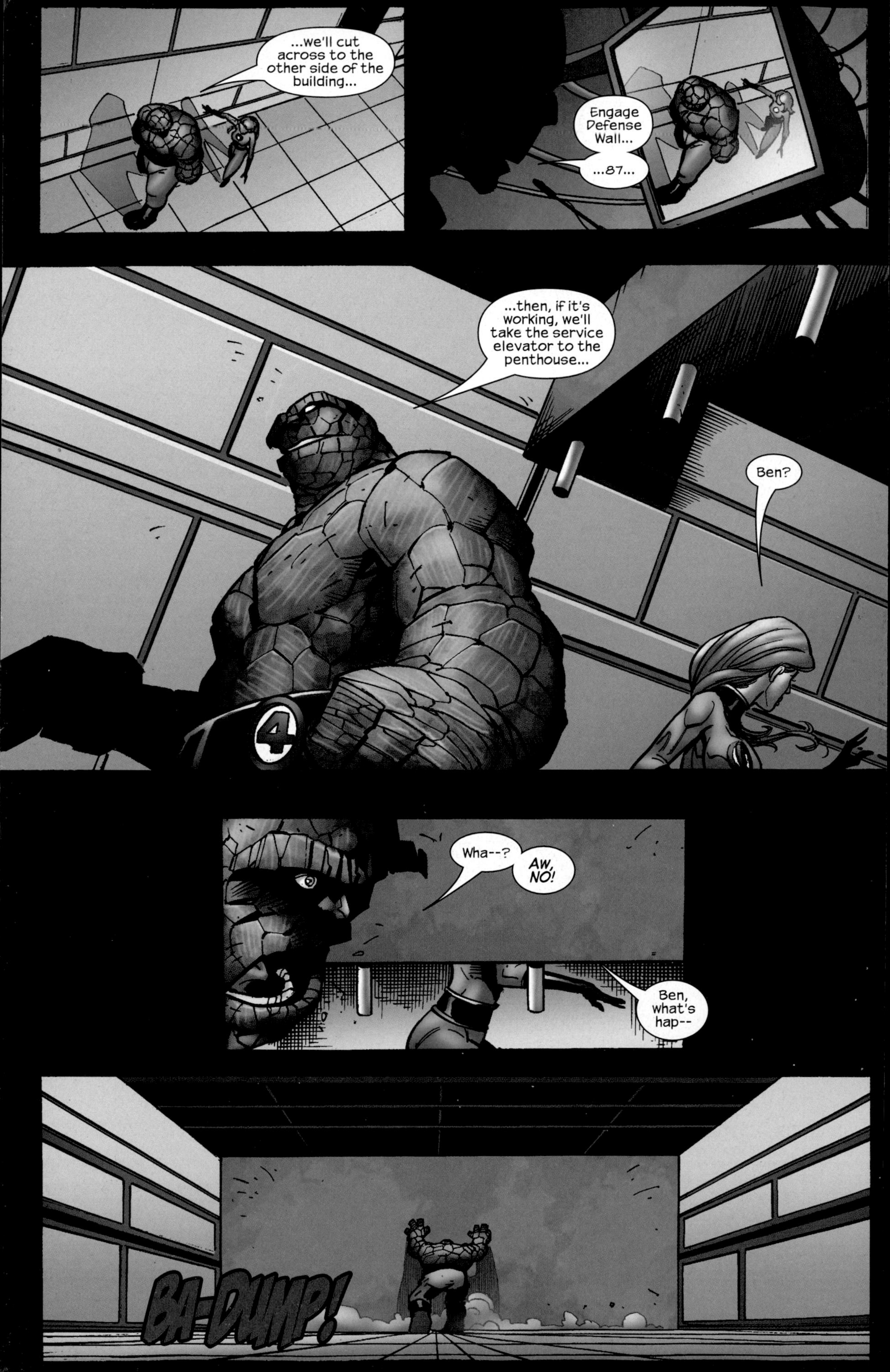
...we'll cut across to the other side of the building...
Engage Defense Wall...
...87...
...then, if it's working, we'll take the service elevator to the penthouse...
Ben?
Wha--?
AW, NO!
Ben, what's hap--
BA-DUMP!

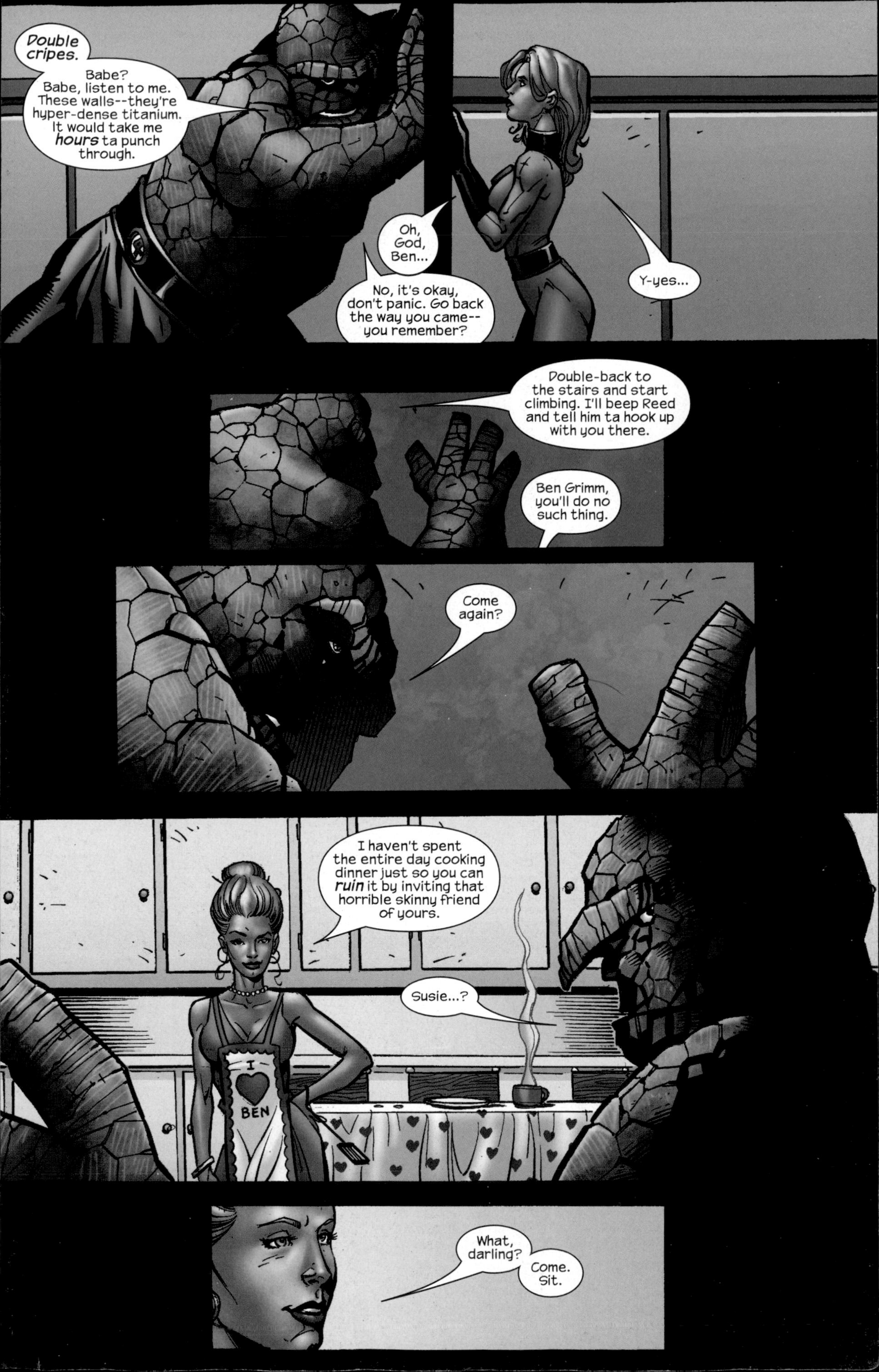
Double cripes.
Babe? Babe, listen to me. These walls--they're hyper-dense titanium. It would take me *hours* ta punch through.
Oh, God, Ben...
Y-yes...
No, it's okay, don't panic. Go back the way you came-- you remember?
Double-back to the stairs and start climbing. I'll beep Reed and tell him ta hook up with you there.
Ben Grimm, you'll do no such thing.
Come again?
I haven't spent the entire day cooking dinner just so you can *ruin* it by inviting that horrible skinny friend of yours.
I
BEN
Susie...?
What, darling?
Come. Sit.

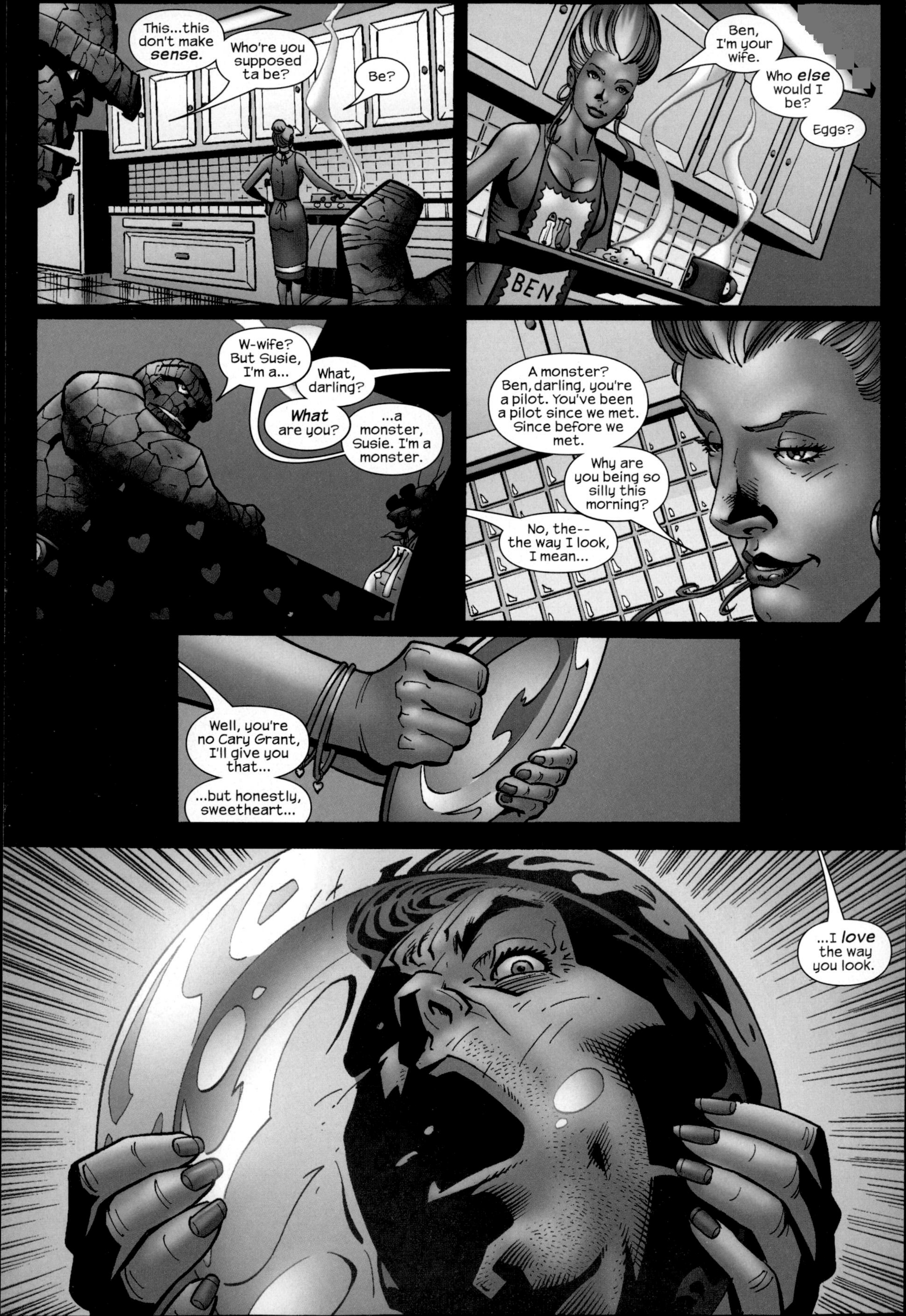
This...this don't make *sense.*
Who're you supposed ta be?
Be?
Ben, I'm your wife.
Who *else* would I be?
Eggs?
BEN
W-wife? But Susie, I'm a...
What, darling?
What are you?
...a monster, Susie. I'm a monster.
A monster? Ben, darling, you're a pilot. You've been a pilot since we met. Since before we met.
Why are you being so silly this morning?
No, the-- the way I look, I mean...
Well, you're no Cary Grant, I'll give you that...
...but honestly, sweetheart...
...I *love* the way you look.

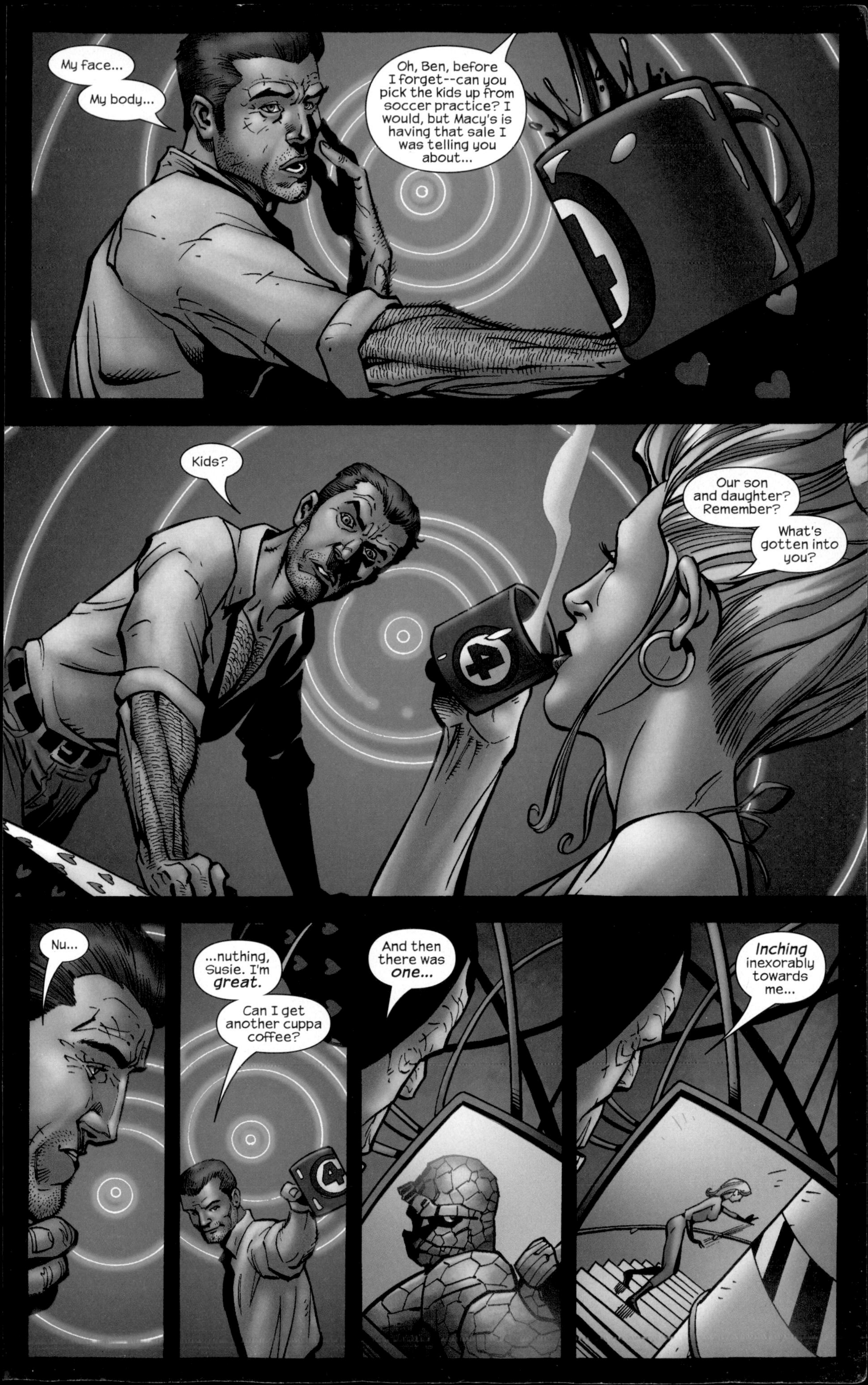
My face...
My body...
Oh, Ben, before I forget--can you pick the kids up from soccer practice? I would, but Macy's is having that sale I was telling you about...
Kids?
Our son and daughter? Remember?
What's gotten into you?
Nu...
...nuthing, Susie. I'm *great.*
Can I get another cuppa coffee?
And then there was *one...*
Inching inexorably towards me...

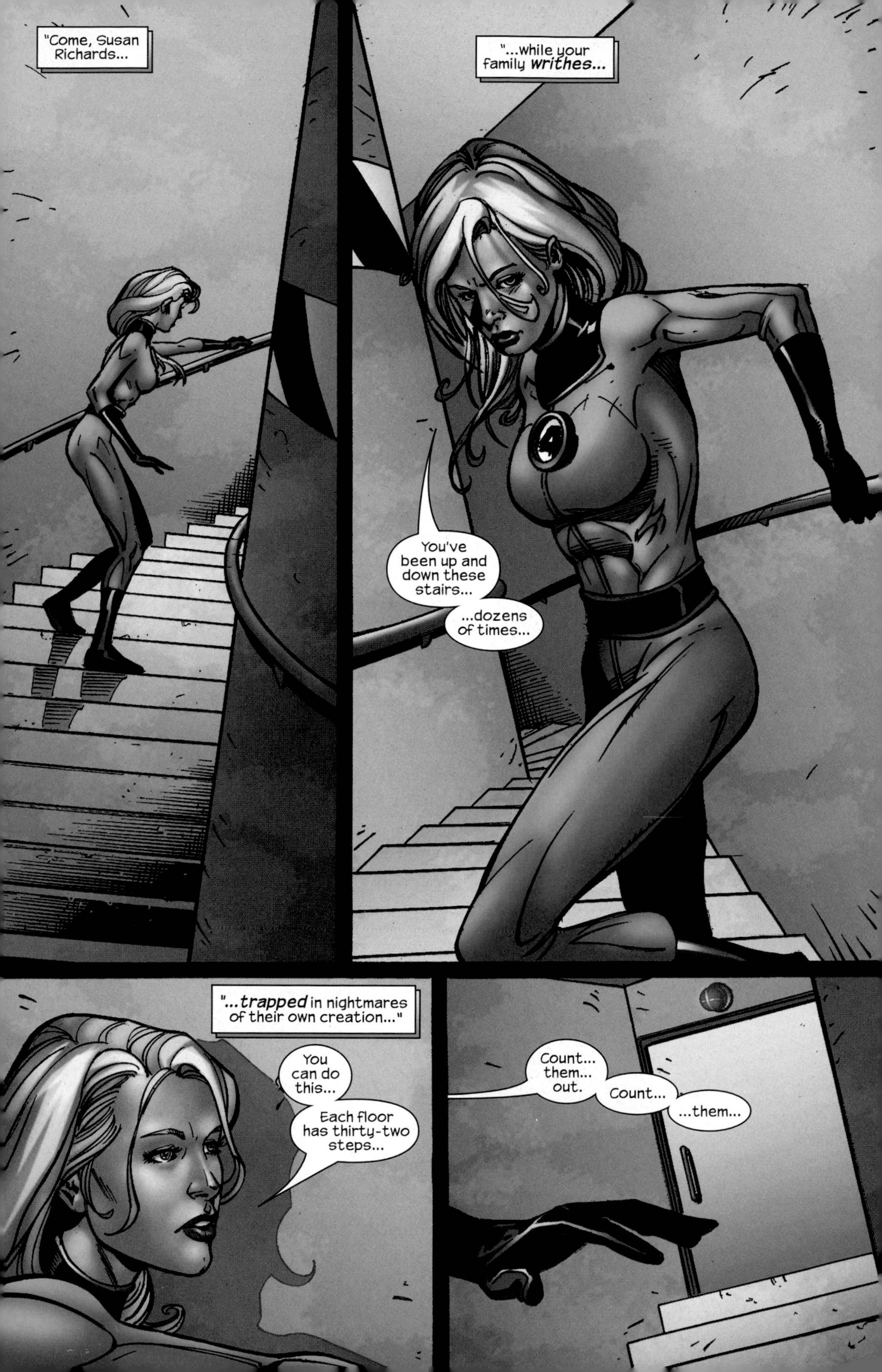
"Come, Susan Richards...
"...while your family *writhes*...
You've been up and down these stairs...
...dozens of times...
"...*trapped* in nightmares of their own creation..."
You can do this...
Each floor has thirty-two steps...
Count... them... out.
Count...
...them...

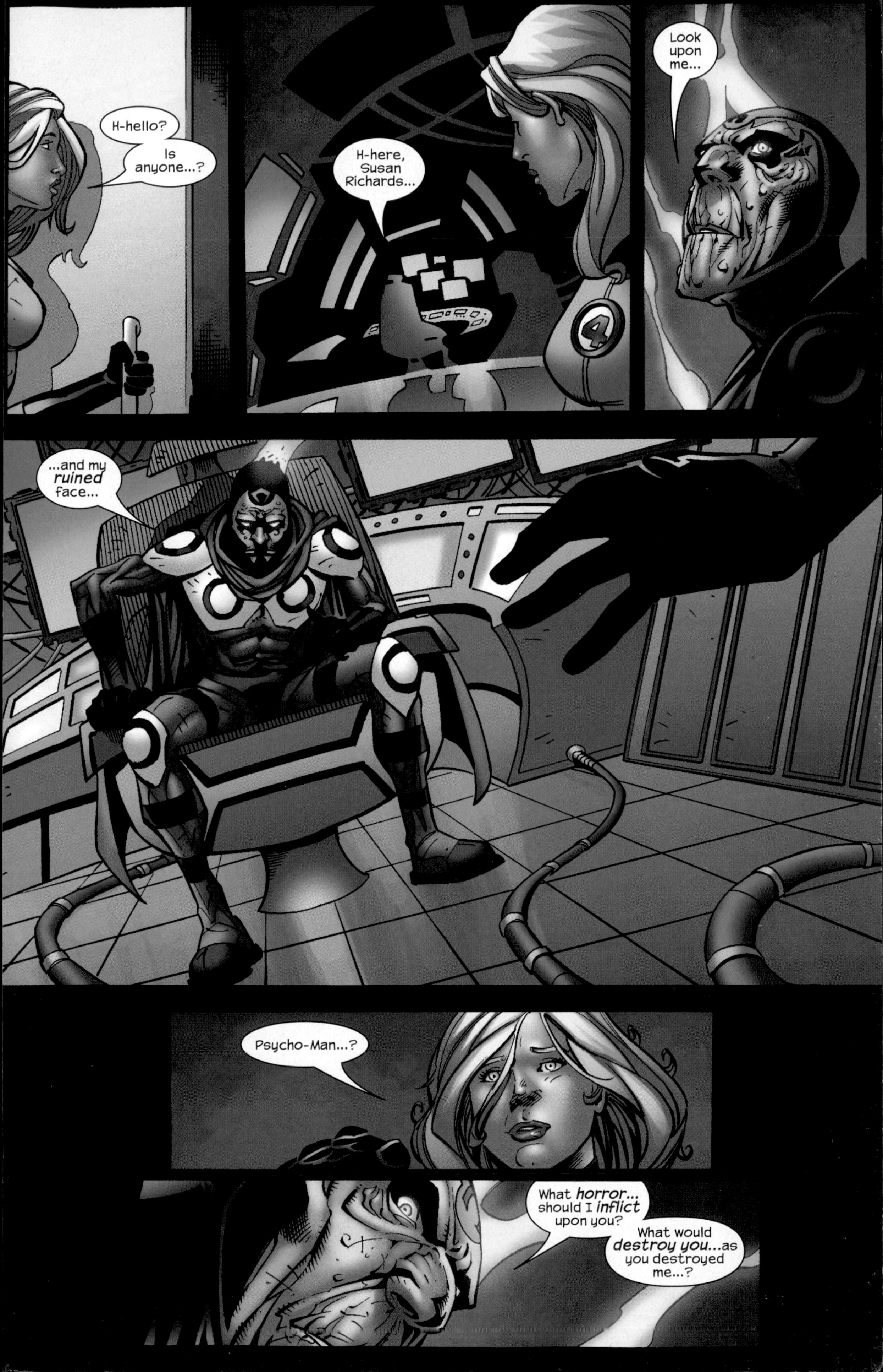
H-hello?
Is anyone...?
H-here, Susan Richards...
Look upon me...
...and my *ruined* face...
Psycho-Man...?
What *horror*... should I *inflict* upon you?
What would *destroy you*...as you destroyed me...?

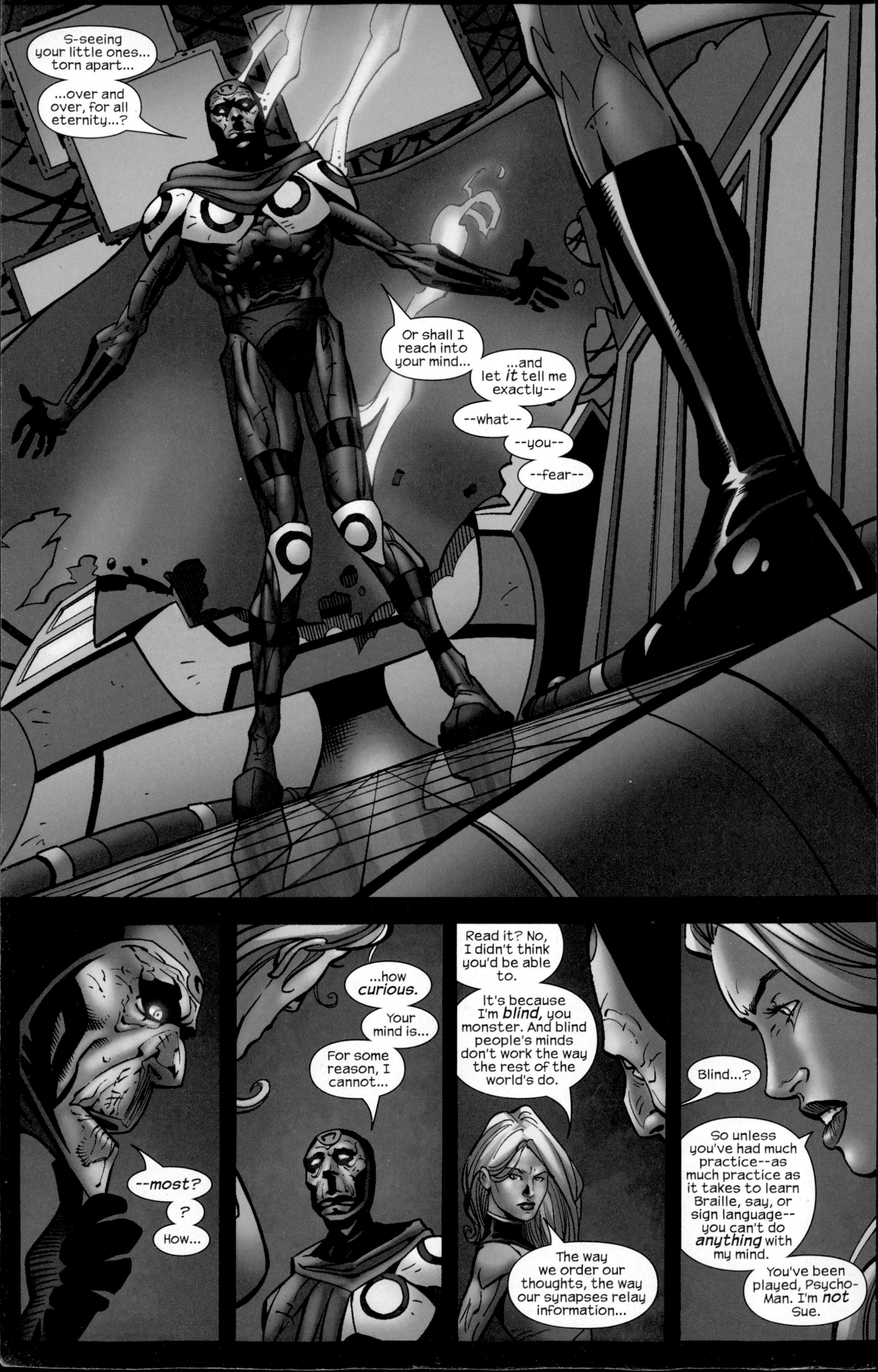
S-seeing your little ones... torn apart...
...over and over, for all eternity...?
Or shall I reach into your mind...
...and let *it* tell me exactly--
--what--
--you--
--fear--
--*most?*
?
How...
...how *curious.*
Your mind is...
For some reason, I cannot...
Read it? No, I didn't think you'd be able to.
It's because I'm *blind,* you monster. And blind people's minds don't work the way the rest of the world's do.
The way we order our thoughts, the way our synapses relay information...
Blind...?
So unless you've had much practice--as much practice as it takes to learn Braille, say, or sign language--you can't do *anything* with my mind.
You've been played, Psycho-Man. I'm *not* Sue.

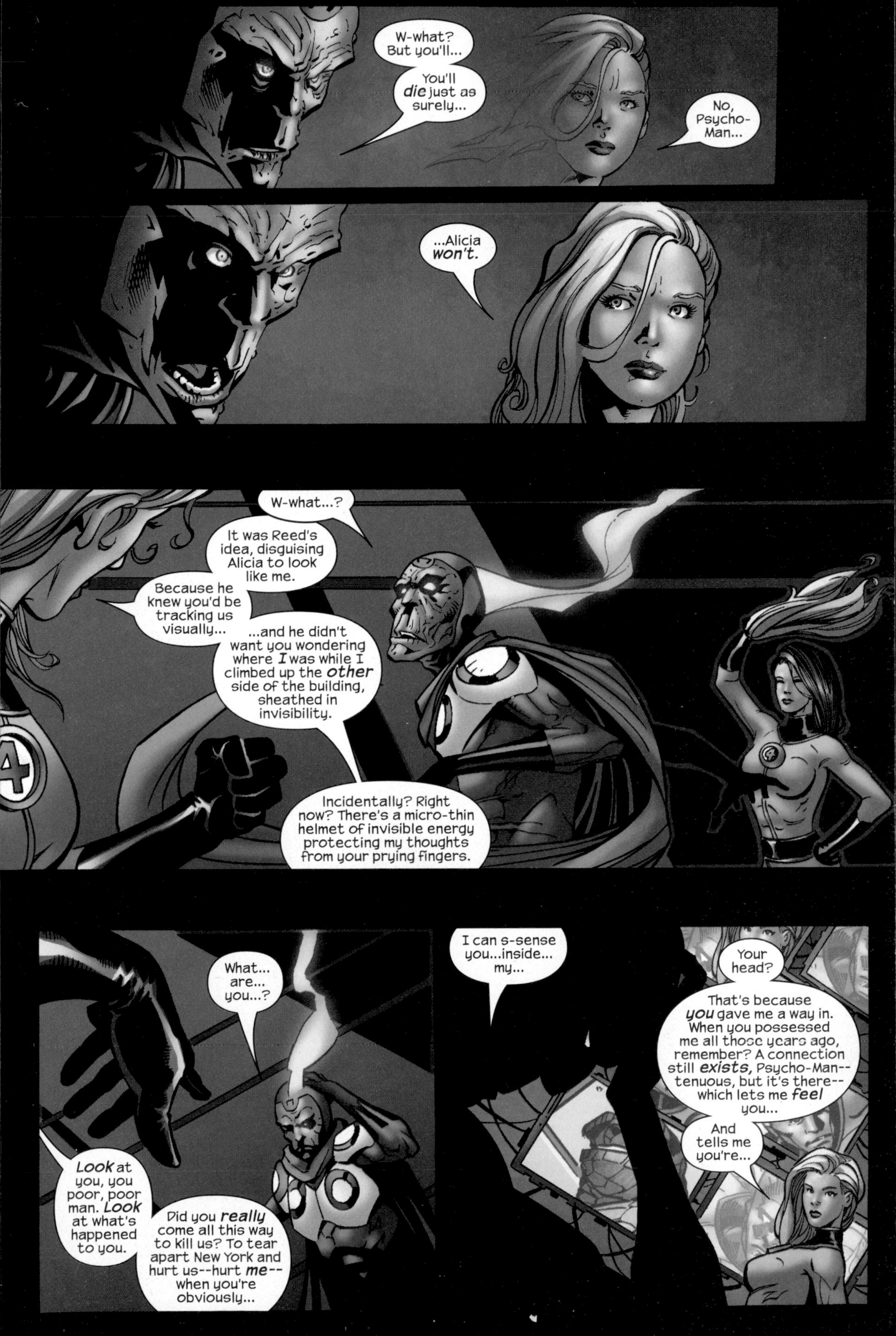
W-what? But you'll...
You'll *die* just as surely...
No, Psycho-Man...
...Alicia *won't.*
W-what...?
It was Reed's idea, disguising Alicia to look like me.
Because he knew you'd be tracking us visually...
...and he didn't want you wondering where *I* was while I climbed up the *other* side of the building, sheathed in invisibility.
Incidentally? Right now? There's a micro-thin helmet of invisible energy protecting my thoughts from your prying fingers.
What... are... you...?
Look at you, you poor, poor man. *Look* at what's happened to you.
Did you *really* come all this way to kill us? To tear apart New York and hurt us--hurt *me*--when you're obviously...
I can s-sense you...inside... my...
Your head?
That's because *you* gave me a way in. When you possessed me all those years ago, remember? A connection still *exists,* Psycho-Man--tenuous, but it's there--which lets me *feel* you...
And tells me you're...

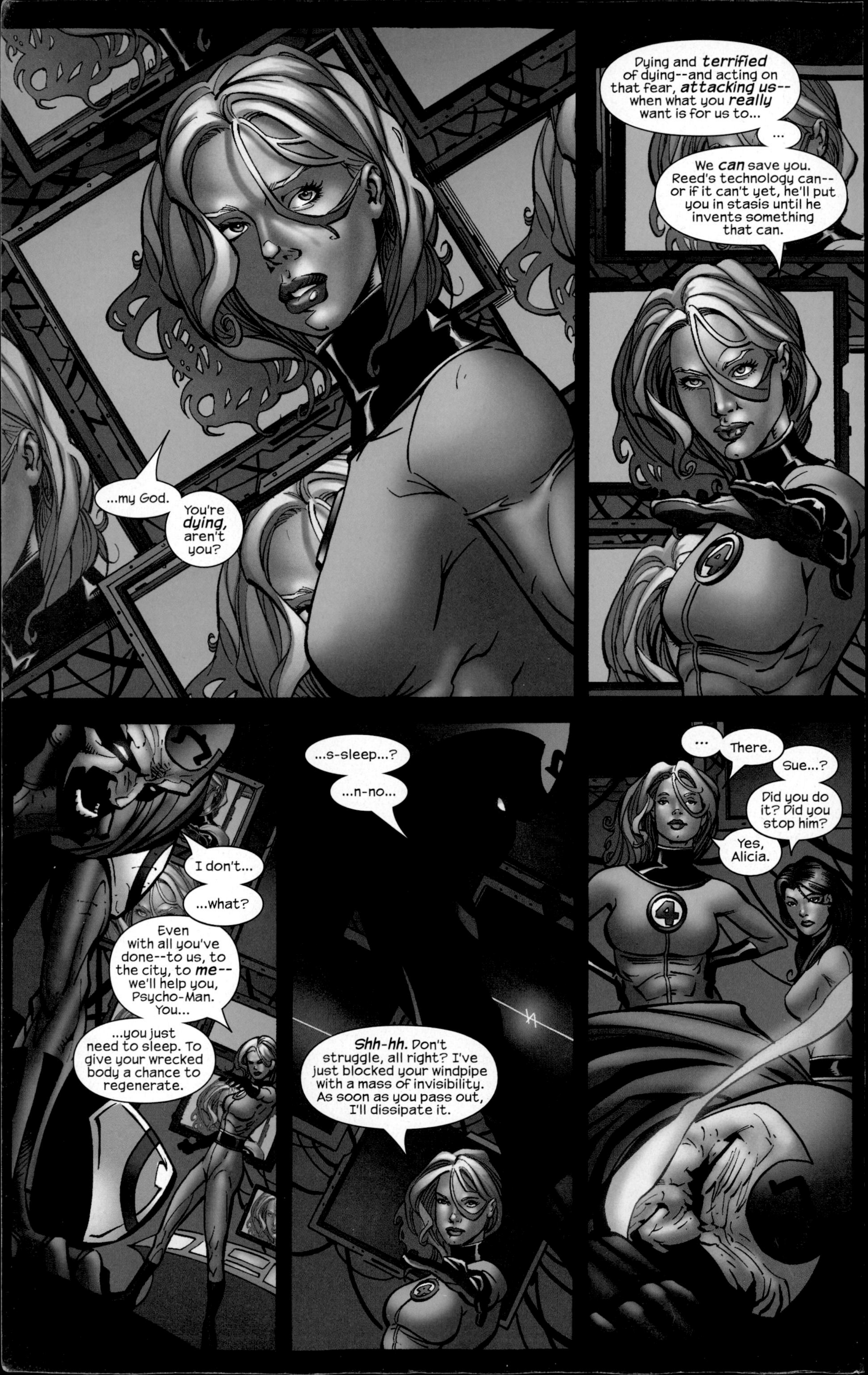
...my God.
You're dying, aren't you?
Dying and terrified of dying--and acting on that fear, attacking us--when what you really want is for us to...
...
We can save you. Reed's technology can--or if it can't yet, he'll put you in stasis until he invents something that can.
I don't...
...what?
Even with all you've done--to us, to the city, to me--we'll help you, Psycho-Man. You...
...you just need to sleep. To give your wrecked body a chance to regenerate.
...s-sleep...?
...n-no...
Shh-hh. Don't struggle, all right? I've just blocked your windpipe with a mass of invisibility. As soon as you pass out, I'll dissipate it.
...
There.
Sue...?
Did you do it? Did you stop him?
Yes, Alicia.

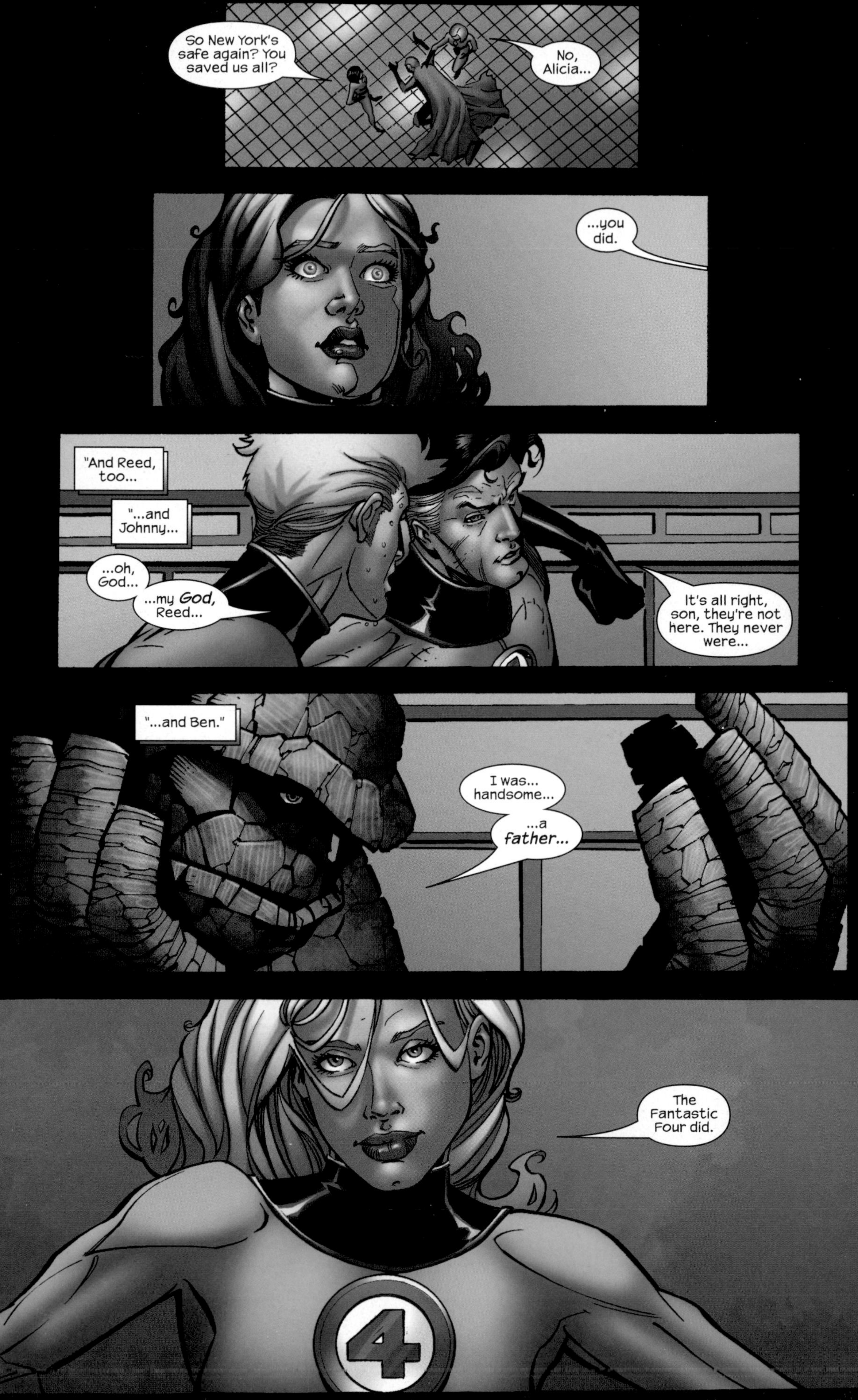
So New York's safe again? You saved us all?
No, Alicia...
...you did.
"And Reed, too...
"...and Johnny...
...oh, God...
...my God, Reed...
It's all right, son, they're not here. They never were...
"...and Ben."
I was... handsome...
...a father...
The Fantastic Four did.

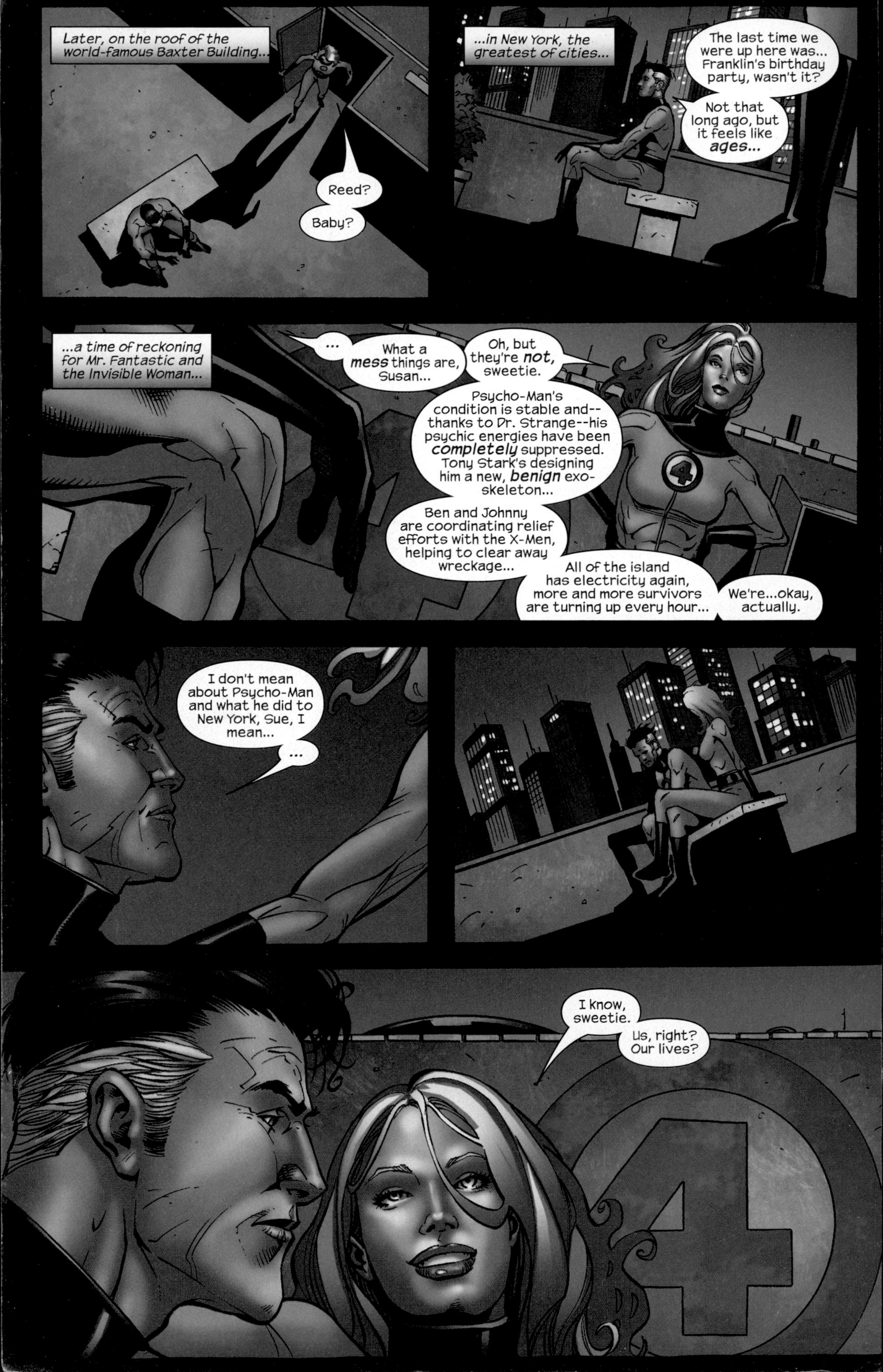

Later, on the roof of the world-famous Baxter Building...
Reed?
Baby?
...in New York, the greatest of cities...
The last time we were up here was... Franklin's birthday party, wasn't it?
Not that long ago, but it feels like ages...
...a time of reckoning for Mr. Fantastic and the Invisible Woman...
...
What a mess things are, Susan...
Oh, but they're not, sweetie.
Psycho-Man's condition is stable and--thanks to Dr. Strange--his psychic energies have been completely suppressed. Tony Stark's designing him a new, benign exo-skeleton...
Ben and Johnny are coordinating relief efforts with the X-Men, helping to clear away wreckage...
All of the island has electricity again, more and more survivors are turning up every hour...
We're...okay, actually.
I don't mean about Psycho-Man and what he did to New York, Sue, I mean...
...
I know, sweetie.
Us, right? Our lives?

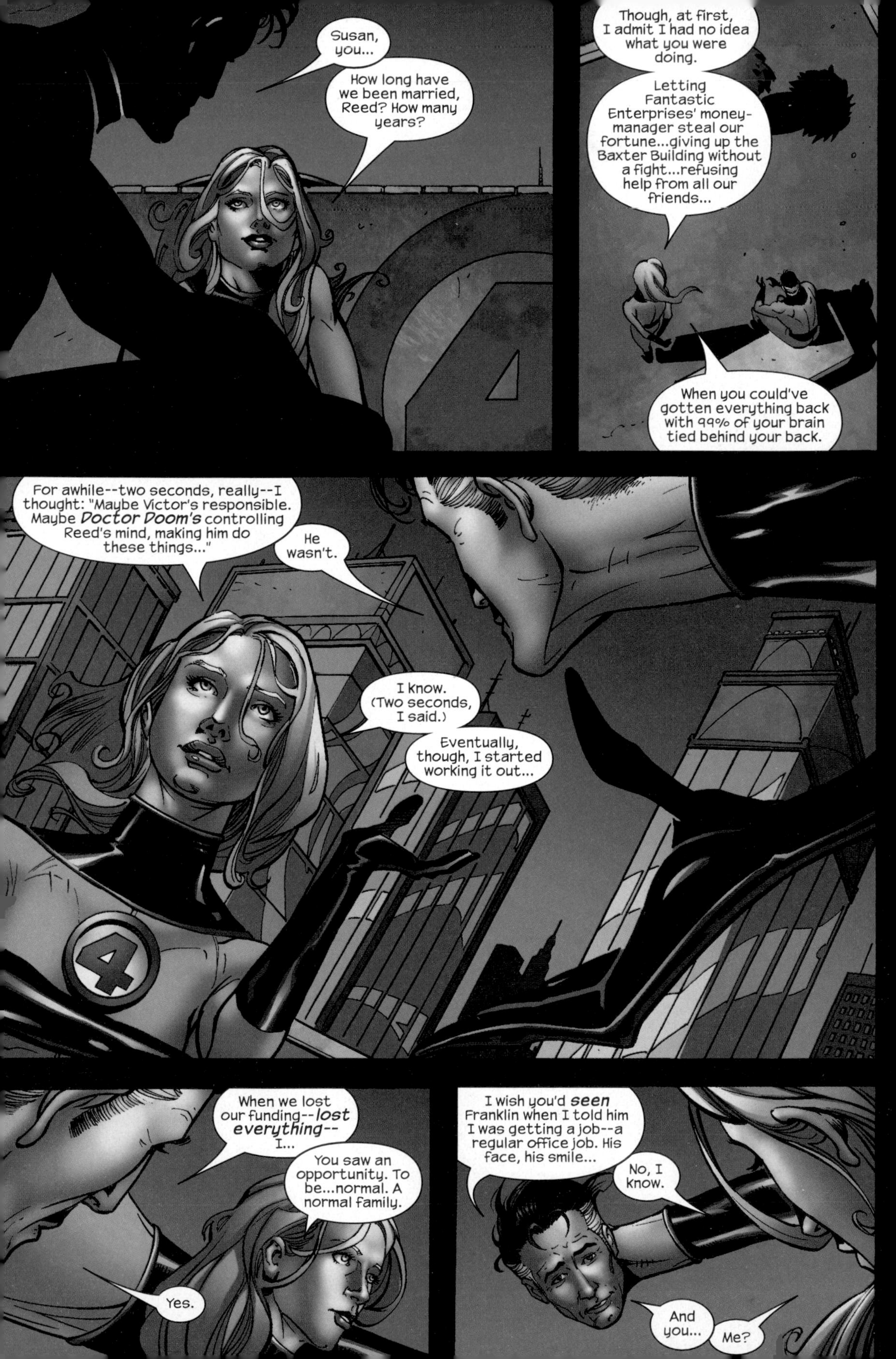

Susan, you...
How long have we been married, Reed? How many years?
Though, at first, I admit I had no idea what you were doing.
Letting Fantastic Enterprises' money-manager steal our fortune...giving up the Baxter Building without a fight...refusing help from all our friends...
When you could've gotten everything back with 99% of your brain tied behind your back.
For awhile--two seconds, really--I thought: "Maybe Victor's responsible. Maybe *Doctor Doom's* controlling Reed's mind, making him do these things..."
He wasn't.
I know. (Two seconds, I said.)
Eventually, though, I started working it out...
When we lost our funding--*lost everything*-- I...
You saw an opportunity. To be...normal. A normal family.
Yes.
I wish you'd *seen* Franklin when I told him I was getting a job--a regular office job. His face, his smile...
No, I know.
And you...
Me?

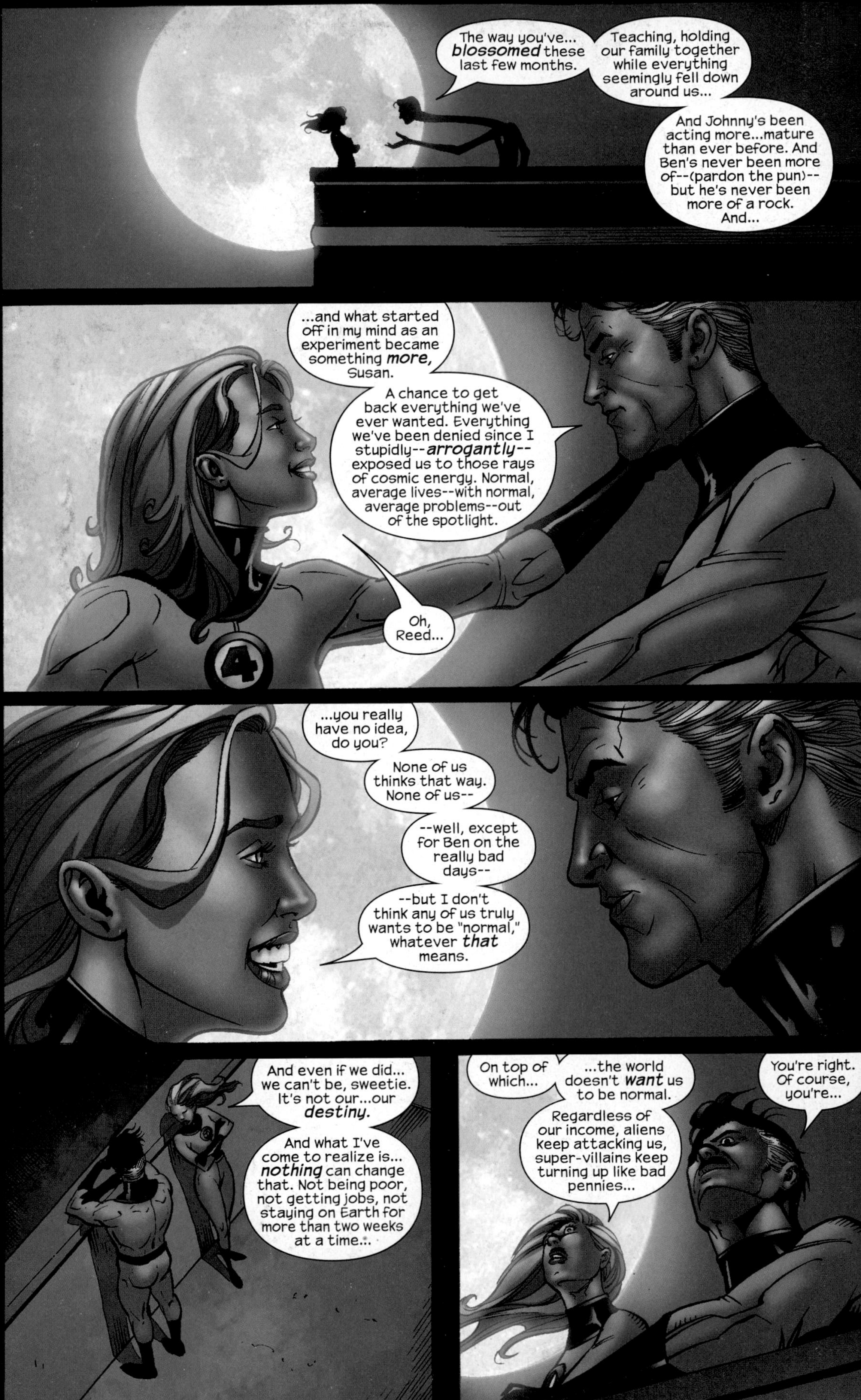

The way you've... blossomed these last few months.
Teaching, holding our family together while everything seemingly fell down around us...
And Johnny's been acting more...mature than ever before. And Ben's never been more of--(pardon the pun)--but he's never been more of a rock. And...
...and what started off in my mind as an experiment became something more, Susan.
A chance to get back everything we've ever wanted. Everything we've been denied since I stupidly--arrogantly--exposed us to those rays of cosmic energy. Normal, average lives--with normal, average problems--out of the spotlight.
Oh, Reed...
...you really have no idea, do you?
None of us thinks that way. None of us--
--well, except for Ben on the really bad days--
--but I don't think any of us truly wants to be "normal," whatever that means.
And even if we did... we can't be, sweetie. It's not our...our destiny.
And what I've come to realize is... nothing can change that. Not being poor, not getting jobs, not staying on Earth for more than two weeks at a time...
On top of which...
...the world doesn't want us to be normal.
Regardless of our income, aliens keep attacking us, super-villains keep turning up like bad pennies...
You're right. Of course, you're...

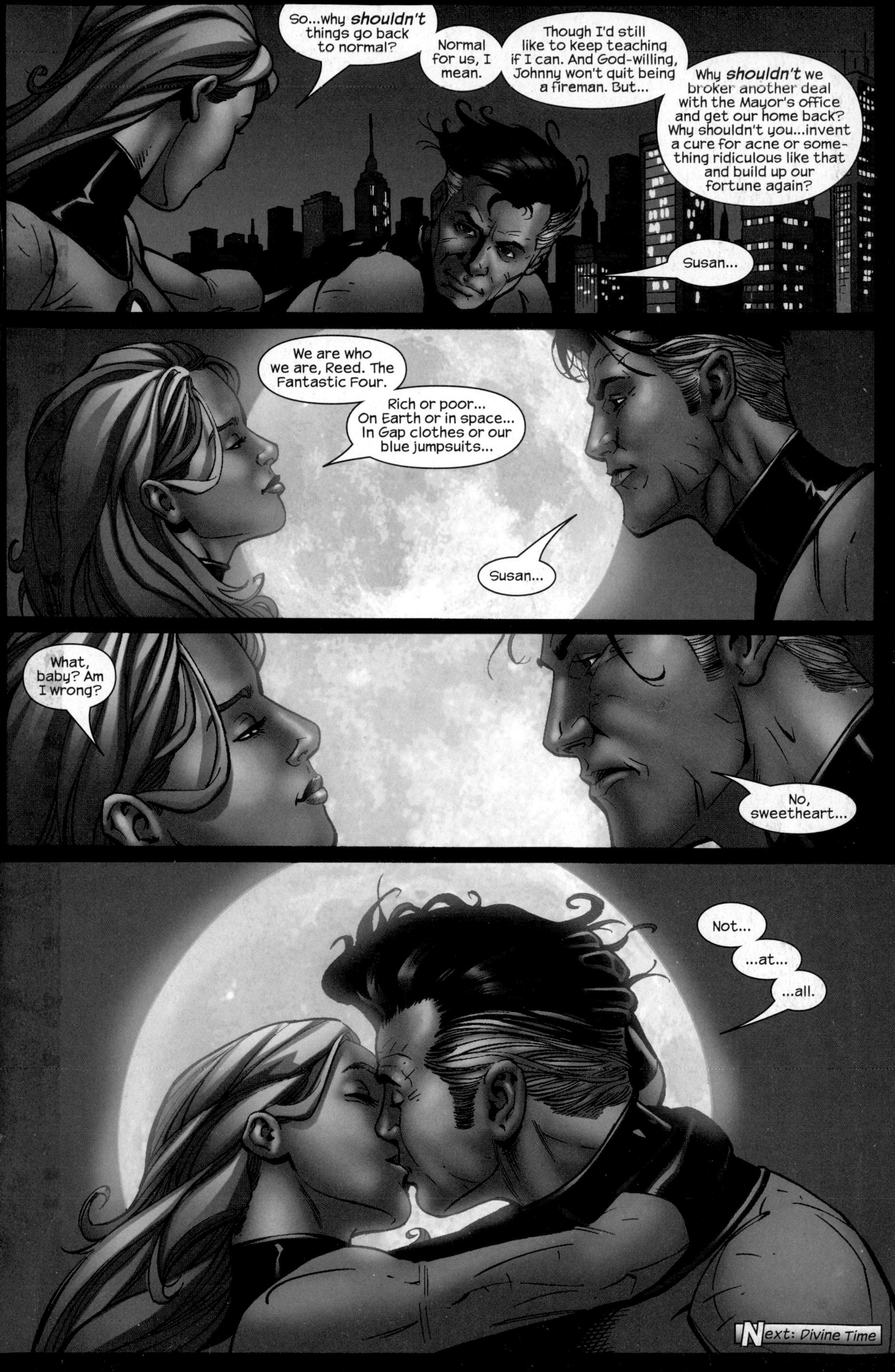
So...why shouldn't things go back to normal?
Normal for us, I mean.
Though I'd still like to keep teaching if I can. And God-willing, Johnny won't quit being a fireman. But...
Why shouldn't we broker another deal with the Mayor's office and get our home back? Why shouldn't you...invent a cure for acne or something ridiculous like that and build up our fortune again?
Susan...
We are who we are, Reed. The Fantastic Four.
Rich or poor... On Earth or in space... In Gap clothes or our blue jumpsuits...
Susan...
What, baby? Am I wrong?
No, sweetheart...
Not...
...at...
...all.
Next: Divine Time

AFTERWORD

I remember the *exact* moment I found out I was going to be working on the Fantastic Four. It was early in May—May of 2003—and I was on my cell phone with my mom and dad, trying to convince them that they didn't need to come to my graduation later that month. "Really, it's not necessary," I was saying, when a second call started to come in.

I recognized the number immediately—a 212-576 number, burned into my brain for all eternity—since I'd been talking to Marvel, on-and-off, for a few months, pitching them on several different projects. Including one that took an offbeat, more grounded, and more human look at comicdom's First Family.

"Mom, Dad—" I said, but then just clicked over.

Marvel said some things to me, I said some stuff back, but what it boiled down to was: "We think this is great so start writing your first script, okay?"

I clicked back over. "Mom, dad—that was Marvel," I said, "Marvel Comics in New York City." (As if there were some other Marvel Comics somewhere else in the world.)

"Oh?" my mom said guardedly. (Tempering her enthusiasm the way mothers and fathers of young playwrights are conditioned to do.)

"Yeah," I said. "I'm gonna be writing the Fantastic Four for them."

Dead silence from my parents for a few seconds, then my dad said: "So I guess that means you're *not* selling those boxes of comic books in the attic?"

And then my mom said: "Sweetie, are you sure you didn't misunderstand? I remember reading 'The Fantastic Four' when I was a teenager—in Spanish. I can't imagine they'd start you out on 'The Fantastic Four.' Maybe you should call them back."

"You're right," I said, then got off the phone with them, then called Marvel again, but no...there hadn't been any mistake: My first professional comic-book-writing gig *was* going to be the Fantastic Four. (The FF's cosmic origin, remembered from a Saturday morning cartoon, started playing in my head...)

I got off the phone with Marvel and walked to my local comic book shop and told the guys there that I was going to be writing a new Fantastic Four comic book.

"*Ultimate Fantastic Four*?" they asked.

"No," I said, setting the first three *Fantastic Four Essentials* on the counter next to the cash register, "the other one." (What would eventually become *Marvel Knights 4*.)

That was almost two years ago. Now I'm writing this afterword for the second *Marvel Knights 4* collection. Truly a dream come true.

I'm as proud of the stories in this book as anything else I've written. They're dedicated to *my* Fantastic Four: my mom, my dad, my brother Raf, and my sister Georgie.

Any similarity they bear to Reed, Sue, Johnny, and/or Ben is *purely* coincidental.

Roberto Aguirre-Sacasa
December 9, 2004